Stress
Survive and Thrive

Robert Hale

Published by
AVICENNA
C/ R. Curtoys Gotarredona, 1, Esc. 2, 2B
07840 Santa Eulària des Riu
Spain

ISBN: 978-84-120109-1-6

Second Edition.

Whilst every effort has been made to trace owners of copyright material, the author would like to apologise for any omissions and will be pleased to incorporate acknowledgements in any future editions.

Preface

I want this book to be informative, useful and readable. Many books about stress management fall into two categories. Some are short, simple books that promise instant results with minimal effort. Others focus on a single aspect or method of stress management, e.g. positive thinking, mindfulness, relaxation, "stress is positive". I believe you deserve more. I believe you need a book with both greater depth of explanation and breadth of coverage which provides a realistic platform for real progress. I am quite open in my belief that nothing of real value comes without a little effort. If you think I am wrong, this book is probably not for you.

Stress is a fact of everybody's life. At best it can stimulate us, energise us and strengthen us. At worst, it can make us ill and contribute to our demise. Most of us learn how to cope more or less well by trial and error. We do our best. Sometimes we do not do very well, and stress affects us negatively and significantly. If this book helps you to cope better with life, even a little, it will have achieved a useful purpose. If further, it stimulates you to go beyond coping, to a position where you can thrive in life, it will have been a success.

If you are stressed, you really don't want to read a dull book. Some of the stuff I have read about stress has been so dull that it made me fall into a stupor. I don't want to make you fall into a stupor, I want you to be sunny and bright and full of life. So I have tried to make this book interesting and easy to read. I hope I have managed to do so, so that you will read it to the end. I think it will be worth it.

Jargon is like the kiss of death to understanding and readability. I have largely banished it from the main text. Apart from one more technical chapter (Chapter 5) which you can largely skip if you like, you will find it only in the footnotes and the glossary, which you may read or not, as you prefer. It will not affect the practical usefulness of the book one bit.

One important kind of stress is not covered by this book, and that is post-traumatic stress syndrome (PTSS). The reason for this is that PTSS has important characteristics that distinguish it from the common kind of chronic stress, and which require more specialised care and management. That is not to say the techniques and ideas presented in this book would not be useful to people who experience PTSS, it is just that they would fall short of being sufficient.

Much of this book is loosely and not exclusively based on psychological approaches that try to help change your thinking and behaviour[1] (which, by the way, is proven to work). Sometimes the way this is put into practice involves you in keeping so many daily diaries and registers that you actually have no time left for living your life. I want you to enjoy your trip, not to be submerged in paperwork. I only suggest you keep two diaries for a week each, which is not a great deal to have to manage.

Ultimately, the aim of this book is to help you lay the groundwork for you to thrive in your life. To thrive I take to mean to grow, develop as a person, prosper (not necessarily in materialistic terms but not excluding that either), and feel fulfilled and happy. You can only do this if you get beyond just "coping". What I mean is that I would like you to be so good at handling your life that you become a Master at it. At that point, you will have waved goodbye to chronic stress, as it will have evaporated from your life.

All right, you and I will, in all probability, never be 100% effective at handling life. We will never reach any perfect, sunlit uplands of a zero-worry life. But we have conjured the image of an ideal goal in order to set up a fulfilling journey. So gentle reader, you are about to start your journey towards a better experience of life. Onwards and upwards!

Disclaimer

The information given in this book is in no way to be considered medical advice. This book contains in various sections suggestions for physical, mental and behavioural exercises. Please consult your doctor before starting to do any of the suggested exercises. All of the exercises in this book are usually well tolerated. However, if you should experience pain or any other symptoms while or after doing the exercises, stop doing them and seek medical advice. Do not do any of the exercises if you are feeling unwell. If you choose to use these exercises, you do so at your own risk and under your own responsibility. Neither the author nor the publisher will accept any responsibility for negative events arising from using them.

---

1   "Cognitive-behavioural therapy" or CBT.

Contents

To Eilene for her support, encouragement, and forbearance during the writing of this book.

Introduction

"Why does this happen?" asks Sonia, who has chronic neck and shoulder problems. In her case, as in so many others the cause is repetitive strain (itself a form of stress) combined with time pressure and worry. She talks about how complicated life is nowadays, and how there are not enough hours in the day. I tell her the cause is essentially simple, she has to work too hard and worry too much. Our modern, globalised society is so large and so complex that we all do.

Like Sonia, when suffering from a new health symptom, many of my patients ask me, "Why has this happened?" Usually the broad answer is that it is the impact of stress, in one form or another, whether emotional, environmental, biological or mechanical. One of my answers to the question is, "It's just life".

Modern life is intrinsically prone to generate stress. For example, the human frame and the human mind were not designed to work 8+ hours a day, day after day, year after year. Anthropological studies of pre-agricultural societies (small groups of extended families living by hunting and gathering in a natural environment) show that activities that can be classed as "work" occupy them much less than in modern societies, with most estimates falling between 3 and 5 hours a day on average[2]. The rest of their time is spent at leisure, much of which is resting and sleeping, the latter even during daytime.

Another major source of stress in modern societies – relationship troubles – is attenuated in small pre-agricultural societies because these societies usually have strict rules of behaviour that govern relationships. Family life, I suppose, has always had its share of strife. Certainly, I have never encountered a perfectly functional family, except of course the Waltons[3]. (And even there, John-Boy had his moments.) Nevertheless, in past times the opportunities for, and risks/benefits of radical change within one's social relations were weighted in favour of social stability. Such social limitations can bring their own stresses, but that must be measured against the stress caused by the vast confusion of choice that has developed over the last 150 years. Stress counsellors use the adage, "Accept what cannot be changed", and in simple small scale societies, the rules of relationships being inviolable, the anxiety of a potential choice against convention was not a factor. There was no choice but to accept!

Of course, abundance of choice now affects all areas of modern life, not only in relationships. It is most obvious in our role as "consumers". There are so many different things we can "consume", and so many different varieties of each. There is marketing and peer pressure upon us to "consume" as many things as possible, which generates in us not only the anxiety of the

---

2   Sahlins M. 1972. Stone Age Economics. New York: Aldine.
3   "The Waltons" was a feel-good 1970s American television series featuring a poor but close-knit family in rural Virginia in the 1930s and 40s, created by Earl Hamner, Jr., and based on his 1961 novel Spencer's Mountain.

choice, but the potential for fault lines of an economic nature to weigh upon us, too. People in pre-agricultural societies do not live with the pressure of being commercial consumers.

A fourth major source of stress is change, and more particularly the pace of change, which is accelerating in an almost exponential way; to the point now where many people, particularly those over the age of 50, are finding it increasingly difficult to manage. New technology can do more things faster, and humanity, for some idiosyncrasy innate in its psyche, feels obliged to use all of that new capacity for the promise of increased wealth and/or status. So we have to be "connected" "24/7" and "upgrade" promptly for fear of poverty, or ridicule and social exclusion, and suffer the consequences of the stress of keeping up with it all. The ever-accelerating race to be or to appear as worthy as one's peers may give some a superficial sense of achievement and worth, but enslaves the many and makes a lot of people ill.

This is not an advertisement for the caveman way of life. You may not wish to live in a cave or a wooden hut, running around barefoot in the forest with no access to a good dentist or the Internet. That is no bed of roses, either! Pre-agricultural societies have to cope with difficulties of their own, without our technological advantages – bad weather, wild animals, insecurity and disease. However, they have had millions of years to evolve organic ways to deal with these. We have had only a few decades to adapt to the stresses of modern relationship dynamics, consumerism, and the pace of change, and only a few thousand years to adapt to the hard work of ploughing the fields and scattering.

For these reasons, I believe modern societies are much more vulnerable to stress than pre-agricultural ones. The human being was not designed for such a labour and thought-intensive lifestyle as the one we lead today, so certain kinds of physical and mental disorders are to be expected to occur with greater frequency. That being the case, we have to learn and hone a much larger and more sophisticated repertoire of protective measures against these forms of stress than simpler societies need to do.

Pre-agricultural societies had their witch doctors (shamans, medicine men, wise women, etc.), versed in special knowledge, including how to ward off misfortune, illness, and the evil eye; and how to engender courage and fortune in the hunt or in battle. Today we have doctors, clerics, psychologists and counsellors. But I think the most effective way in which we can ward off the effects of the modern evil, stress, and to live peaceful, happy and fulfilling lives, is to be our own witch doctors. We all need a repertoire of techniques and incantations, different for each one of us and each to his or her own, but always adhering to a few basic principles.

So what *can* Sonia, you or I, as individuals, do to protect ourselves? Read on...

Part 1: How stress works

1. A burden that strengthens, a burden that harms

Good stress and bad stress – Stress and strain – Definition of stress – Stress and anxiety - All too much - What to do - Negative to positive

In Thornton Wilder's 1927 classic novel *The Bridge of San Luis Rey*, the orphan Pepita, who has become the Abbess's protégé, is sent to the grand house of a lonely, aged aristocratic lady, to be her companion:

> She had never been taught to expect happiness, and the inconveniences, not to say terrors, of her new position did not seem to her excessive for a girl of fourteen. She did not suspect that the Abbess was even there hovering about the house, herself estimating the stresses and watching for the moment when a burden harms and not strengthens.[4]

Look at that last phrase, "when a burden harms and not strengthens". This carries the essence of what we know about stress. It implies, rightly, that stress is not in the weight of the load but in its effect upon us. To carry a burden requires an effort from us. An effort which tests us but which is within our capabilities can make us stronger, but if the effort required is too great for us, we can be harmed by it. Most often, in popular speech, we use the word "stress" for the burden that harms. Kelly McGonigal has argued that this negative popular perception is detrimental to our health in itself[5]. So it is important to highlight here at the start that stress may have both positive and negative effects depending on the nature of the situation and our attitudes and responses to it.

Physical trainers know that in order to increase your muscle strength and stamina you must do physical exercises which are challenging to your body. The exercise is a positive stress – the burden that strengthens. Let us take running with a weighted rucksack as an example. Trainers also know that if you try to carry too much weight, over too long a distance or for too long a time, or you do not pace yourself properly, or you do it too frequently without sufficient rest and recuperation, or you are feeling unwell before you start, you will quickly become exhausted and risk injury. That is negative stress – the burden that harms.

Before 1950 few people except physicists and engineers talked about stress. To them it was a physical concept relating to materials. If you place a plank of wood between two work benches, with its ends resting on them, then place a heavy block of concrete onto the middle of the plank where it is not supported, it will bend or, depending on the kind of wood, the dimensions of the

---

4   Excerpted from *The Bridge of San Luis Rey* by Thornton Wilder. Copyright Thornton Wilder 1927.

5   McGonigal K. 2015. The upside of stress: Why stress is good for you (and how to be good at it). 2nd edition. Avery.

plank and the weight and shape of the concrete, it could even break. The weight of the concrete provides the stress on the plank, the deformation (bending) of the plank before it breaks is called the strain.

Before the middle of the 20th century, if you wanted to talk about anxiety or health complaints relating to heavy work demands, relationship troubles or economic difficulties, you would not have used the word "stress". You might instead have said you felt "under pressure", "a bit run down", "at the end of your tether", or some such expression. But "stress" then began to be used to describe the body's responses to challenging situations, thanks to the ground-breaking work of a Canadian scientist called Hans Selye.

Selye was a physiologist and as such he was particularly interested in how stress affected the body. (We will talk a little about his ideas later.) Yet the workings of the mind are fundamental to stress, and many of the people who subsequently studied stress have been psychologists. I have adapted our working definition of stress (which you should keep in mind while reading this book) from the work of a psychologist who has been prominent in the field, R.S. Lazarus[6]:

> **"I experience stress when I feel that I cannot cope with the demands put upon me and the dangers I am exposed to."**

A "demand" is any event or situation to which a living organism must in some way adapt. Adaptation clearly requires some sort of response from the organism. In place of "demands", we could just as well use the word "challenges".

To "cope" with an event or situation means to respond appropriately to bring about a satisfactory outcome. This may mean a return to the *status quo*, or an improvement in one's life, or even "least bad" damage limitation.

Stress and anxiety

Are stress and anxiety the same thing? No, stress is a process with inputs and outputs. An extremely common output (response) of the stress process is anxiety. Anxiety can manifest itself mentally as nervousness, being "on edge", worry, and bodily as physical symptoms of many and varied kinds.

All too much

Sometimes when we are stressed we might say something like, "It's all too much". But too much for what? The answer is that we feel it is too much for us to deal with. As the above

---

6   Lazarus put it: "Stress arises when individuals perceive that they cannot adequately cope with the demands being made on them or with threats to their well-being." (Lazarus RS. 1966. Psychological stress and the coping process. New York: McGraw-Hill.) Lazarus and his co-worker S. Folkman later developed the Transactional Model of Stress. They described stress as "...an imbalance between the demands imposed on the organism, and the capacity of the organism to cope with those demands." (Lazarus RS, Folkman S. 1984. Stress, Appraisal, and Coping. New York: Springer.)

definition suggests, when our ability to cope is inadequate for the pressures we feel upon us, we feel stress.

But why should our ability to deal with the situations in our life be inadequate? There are two possible reasons:

1. Either the challenges we face place extraordinarily high demands on us.

2. Or something about us limits our capacity to meet the challenges that we would ordinarily and frequently expect to face in our daily life.

In other words, either the burden is unusually great and therefore difficult to bear, or we are not strong or well-equipped enough to bear life's ordinary burdens. The first reason may arise if we suffer some kind of major traumatic event: the death of a close family member, serious illness or injury, divorce, being witness to horrific events, losing one's home, and so on. It could also arise if the challenges we face are ordinary ones, but are extremely numerous or concentrated. Maybe we work in a high intensity industry and our boss is a tyrannical, workaholic maniac. Or maybe, just through a rare coincidence in the positions of the stars and planets (!), a very high number of important and urgent tasks have coalesced around us.

But what about the second reason, something limiting our capacity to effectively respond? What could that be?

a) A lack of something essential.

- Physical health / conditioning.
- Practical skills.
- Emotional awareness.
- Thinking skills.
- Material resources.
- Help.

b) An inappropriate reaction.

- Knee jerk responses.
- Limited/unhelpful beliefs and thinking patterns.
- Habitual negative emotions.

In a phrase, we are talking about resources and resourcefulness. We will look these things in more detail later.

What to do?

Our working definition of stress that I introduced earlier in this chapter has an important implication. If stress arises when the challenges we face are greater than our capacity to cope with them, we have only a few options:

- Ignore, deny, or forget the challenge.

- Reduce or avoid the challenge.

- Act upon the challenge and/or improve our capacity to respond effectively to the challenge.

The first option – not good – it is liable to result in a bigger problem to deal with later down the line. The second option – better - but we may miss out on the positive outcomes of facing up to a challenge. It may be an activity we get some enjoyment from. Moreover, facing up to a challenge is an educational experience which makes us stronger. The third option – the best – is the road to self-development and a better life!

Our capacity to respond effectively to challenges requires the use of certain resources that we possess, such things as knowledge, experience, skills, intelligence, our personality, attitude, physical health, and the support of friends, family and society; money, too, is often helpful.

Our response to a situation includes our emotions, thoughts, and sensations, physiological changes (changes in the workings of the body), and changes in our actions (our behaviour). When we are having difficulty coping, our responses at many levels indicate that we are stressed:

- Physiological, e.g. our blood pressure goes up.

- Sensations, e.g. we are more sensitive to pain.

- Emotional, e.g. we feel anxious.

- Thoughts[7], e.g. we may think the world is against us.

- Behavioural, e.g. we may react to people angrily.

Turning negative to positive

With the above description of stress, we are talking about a negative situation, that is, that life's demands are exceeding our capacity to cope. However, it has often been said that there is both positive stress and negative stress – the burden that strengthens, the burden that harms – and that is true. In fact, many of the techniques and strategies suggested in this book are aimed at turning the negative into the positive. So that instead of allowing challenging situations to harm us, they may nourish our development as people. Managing stress successfully means avoiding,

---

7   Thoughts: technically called "cognitions" or collectively "cognition".

reducing, or eliminating its negative impact, and further, even transforming its impact to make it positive.

If we want to be able to deal better with our stress, it is fundamentally important for us always to remember that stress is not an external event or situation that happens to us. We may understand this more easily if we consider that the same event or situation may be stressful to one person but not to another. And it may be stressful to us at one time but not at another. So we can see that the event or situation is not in itself the stress; but it may or may not induce stress within us, depending on our own current circumstances: our attitude, character, available resources, general coping skills, and other things that have been happening to us. Stress is a tension within us caused by an *interaction* between us and the outside world, and both we and the outside world are complex and many faceted things!

Main points

- Stress is not what happens to us.
- It is a tension caused by an *interaction* between us and the outside world.
- Stress is due to a mismatch between the demands placed upon us and how well we feel able to respond to them.
- Either the demands are too great or our capacity to respond to them is inadequate.
- How things affect us depends on our attitude to them.
- Our capacity to respond depends on our resources and our resourcefulness.

2. What does it feel like and how much of it do I have?

Feeling stress - Recognising stress - Assessing stress

Restless Anxiety, forlorn Despair,

And all the faded family of Care.

- Sir Samuel Garth (1671-1719)

Often we know intuitively when we are stressed because of the characteristic feelings it gives us. Typically, and talking about our feeling in general, we may say we feel:

- Nervous.
- Anxious.
- Tense.
- Stressed out.
- Under pressure.

But...

- The feelings associated with stress are not the same for everybody.
- They may be different according to the intensity and duration of our stress.
- Other people can observe things about us when we are stressed of which we may be unaware[8].
- If we are subject to persistent low grade stress, we may become so used to it we do not realise we are particularly stressed.

So, how can we recognise that we are stressed?

Recognising stress

Stress manifests as changes in the way we think and process information ("cognition"), in our emotions, in how we feel physically, and in how we act - our behaviour - as shown in the table below. The symptoms of stress are many and varied; so only some of the most common ones are listed.

---

8   Strictly, symptoms are what we feel within ourselves. What other people can observe are called "signs". For simplicity, I will use the word "symptoms" for both.

Symptoms of stress	
Thinking and information processing Poor concentration Poor attention span Poor memory Poor judgement Negative attitude / outlook Constant or frequent worrying Racing thoughts	**Physical** sensations[9] "Butterflies in the stomach" A sensation of having a lump in the throat Dry mouth Cold hands and feet Feeling hot Sweating Nausea Dizziness Diarrhoea or constipation Desire to urinate Loss of interest in sex
Emotions "Nervousness", Agitation Irritability Mood swings Unhappiness (covers many emotional states: sadness, bitterness, fear, despair, loneliness, feeling overwhelmed, etc.) Being overly emotional Reduced enthusiasm Reduced self-confidence Reduced self-esteem	**Behaviour** Tics: twitches and involuntary movements Fidgeting, fiddling, nail-biting, finger-drumming, pacing Yawning Clenching or grinding teeth, especially while asleep Changes in speech (too fast, too loud, too hoarse, stumbling over words, stammering) Defensiveness Hostility Aggressiveness Over-reacting Eating more or less than usual Change in activity level Change in sleeping habits Isolating oneself Drinking or smoking more than usual

Table 2.1: Symptoms of stress.

The effects of stress also extend to our social relations and functioning, with important implications for family, friends and work. A stressed person may be less interested, able to appreciate, or tolerant, of the needs of other people. They may be hostile and aggressive, or withdrawn. They may be less able or inclined to respond appropriately and proportionately in social situations, for example by over-reacting or by being uncommunicative. They may neglect their appearance. They may show poor judgement in dealing with other people, forget or make

---

9   Only short-term symptoms are listed here. Chapter 5 is about the long-term effects of stress.

mistakes with practical tasks, or be indecisive when clear decisions are needed. They may be accident prone due to poor attention and reduced fine motor skills. In short, the stressed person is more likely to perform badly in his or her roles within the family, among friends, at work, and in the wider society.

How stressed am I?

Various methods have been developed to assess how much stress people have experienced or are experiencing. Many of them use questionnaires. The three listed below are widely used and can easily be accessed on the Internet. In fact, I would encourage you to look them up and see how you measure up!

1. One popular tool is a simple and reliable questionnaire devised by Sheldon Cohen[10] of the Laboratory for the Study of Stress, Immunity and Disease at the Carnegie Mellon University in Pittsburgh (USA). It is called the *Perceived Stress Scale* (PSS), and was designed to compare stress levels in groups of people. Its reliability and validity have been tested as good. It can be accessed on various online sites.

   The PSS presents a series of questions which aim to assess how frequently an individual has experienced certain emotions and thoughts, or acted in certain ways, over the last month. The questionnaire asks the subject to score each question (or "item") on a scale from 0 to 4, thus: 0 (never), 1 (almost never), 2 (sometimes), 3 (fairly often), 4 (very often). Some adapted examples of the kinds of experiences the PSS refers to are:

   ○ Being upset by an unexpected event.

   ○ Being unable to control important things in your life.

   ○ Feeling nervous or stressed.

   ○ Not feeling confident about handling personal problems.

   ○ Feeling that things were not going your way.

   ○ Feeling unable to cope with all the things you had to do.

   ○ Feeling unable to control irritations in your life.

   ○ Feeling you were not on top of things.

   ○ Being angered by things outside your control.

   ○ Feeling that difficulties were piling up so high that you could not control them.

---

10 (1) Cohen S, Kamarck T, Mermelstein R. 1983. A global measure of perceived stress. Journal of Health and Social Behavior 24(4):385-396. (2) Cohen S, Williamson G. 1988. Perceived stress in a probability sample of the United States. In Spacapam S, Oskamp S (Eds.). 1988. The social psychology of health: Claremont Symposium on applied social psychology. Newbury Park, CA: Sage.

Notice that many of the examples are similar. They focus on feelings of being upset, nervousness, lack of confidence, lack of control, irritation, anger and inability to cope; with events or situations that are unexpected, random, problematic, or too numerous.

The PSS is not meant as a diagnostic tool. However, we would not go far wrong if we said that if overall you think you have experienced such feelings anything more than "sometimes" (an average score of 2) during the last month, your stress level is probably higher than it should be for you to be able to thrive.

2. Another tool is the ***Holmes and Rahe Stress Scale***[11], which lists a series of major life events, weighted according to their relative importance. The weightings have been generated from research about what people who have experienced these events actually feel about them.

    Further research indicated that one could calculate the total impact of stress on one's health from major life events[12]. A total score is found by marking the events of the Holmes and Rahe Stress Scale which have affected you during the past year, then adding up the values of those events. If any event has happened to you more than once, you multiply that event's value by the number of times it has happened to you, before adding up the total. The result is interpreted in terms of the risk of developing a stress-related illness in the near future.

3. The Holmes and Rahe Stress Scale is made up of major life changes, but most everyday stress is caused by more minor hassles. Kanner and colleagues (1981)[13] created a ***Hassles Scale***, including items concerned with things like losing things, traffic jams, arguments, disappointments, body weight and physical appearance[14]. They found the Hassles Scale was better at predicting psychological well-being (with problems such as anxiety and depression) than Holmes and Rahe Stress Scale.

Each measure has its own strengths and limitations. The PSS assesses more recent stress than the Holmes and Rahe Stress scale and asks you about your actual feelings rather than the things that have happened to you. The Hassles Scale assesses current stress and irritations/frustrations

---

11   Holmes TH, Rahe RH. 1967. The Social Readjustment Rating Scale. Journal of Psychosomatic Research 11(2): 213-218.

12   Rahe RH, Mahan JL, Arthur RJ. 1970. Prediction of near-future health change from subjects' preceding life changes. *Journal of Psychosomatic Research* 14(4)401-406.

13   Kanner AD, Coyne JC, Schaefer C, Lazarus RS. 1981. Comparison of two modes of stress measurement: Daily hassles and uplifts versus major life events. *Journal of behavioral medicine* 4(1):1-39.

14   McLeod SA. 2010. SRRS - Stress of Life Events. Retrieved from www.simplypsychology.org/SRRS.html on 16/09/2015.

rather than life changing events. We will be talking more about short-term and long-term stress, and major life changes versus daily annoyances in another chapter.

Main points

- Often we intuitively know what stress feels like for us.
- Stress symptoms differ for different people and different kinds of stress.
- Stress affects our cognition, emotions, physical body and behaviour.
- Methods have been developed to assess how much stress we have experienced or are experiencing.

3. When the muck hits the fan

Apollo 13 – Inputs and outputs - A threat announces itself – First feelings and thoughts – Major or lesser stress – Weighing up our options - Kit for coping – A test or a hammer blow – The transactional model

> *Houston, we've had a problem.*
>
> - Commander Jim Lovell, Apollo 13

Houston, we have a problem!

On Monday 13th April 1970, the crew of Apollo 13, more than four fifths of the way to the moon, heard a loud bang, followed by power fluctuations and the firing of their craft's automatic steering thrusters. Moments later, after carrying out some initial checks, Commander Jim Lovell radioed mission control at the Kennedy Space Centre in Houston with the words, "Houston, we've had a problem". It transpired that one of the craft's oxygen tanks had exploded. The mission to land on the moon was aborted. The craft swung round the moon in orbit and successfully returned to Earth, damaged but with the three-man crew safe. I remember as a 9-year-old child following television reports of its progress back to Earth, almost biting my fingernails with anxiety. Can you imagine a situation as potentially dramatic as that one for the people directly involved? 200,000 miles from home, out in the vast, black nothingness of space, uncertain of the seriousness or implications of the damage to their craft. Yet the crew did not panic, they kept their cool, analysed their situation calmly, and worked with the technicians and engineers back on Earth to resolve the situation happily. In the recording of their radio transmissions just after the accident, Lovell sounds as cool as pie. As astronauts, he and his fellow crew members had been selected for their capacity to cope with stress, and given extensive training in dealing with stressful challenges. That is a best case scenario. You and I are not so select!

A question of inputs and outputs

In fact, our effectiveness (or lack of it) when dealing with unforeseen and dramatic situations is probably much more haphazard than that of the Apollo 13 astronauts. But the basic process is the same. It is a process with many inputs and a range of outputs, and most importantly, what goes on in the space in between. Let us go through a simplified version.

Let us say you are coasting through your life at the moment on cruise control. Then... Bam! All of a sudden, a situation arises. Suddenly things are not going your way, and badly so.

The reference to cruise control might be more than a metaphor. You and I are probably never going to have space craft trouble, so let us look at vehicle trouble closer to home. In December 2009 a man in Melbourne, Australia, was driving along a busy motorway with cruise control set at 50 miles per hour. As he approached his motorway exit, he tapped the brake pedal with his foot, an action which would normally turn off cruise control, but nothing happened. The car kept on going at the same speed![15] Can you imagine?! What were his first feelings? Can you imagine the rush of adrenaline through his body, the jolt in the pit of his stomach and the jump of his heart?

A threat announces itself

This is our first awareness of a potential threat. Our minds are constantly processing information about the world around us, which is conveyed to the mind via the senses. Much of what happens to us in our daily lives we are familiar with, and we have attained mastery over how to deal with it. However, situations can arise which, for one reason or another, we assess as being a "problem". We perceive a threat. Anything which potentially knocks us out of our easy cruise through life, even a little way, may be considered a challenge or a "threat". The difference between the unproblematic run-of-the mill situation and the potentially difficult situation is largely an unconscious process. We only become aware of it if our appraisal is negative (i.e. we perceive a threat), through an emotional feeling such as fright, apprehension or unease, and perhaps bodily sensations such as feeling our heart "jump".

In a word, we feel a sense of alarm. Various aspects about the situation and about ourselves can make the difference between tranquillity and alarm:

- The nature, magnitude, proximity, meaning and duration of the event or situation.

- Our prior state of alert. Some people are more easily alarmed than others, and you may be more easily alarmed on some occasions than on others. This in turn depends on a series of factors such as heredity, formative experiences, past adult experiences, cultural background, beliefs, values and goals, and recent events.

- Your own general feeling of vulnerability or invulnerability. This too depends on other factors such as self-esteem, past experiences, and your perception of your effectiveness in coping with problems in general or of this kind.

In any case, once we have felt the alarm, we begin to have our first thoughts about the situation. What do you imagine might have been the first coherent thoughts of the driver in the cruise control situation described above?[16] He had never experienced anything like this before and it is an immediate emergency. What did he think?

---

15 http://www.dailymail.co.uk/news/article-1236020/Horror-ride-driver-stuck-50mph-cruise-control-30-minutes-slow-traffic.html (accessed 12/11/2015).

16 This is called "primary appraisal". It arises as an unconscious process. Basically, it tackles the question, "What does this mean?"

Maybe:

- "This must be some mistake, or a minor malfunction. Try again. No. What about touching the accelerator? No!"
- "It doesn't work! I can't get out of cruise control! *****! This is a problem!"

Weighing up the threat

This is what our car driver did just after thinking "This is a problem!" He probably thought:

- "How bad is this?"
- "Is my life is in danger here?!"

The answers will depend on how damaging to us the threat could be, how imminent it is, how familiar we are with this kind of thing, and how confident we are in our own abilities to resolve the situation without major harm. We may find ourselves thinking, in the worst case, "I'm going to die!" or "I am completely overwhelmed by this", or more positively, "This is a difficulty, but I am well capable of dealing with it." In the first case, our anxiety will be great and (assuming our prediction of an early death proves premature!) prolonged; in the latter case it will be lesser and more quickly resolved. There are obviously gradations of response, so there is no clearly drawn line in the sand to tell us what is "major" and what is "lesser" stress. Weighing up the threat can be a very rapid process, as in our runaway car example. Other kinds of situation might necessitate longer reflection.

Back to the man in the runaway car. He thinks:

- "This is potentially catastrophic!"
- "I might be killed!"

Weighing up our options

Once we have become aware of a threat, and quickly assessed its importance, we consciously weigh it up and consider our options[17]. In the example situation above, after the first realisation that you had a serious and dangerous problem, what would you have thought about it?

- "Can I do anything about this?"
- "What can I do?"
- "Shall I do this or shall I do that?"
- "What should I try first?"

---

17   This is called "secondary appraisal". It is largely a conscious process.

Can anything be done? Your answer to this question will be influenced by such things as your previous experience of this kind of event or situation, whether or not you feel any sense of control, the strength of your self-esteem, whether you feel your habitual ways of dealing with difficulty will be up to the task, and whether you possess the resources you need (time, money, tools, knowledge, skills, help, etc.). What would you have done in the runaway car example above?

What the driver did is this. He tried slamming his foot on the brake pedal, pulling the handbrake and turning off the ignition, all to no avail. But he possessed a vital resource, his mobile phone, which probably saved his life. He used it to call the police, and a police vehicle was sent to attempt to clear the way before him. He followed the police car along the motorway at a constant speed for miles. But the motorway ended and became a highway, and the traffic slowed. As they weaved in and out of the slow moving traffic, he became increasingly convinced that he must eventually crash. After 25 miles the traffic jammed, and he knew a crash was inevitable, but he attempted even then to make the best of a terrible job. In his own words:

> *"There was traffic in every lane. I just didn't have anywhere to go. I just put all my weight on that footbrake, pulled on the handbrake again, swerved on the wrong side of the road to avoid running into the back of everyone, went over the concrete road island and bounced a bit. I could hear the tyres skidding on the road for what seemed like for ever. When I opened my eyes, I was bonnet-to-bonnet with the car in front of me."*

Not surprisingly, he was taken to hospital suffering from shock.

Kit for coping

I have mentioned our capacity to deal with things, to cope. What things provide such capacity? We can call these things "coping resources". Coping resources are the things at our disposal which can facilitate our efforts to meet the demands of a situation. Material resources are external to ourselves and are useful instruments like money and time. Personal resources are internal attributes, whether innate or acquired by learning, such things as intelligence, a positive attitude, or particular skills. Social resources are the support available from our loved ones, the people around us, the community in which we live, the authorities, and charitable organisations. Spiritual resources clearly depend upon our beliefs, so could perhaps be considered a "personal resource". However, while to a non-believer, another's belief in God is just a belief, to the believer God is real whether the non-believer believes it or not! So, given that our beliefs may include a transcendental, supernatural intelligence that we regard as being higher than ourselves and the concrete, practical world in which we carry on our daily lives, I choose to consider this as a different order of help!

YOU MAY NEED...	
Material	Money, time, tools, information.
Personal	Personality traits, attitude, intelligence, way of thinking, education, experience, beliefs, skills, knowledge, values, aspirations, goals, affinities, talents, self-knowledge.
Social	Friends, family, organisations.
Spiritual	God...?

Table 3.1: Coping resources

In truth, it is not just the *actual* availability (or possession) of these resources that counts, but our *perception* that we possess them or have access to them, and that we can use them effectively. That is, in order for a resource to be useful to us, we have to see that it is available to us and understand how to use it properly.

Lest we forget the burden that strengthens

Without meeting challenges, can anybody live a life that is fulfilling to themselves and valued by those around them? Challenges which we overcome have the potential to be life enhancing: we learn from them and are more capable of facing similar challenges in the future. However, if the difficulty of a challenge overwhelms our capacity to cope, the outcome can be devastating. Stress is therefore more likely to be positive if the nature and degree of the threat provides a mild to moderate test of our capabilities, but not a hammer blow to them.

The transactional model

The outline of the stress response given above derives from the ideas of two psychologists, Richard Lazarus and Susan Folkman. It forms part of their "Transactional Model" of stress, summarised in the diagram below.

Fig. 3.1: The transactional model of stress (after Lazarus & Folkman, 1984[18])

18   Lazarus RS, Folkman S. 1984. Stress, Appraisal, and Coping. New York: Springer.

Main points

- Stress is not what happens to you, it is what happens *with* you when you attempt to meet a challenge.

- Three stages are involved in assessing the challenge: we first become aware of a potential threat (it announces itself), we weigh it up, we weigh up our options.

- How a challenging event or situation affects you, depends upon an array of things:
  - About you: your background, personality, experience, beliefs, values and self-belief.
  - About the situation: its nature, proximity, magnitude and duration.
  - About your resources: the material, personal, social and spiritual help available.

4. Nobody knows the trouble you've seen

Stress is personal and nuanced – Bothers and earthquakes – Lightning bolts and desert crossings – Stress responses – the General Adaptation Syndrome – The problem of the mind

Nobody knows the trouble I've seen

Nobody knows my sorrow

Nobody knows the trouble I've seen

Glory hallelujah!

- Traditional African American spiritual song

Nobody knows the trouble you've seen. It is a very personal matter. We can know the facts about what has happened to you, we can observe your behaviour and you can tell us about your emotions. But there are no words you can use which will convey to us exactly how your stress feels to you or what it means to you, and we cannot measure those things with a ruler or any kind of electronic device. Stress is a highly nuanced experience which is different for everyone.

Yet we do have general descriptions of stress which can help us to gain some practical understanding which will be useful to us in our mission to manage it better. Despite the complexity of stress, it is their very simplicity which enables us to get a handle on it.

Bothers and earthquakes

Stress can be generated by many different kinds of events and situations, but we may talk about all of them as being either daily hassles or major life changes. I will call the former "bothers" and the latter "earthquakes".

I remember an advertising campaign run by British Rail years ago showing side-by-side graphs of the heart rates of a train passenger and a car driver during a journey from, I believe, Leeds to London. The heart of the car driver beat faster on average and with greater variations in rate than that of the train passenger. Train travel, obviously, was being sold as a more relaxed alternative to the stress of driving. Driving a car can be a bother.

Now, as I write, thousands of Yazidi people, a small ethnic group living in northern Iraq, are besieged on a barren mountain range with no shelter, food or clean water, having been forced to flee from their villages by a heavily armed and brutal insurgent group. "Convert to our faith or be killed", they had been told.

It might seem amazing that the same word - "stress" - may be applied to two situations which are seemingly incomparable in impact and scale. If a potential danger suddenly occurs on the course of our car journey, we feel temporarily alarmed. If we were forced to trudge under an angry sun, hungry and thirsty, towards a precarious mountain refuge, leaving butchered relatives back in our village, we would feel a good deal more than "alarmed": we may feel terrified, we would certainly feel shock.

Yet there it is. The body and the mind have, up to a point, common patterns of response to threats of whatever kind, though the intensity, duration, and outcome will differ. For example, many of the people who suffered such brutal persecution in Iraq may go on to develop Post-Traumatic Stress Disorder. This occurs when one has been witness to or involved in horrific events of great magnitude, not minor bothers. But because of some basic similarities in the stress response, we can use the word stress about both situations, although they are opposite extremes in terms of intensity and severity. One is just a "bother", the other a metaphorical "earthquake"[19].

Lightning bolts and desert crossings

Another basic distinction between different kinds of stress can be made by saying whether it is brief or drawn out, and whether it is very intense or not. I will call brief, intense stress "lightning bolts" and drawn out, less intense stress "dessert crossings".

Imagine a situation of sudden alarm. You close the door of your home and suddenly realise your key is still inside. There is nobody else at home. What do you feel? You feel a bolt (no pun intended), don't you? It feels like a sudden shock, doesn't it? It is a bolt of recognition, adrenaline and nervous discharge!

Alternatively, your husband, wife or long-term partner tells you out of the blue that they have been having an affair and decided to leave you. What do you feel? The bolt is powerful, emotionally it could knock you over. It rams into your solar plexus leaving you stunned.

The first of these situations is a bother, the second an earthquake, but there is something they have in common: they are both sudden and involve alarm and shock. They are both lightning bolts, differing in degree, the first minor, the second major. Technically they are both called "acute" situations.

Desert crossings are different. They are a long, hard slog. You have a long way to go under difficult and uncomfortable circumstances. You may not be sure of your direction, your destination or your goal, or indeed whether the desert will ever come to an end. For example, if you suffer continual harassment, bullying or "mobbing"[20] at work, but you cannot quit because in the current economic climate it would not be very easy to find another job, you are on a desert crossing. Technically, desert crossings are called "chronic" stress.

---

19 Much stress literature terms these "daily hassles" and "major life changes". I find it less arid to call them "bothers" and "earthquakes" instead.

20 "Mobbing" means bullying by a group of people.

More about lightning bolts (aka "acute stress")

When you suddenly realised you had just locked yourself out of your own home, you will have experienced a sudden feeling of alarm, perhaps a lurch in the pit of your stomach, your heart jumping, a bolt of excitement coursing through your body, an impelling need to act. Afterwards, when you have realised how you may resolve the situation without too much hassle (maybe a trusted person has a copy of the key) you feel relief. You may realise you have been perspiring, and it may take a little time for your heart rate to slow down to normal. But return to normal it will, just as it should. For a brief time, you have been under stress, but such brief, immediate responses are essential for survival, both for the individual and for the human race, so they are entirely appropriate in emergency situations.

Acute stress involves short-lived, relatively intense responses to recent events. In general, they are normal and physiological, not pathological. That is, they are not a problem because they serve a purpose. During these reactions some bodily processes are accelerated, and others are damped down:

- The heart beats faster and more powerfully, and the muscle fibres in the walls of the smaller arteries contract, reducing their diameter. The effect of these two changes is to increase blood pressure.

- The airways (bronchi) dilate, allowing more air to pass through.

- Gastrointestinal activity (movement, secretion) is reduced.

- Sweating is increased.

- The body's storage sugar (glycogen) is broken down into glucose, a simple sugar which is the fuel of our cells.[21]

These are the very adaptations we need in an emergency situation. Emergency situations have been called "fight or flight" situations[22]. The urge to show aggression or to escape when faced with a challenge are primitive urges. They are what a wolf, a wildcat or a stag would do. While humans have the mental apparatus to override these urges, the involuntary processes of our bodies still respond to them.

In such situations the body needs to be primed for action. Increased tone and activity of the heart and blood vessels ensure that the muscles and vital organs receive an efficient supply of oxygen and nutrients, and that waste products are quickly cleared from the system. Blood, however, is diverted away from functions with less immediate priority, such as digestion. If you

---

21 The physiological breakdown of complex chemicals to simpler ones in our bodies is called "catabolism".

22 The "fight or flight" response has also sometimes been called "fight, flight or freeze" because "freezing" i.e. suspension of thought and activity, is one response to critical situations. However, it is important to remember that "fight" or "flight" would be adaptive (e.g. life-saving) more often than "freezing", unless of course, you are a possum.

are being chased by a tiger, digesting your own lunch is the least of your priorities, and for the tiger, digestion will happen all in good time (the later the better from your point of view!) You will both be breathing hard as you run, as the blood must take up more oxygen from the lungs and expel more carbon dioxide. Dilated airways allow for the increased flow of air to and from the lungs. Finally, increased breakdown of storage tissues into ready fuels means increased available energy to run with. A by-product will be heat, which needs to be efficiently dissipated by perspiration if your body is not to overheat[23].

Although acute stress responses are generally functional (i.e. good for us), there are occasions in which there is a mismatch between the response and the situation. A response should be proportionate, neither a damp squib nor a wild over-reaction. Disproportionate reactions cause us problems, and are therefore dysfunctional (i.e. potentially bad for us).

Excessively intense reactions can happen if a person has become hyper-sensitive to threat. The saying, "Once bitten, twice shy", sums up this situation nicely. Sensitisation to a threat can have survival value. If you are once bitten by a snake, you would do very well to be wary of snakes in general. But not so dogs, in general. So it does depend upon the context, and our appraisal of the context. To be generally wary of snakes, if we are not a poisonous reptile expert, is a sensible strategy. But to be petrified of all dogs is unreasonable, as well as being disabling, as we will often encounter pet dogs. Sometimes people do become unrealistically sensitive and intensely responsive to mild threats which most people would say should not merit such a reaction.

More about desert crossings (aka "chronic stress")

In medicine and psychology, the word "chronic" means simply that the condition is long-lasting. This contrasts with "acute" conditions. Acute symptoms are intense and relatively short-lived, chronic ones are milder but drawn out. Many illnesses have an acute stage which, if for some reason does not end in resolution, leads to long, drawn-out and less intense illness (chronic illness). Other illnesses are chronic by nature, but may involve periodic acute exacerbations.

---

23 The bodily changes described here are triggered by the activation of two important control systems, one nervous and one hormonal. On the one hand, a part of the nervous system is activated which helps to regulate many bodily processes. It is called the sympathetic nervous system or SNS. The SNS works to regulate these things in concert with its partner, the parasympathetic nervous system (PNS). These two are complementary in that their actions are opposite and balanced according to the needs and priorities of the moment. Together, they comprise the two divisions of the autonomic nervous system (ANS). An example of a bodily change mediated by this system in response to stress is the heart rate. With the heart rate and some other bodily processes, the SNS acts as the accelerator, the PNS as the brake. The alarm we feel when we are acutely stressed activates the SNS, which causes the heart rate to increase. At the same time, adrenaline is released from the inner part (the medulla) of the adrenal glands (secretory organs situated on top of the kidneys). Adrenaline is a hormone, a chemical messenger, which influences physiological processes in much the same way as the SNS. In fact, the SNS and adrenaline potentiate and augment each other's effects.

The same happens with stress. We have discussed acute stress above. It is characterised by intense reactions, which occur in response to sudden emergencies. Chronic stress, on the other hand, involves adaptive responses to ongoing situations which are not going away soon. Typical situations of this kind are an unhappy marriage, mobbing or bullying at work, and debts or other long-term economic pressures.

The bodily adaptations required in these situations differ from those needed in sudden emergencies. When the organism is under constant pressure to perform, to meet extra demands, it requires a constant supply of fuel for energy production, and it needs a means of up-regulating its general responsiveness. Sound complicated? Let me explain. The activation of bodily processes that occurs in acute stress favours the rapid but relatively inefficient breakdown of the body's sugar store (a chemical called glycogen). However, long-term and constant challenge requires longer-lasting, more constant, more efficient energy production. Then, fat stores and muscle tissue have to be broken down to produce fuel (fatty acids and sugars) in the blood, calcium is taken from bone to serve in metabolic reactions, and sodium is retained in the body to increase blood volume and hence help to keep the blood pressure up.

A long-term situation of stress implies that we must always be on at least amber alert. Therefore, to cope with chronic stress the general responsiveness of the body must be up-regulated, so we can respond quickly to the problems we expect to meet. To understand how this works, think of the control switch that sets the temperature of a heating system in a home (the thermostat). You may decide that a room temperature of 18°C is fine during the night when you are tucked up in bed, but that during the day if you are at home you need 21° to be comfortable. So you up-regulate the system using the control switch (or set it to do so automatically) first thing in the morning and down-regulate it at night. Your body has systems to up or down-regulate its processes in a similar way. We could call this system an "activity-stat" instead of a thermostat[24]. Chronic stress requires a resetting of the "activity-stat" for various bodily processes.[25]

Chronic stress responses are still generally functional (that is, appropriately adaptive to the situation), but they are a "Plan B". Plan A was to resolve the situation quickly. If this cannot be done, we resort to Plan B. Plan B is not as satisfactory as Plan A: it is a "least-worst" strategy involving bodily changes which are quite costly in terms of energy and "wear and tear". The organism under chronic stress can be compared to a car engine running on an over-fine fuel

---

24 Technically this process is called "allostasis". While homoeostasis refers to the regulation in response to second-by-second changes, allostasis refers to the long-term regulation of homoeostasis itself, in response to long-term changes in the environment.

25 Physiologically, under chronic stress the outer part of the adrenal gland, the cortex, secretes more of its steroid hormones. Cortisol is one of these, sometimes known as the "stress hormone", part of whose function is to ensure the prolonged and regular provision of resources. One such action is to keep blood sugar levels raised. Another function which is up-regulated is the baseline tone of the sympathetic nervous system (SNS).

mix: you have to use more throttle to achieve the same power, the engine overheats, and its components wear out sooner.

Selye's General Adaptation Syndrome

Nobody knows the trouble you've seen because stress is as varied as are people. But a useful idea has been developed which can explain all of them and that can be written on the back of a postcard.

I have mentioned previously the name of Hans Selye, the physiologist who did ground-breaking work on stress. In 1936 he described the generalities of the body's response to stress, which he would go on to name the *General Adaptation Syndrome* (or *GAS)*. The GAS model proposes three stages of physiological stress, as outlined in the table below.

In the light of the preceding paragraphs we can now see that what Selye was describing are our responses to lightning bolts and desert crossings (acute and chronic stress). While Selye was principally interested in bodily responses, the same general scheme is equally valid for mental ones. The names are apt: we feel alarmed by a sudden threat, long-term difficulties test our stamina (another word for our capacity for resistance), and we may feel mentally and physically exhausted by the effort of living with stress for long periods.

A common misconception is that stages 2 and 3 are inevitable results of the previous stages: they are not. If a challenging situation is quickly resolved, there will be no need for "resistance". Similarly, exhaustion is not an inevitable result of chronic stress, because life circumstances may change, eliminating the stress, or your abilities to deal with stress may improve. However, there is little doubt that unresolved chronic stress shortens life. The exhaustion phase, if there is no recuperation, results in serious illness and/or early death either from that illness or generally accelerated ageing.

I think rather than to call these three phases of stress "stages", it will be better for us to call them "modes". That is because "stages" suggests a linear process that proceeds uninterrupted over time. However, it is not so clear cut. It is a common thing for people to be under chronic stress but to experience periods of heightened stress over and above that baseline. In that case their bodies and minds are "resisting" the ongoing situation but during short periods of heightened stress they produce "alarm" responses. They are not hopping from one "stage" to another, but they are displaying different modes of coping at different times, according to the circumstances.

General Adaptation Syndrome		
Stage	**Name**	**Description**
1	Alarm	Response to a short-lived emergency: "fight or flight" reactions.
2	Resistance	Adaptation to long-term demands: prolonged bodily changes.
3	Exhaustion	The body's adaptive capacity is exceeded due to exhaustion of resources, and wear and tear.

Table 4.1: The General Adaptation Syndrome

The problem of the mind

At this point one might ask, "Much of this chapter refers to the *body's* responses, but what about my emotions and thoughts? If I am emotionally stressed but there is no physical danger to me, why should my body change?"

One answer is that, in fact, the body-mind response is integrated and coordinated. Whenever challenges, whether physical, emotional or social, are perceived by the brain, responses are produced simultaneously in different spheres: bodily (e.g. increased cardiovascular tone), mental (e.g. anxiety) and behavioural (e.g. seeking help). The regulation of the body by the mind is mediated by deep and ancient parts of the brain[26], which communicate with the body through the hormonal and nervous systems. Generally, the psychological, physical and behavioural changes will all be geared towards the same general plan: fight, fly or resist.

We could argue, "But is it always coordinated in the right way for all circumstances? Why should my heart beat fast when I have an argument with my boss? I do not need to hit him or run away. I need to stay calm and think clearly."

Yes, and one problem is that the organism does not distinguish very well between different kinds and sources of stress. That is why Selye called his model the *General* Adaptation Syndrome: it describes a general, universal kind of response to *stress of all kinds*. During the great majority of our evolutionary time-span, up until relatively recently, concrete and physical sources of stress have posed a far greater threat to our survival and that of our species than psychological ones. Put simply, our ancient automatic stress responses have not had sufficient time to evolve more nuanced biological responses to modern life. And that is why psychosocial sources of stress can make us physically ill.

---

26 The hypothalamus and the brain stem.

Fortunately, there is a way to make up for this evolutionary peculiarity and circumvent automatic but inappropriate responses. The ways to do that are called thinking and learning, and happily, evolution has also provided us with some awesome thinking and learning equipment.

Main points

- Nobody knows the trouble you've seen. Your own experience of stress is unique.

- Contexts in which stress develops can be daily hassles ("bothers") or major life-changing events ("earthquakes").

- Stress may be sudden and intense ("lightning bolts") or long and drawn out but less intense ("desert crossings").

- Selye's *General Adaptation Syndrome* describes three stages of stress: alarm, resistance and exhaustion. We shall call them "modes".

- Stress involves mental, physical and behavioural changes.

5. Does stress affect our health?

Good stress, bad stress - Emphasising the positive - Function of stress - Why things go wrong - Some physiology - Effects of stress - What makes the difference?

> *Peril, loneliness, an uncertain future, are not oppressive evils, so long as the frame is healthy and the faculties are employed; so long, especially, as Liberty lends us her wings, and Hope guides us by her star.*
>
> - Charlotte Brontë (1816-1885)

Stress can be both positive and negative

We have said that stress may have both beneficial and harmful effects. It is important to know that our responses to stress potentially have survival value. If we find ourselves in a hazardous or risky situation, we may need to take rapid action or make an instant decision. The mental and bodily effects of acute stress help us to do these things. They can make the difference between life and death, success and failure, and all the less dramatic consequences in between. Moreover, in achieving successful outcomes in our endeavours, even in the face of adversity, we become more competent at the art of living and are therefore more likely to live fulfilling, meaningful lives. In that case we can say that the stress response is adaptive and functional. But if our mental and bodily responses to a situation are excessive, insufficient or inappropriate, that value for our survival and fulfilment is compromised, even to the point of being harmful to us.

Long-term stress - the kind of stress we are mainly concerned with in this book - is adaptive, too, and so from one point of view could be said to be "positive". Yet here as well, it is a question of degree: the degree to which we are able (or feel we are able) to meet the challenges continually facing us. Very often, a small mismatch over a long period of time is found to be wearing on both body or mind. If that happens, chronic stress has harmful effects.

Emphasising the positive

A new aspect of stress has been proposed which is called the stress mindsets theory[27] [28]. A mindset is a set of beliefs about a subject.

> *One's stress mindset... (is) ...the extent to which one holds the belief that stress has enhancing consequences for various stress-related outcomes... (referred to as a*

---

27   Crum AJ, Salovey P. 2013. Rethinking Stress: The Role of Mindsets in Determining the Stress Response J Pers Soc Psychol. 104(4):716-33.

28   McGonigal K. 2015. Op. cit. (Footnote 5.)

"stress-is-enhancing mindset") or holds the belief that stress has debilitating consequences for those outcomes (referred to as a "stress-is-debilitating mindset").

(Crum and Salovey, 2013[29])

The "outcomes" that Crum and Salovey refer to include performance and productivity, health and well-being, and learning and growth. Their research suggests that the stress-is-enhancing mindset is associated with fewer psychological symptoms and better work performance, that mindsets can be changed rapidly by simple interventions and that a change to a stress-is-enhancing mindset brings positive changes in mental well-being and work performance. They further found that this positive effect seems to be produced both by changes in behaviour and changes in the way the body responds to stress.

In simple terms, they suggest that if you think that stress is good for you, you are less likely to be affected negatively by it, and more likely to experience positive consequences from it.

The researchers acknowledge that this is not the "be all and end all" of it, but it is one factor that influences how we respond to stress. The take-home message is that a positive attitude helps, including a positive attitude to your stress, remembering that it has a function and is there for a reason, and if channelled well, can be enhancing to one's life.

A major part of this book is about changing mindsets, in terms of a change in our beliefs and attitudes to adversity in life. Which, let's face it, is going to be a constant challenge whatever our role in life!

Function

The word "function" will pop up in different guises throughout this book. It refers to the purpose of something. To say our stress is of functional value is to say it has a purpose. How is that?

Human beings have evolved over millions of years, and for most of that time we have been subject to unmitigated natural selection. What does natural selection mean? In a nutshell, hereditary characteristics which are harmful to survival and reproduction have tended to become extinct from our species, while those that promote survival and reproduction have multiplied - they have become built into the "standard model" of our time. Our stress response is a product of that selective process: it is the latest version of a system designed to ensure our survival as a species, which in turn requires the survival and reproduction of healthy individuals, hopefully like you and me.

As we have already seen, our responses to acute stress are designed as a rapid reaction system to sudden threats to our life, health, well-being or the people or things we hold dear. Our responses to chronic stress are purpose built to keep us performing reasonably well and in

---

29 Crum AJ, Salovey P. 2013. Op. cit. (Footnote 27.)

health when the demands upon us are persistent. Overcoming challenge is an unavoidable part of life and a necessary part of living a meaningful and fulfilled life. Our stress responses enable us to do this.

Why things sometimes go wrong

So, if there is functional value, how can there be harmful consequences? Let me answer in a few different ways.

We are not perfect beings, not the finished product, and we never will be. Our evolution goes on. The process of natural selection requires that there should be variety in the gene pool of our species. So, for the survival, growth and further evolution of human kind, each human being has to be different. Since we are all different, some people's stress responses will be "better" than other people's in this particular time and place. Moreover, modernisation has vastly changed the demands placed upon us as a species much more rapidly than we can adapt through evolution by natural selection. For these reasons, our individual stress responses are not perfect!

There can be harmful effects if our bodily and psychological responses are not well adjusted to needs. They may be exaggerated or suppressed, or they may not be nuanced enough, not as finely tuned as they might.

The body's adaptation to long-term stress is functional, but that does not mean there are not trade-offs. The main trade-off is one of increased stamina against reduced efficiency and reduced short-term adaptability. We can go on a long time with this trade-off but in the end it can wear us out.

Nevertheless, the fact that these things are influenced by our genes does not mean they cannot be modified. In fact, there is a lot of leeway for change through a process which humans are particularly good at: learning!

This book is mainly about life's desert crossings, that is, the long haul. The chances are that you are reading this because stress has become a problem in your life over the past months or years. You may be finding this experience distressing, and that may be your motivation to change. But do not think that all stress is necessarily unpleasant and harmful, for that is a very long way from the truth.

The rest of this chapter is an optional read. You may choose to read on if you are simply interested, as I am, in how things work. You will read about some of the effects of long term stress, including some of its potential negative health effects. But do not get morbid about it! Bear in mind what I have said: you do not have to experience the negative effects of stress. You are capable by your attitudes and behaviour of protecting yourself from them, and turning your stressful challenges into opportunities to grow.

35

Physiological effects of stress

I want now to delve a little into the workings of the body. First I will introduce the three most important systems that regulate the body's stress response, then we will look at different body systems in turn to see how stress affects them. For each system I will describe in simple terms what changes they undergo when under stress, what is the function of these changes, what are the positive consequences of them, and what are the potentially harmful effects in the long term.

At this point, in order to delve into the workings of the body, I must introduce three technical terms. I have largely banished these beasts to the footnotes and glossary, but this chapter is about the workings of the body (*physiology*) and so a few technical terms are a necessary evil. These refer to things that play such a large role in chronic stress that it will make our lives easier if we just bring them on stage here without further ado. So, ladies and gentlemen, a big round of applause, I give you:

- The sympathetic nervous system, aka SNS;
- Adrenaline;
- The corticosteroid hormones.

The sympathetic nervous system (SNS)

In a nutshell:

- The SNS stimulates various bodily processes and inhibits others.
- In general, it prepares the body for action.
- It works in concert with its sister, the parasympathetic nervous system *(PNS)*, which produces broadly the opposite effects.
- Together the SNS and the PNS form the autonomic nervous system *(ANS)*, one of the major involuntary control systems of the body.
- The SNS is activated when we feel excited, threatened or under pressure.

Adrenaline

We all know the feeling of a jolt of adrenaline, for example when we are suddenly frightened by something or we think of something that makes us anxious. In a nutshell:

- Adrenaline is a hormone (a chemical messenger) secreted by the inner part (the medulla) of the adrenal glands, which are situated at the top of the kidneys.
- It acts to stimulate much the same bodily processes as those stimulated by the SNS.
- Adrenaline and the SNS each make the body more sensitive to the effects of the other.

- Adrenaline is released into the blood stream when we feel, excited, threatened or under pressure.

- Adrenaline is most important in situations requiring rapid, emergency responses.

Corticosteroids

In a nutshell:

- Corticosteroids are hormones (chemical messengers) secreted by the outer part (the cortex) of the adrenal glands.

- One of these hormones is cortisol, the "stress hormone".

- Corticosteroid hormones act to provide a ready supply of chemical resources to the body. The sugar glucose, required as a fuel for energy production, is one such resource.

- Corticosteroids are released into the blood stream when the organism is stressed.

- Corticosteroids are especially important in long-term stress.

The body's stress response involves heightened reactivity of the SNS, and increased levels of corticosteroid hormones in the blood. The autonomic nervous system (of which the SNS is one division) and the hormones[30], form parts of the basic control systems of human physiology, and their actions and repercussions are multi-system and body-wide.

Let us now look at some of the physiological effects of heightened activity of the SNS and the stress hormones, system by system.

Brain and nerves

Bodily changes

An increased reactivity of nerve cells in the brain concerned with attention goes hand and hand with stress.

Function and positive effects

The function of this is to increase our level of attention in relation to a challenging or threatening situation. This can have survival value in dangerous situations. It can allow us to perform better in challenging tasks, and it facilitates learning.

Long-term disadvantages

One disadvantage is that the heightened state of alert can develop into a habit of continual worry (chronic anxiety). Then it can persistently recur, especially when triggered by things

---

30 The hormones and the glands which secrete them form what is called the "endocrine system".

(people, places, events, situations) that we associate with a threat, even when here and now there is no real threat.

Anxiety can also become generalised from a specific context in which it was first experienced, to the whole range of even very mildly challenging situations. Moreover, it can become disproportionate: for example, do you know people who (or do you yourself?) jump whenever the telephone rings?

Long-term anxiety is a frequent cause of insomnia. Good quality sleep is fundamental for our general psychological and physical well-being. Disturbed or poor quality sleep leads to daytime tiredness, poor concentration, fatigue and increased vulnerability to further stress.

Long-term anxiety can also lead to depression, with its attendant withdrawal and sadness. Both anxiety and depression are often accompanied by a host of physical symptoms for which there is no specific medical diagnosis. These can occur due to a psychological mechanism in which emotional unease is transformed into symptoms felt in the body[31]. Symptoms can occur too, due to biological mechanisms such as increased sensitivity to pain, defensive muscle contraction and postural changes.

In anxiety and depression, increased sensitivity to pain occurs because of changes in the levels of various signalling chemicals[32] in the nerve fibres which carry pain information to the brain, and which relay that information within the brain itself. The brain is essentially a highly concentrated and organised bundle of nerve cells. Nerves carry information. The information conveyed by nerves includes signals that a tissue is under strain or damaged. The brain processes this information and, according to its gravity and meaning, may or may not produce a sensation of pain. The sensitivity of the nerve fibres in the body which convey this kind of information is regulated by the brain, and this regulation is in turn affected by the balance of the different signalling chemicals in the brain.

Chronic stress can also cause changes in appetite (either a decrease or an increase), leading either to weight loss or weight gain, either of which may exacerbate other problems. Weight loss will cause feelings of lacking energy, while excessive weight is a contributory factor in various health conditions such as heart disease, high blood pressure, diabetes, and osteoarthritis.

The long-term heightened activity of the SNS which occurs when we are chronically stressed is costly. It favours the breaking down of the body's tissues to produce ready energy sources[33]. Over the long term, if the body is not to waste away, the systems that build up the body[34] must be up-regulated, too, in order to balance things out. In effect the whole cycle of building up and breaking down, or *turnover*, is accelerated. As explained above, the SNS has a sister, the PNS, which acts in opposite ways to the SNS. The PNS favours building up the body, and its activity

31 This is called "somatisation".
32 "Neurotransmitters".
33 A process called "catabolism".
34 "Anabolism", the opposite of catabolism.

38

ideally should complement and balance that of its hyperactive sister. But a problem occurs because while the balance between the two is naturally sensitive and precise when both are functioning at normal (i.e. unstressed) levels, it becomes less so when both are under increased demands. Thus, all of the bodily processes which these systems control can become less well regulated: heart function, blood pressure, and digestion, to name but three. Symptoms that may be experienced include palpitations (the awareness of the heart beating heavily while at rest), unstable blood pressure, frequent abdominal bloating, and constipation.

Finally, cortisol, a corticosteroid hormone from the adrenal glands, is released into the blood stream in increased amounts when the individual is chronically stressed. Research has shown that long-term exposure to high levels of cortisol permanently affects certain areas of the brain, leading to a decline in intellectual capacity and memory.

Muscles, bones and joints

Bodily changes and their functions

A dog showing aggression will raise its hackles. This is a natural, defensive reaction for mammals (of which humans are one species) to tense the muscles of their shoulders, neck and jaw when they are in aggressive, fearful or anxious mood. This serves two purposes: firstly, to pre-tense the muscles needed for action, especially defence or attack, in case they are needed for rapid deployment; and secondly to send a signal to a potential adversary, "Watch out!" or "Don't hurt me!"

Long-term disadvantages

Modern humans are not wild animals and bare aggression is no longer an acceptable or useful form of human interaction in most peacetime situations. However, this evolutionary trait remains with us. In the chronically stressed person it can cause upper back and neck pain, shoulder problems, headaches, jaw and dental problems.

Why dental problems? Some people have a tendency to tense their jaw muscles, clench or grind their teeth while sleeping, and this tendency increases with anxiety. In the long term this can result in worn or broken teeth, asymmetrical closure of the jaws (e.g. while chewing food), and problems with the joints of the jaw joints just in front of the ears.

Long-term tension in the neck and jaw muscles promotes and accelerates degeneration of the joints as they have to work under compressive forces. The result is osteoarthritis of the spinal joints, reduced space between the vertebrae, degeneration and rupture of the disks between the vertebrae, and osteoarthritis or damage to the cartilage in the jaw joint.

Postural changes typically occurring in the neck and upper body as a result of tensing the muscles involved in the stress response include: carrying the shoulders high, rounding of the shoulders, carrying the head projected forwards and sunk into the shoulders. These changes, too, promote wear and tear of the spinal joints as well as of the tendons around the shoulder joints.

No postural change anywhere in the body leaves the rest of the body unaltered, as postural compensations occur to make sure we stay capable of standing more or less upright and straight. Your head is heavy - around 4.5 Kg - and if it were carried forwards without something else happening elsewhere its weight would cause you to topple forwards onto your face! The compensations are different in the short and long term. In the latter case, commonly the middle of the back develops an excessive forwards curve[35] and the bottom of your back an exaggerated backwards one[36], amongst other changes. I have already explained that a compensation is a "Plan B", a "least-worst" resolution, that brings with it some disadvantages. In the case of the musculoskeletal system these are increased mechanical stress, susceptibility to strain, and accelerated wear.

In the previous chapter, we mentioned how cortisol provides increased blood calcium for use in metabolism. Where does it get it from? It removes it from the body's calcium store, the skeleton. This may result in weak bones (osteoporosis). Osteoporosis is not strictly a disease of calcium metabolism, it is a disease of bone metabolism as a whole. The latter involves the maintenance of a protein matrix which is hardened by calcium phosphate and also contains many other minerals. But it seems that chronically high cortisol levels do promote the global weakening of bone. Although mild to moderate osteoporosis usually causes no pain, it renders the individual at increased risk from bone fractures should she or he fall or have an accident. Such fractures chiefly affect the spine, the hip and the wrist. Those involving the former two can be particularly devastating.

Heart and blood circulation

Bodily changes and their functions

Stress affects the heart and blood vessels in two main ways: it increases the heart rate and it raises the blood pressure. Increased activity of the SNS makes the heart beat faster and more powerfully. Blood pressure is raised by the combined effects of the SNS and the hormones from the adrenal cortex. Increased activity and tone of the heart and blood circulation supplies the blood needed for the increased muscle activity that may be necessary in situations requiring a physical response.

In addition, long-term stress increases cholesterol production by the body. It is known that cholesterol is used in the production by the body of cortisol. Interestingly, this raises the

---

35 "Hyperkyphosis".
36 "Hyperlordosis".

possibility, though unconfirmed, that high cholesterol may actually be a functional adaptation to chronic stress.

Both stress and anxiety seem to increase the blood's tendency to clot. More rapid blood clotting may be an advantage in situations of danger which present the risk of physical injury.

Long-term disadvantages

Increased reactivity of the heart may be experienced as a thumping sensation in the chest, known as palpitations. These are generally harmless. However, if you are otherwise predisposed (for example genetically or due to congenital defects or previous heart disease), you might experience disturbances of the rhythm of the heartbeat[37], which can be serious.

High cholesterol levels have long been considered a risk factor for heart disease, while an increased tendency of the blood to clot is a known trigger of heart attacks.

High blood pressure and sticky blood raise the risk of suffering a stroke either from a bleed in the brain or from a blockage, caused by a clot, of the blood supply to a part of the brain.

Guts

Bodily changes and their functions

The gastrointestinal tract is particularly sensitive to stress. In situations of acute stress relating to some urgent challenge, SNS activity shuts down digestive processes such as gastrointestinal movement and the secretion of digestive juices. In such situations, the body selects action as the priority, not digestion, so important resources like blood flow and nerve traffic are switched away from the digestive organs to other, priority organs - the brain, the muscles, the airways and lungs.

Long-term disadvantages

In long-term stress, of course, digestive function must continue. For this to happen some degree of balance between the SNS and the PNS must be restored. Nevertheless, frequently the high degree of balance necessary for the precise control and coordination of digestive function according to hour-by-hour needs is disturbed. The result then is chronic disorder of digestive function, altered gut flora, and reduced regenerative capacity.

Together, these effects may cause chronic symptoms such as heartburn, bloating, constipation, and irritable bowel syndrome, and may lead to intestinal yeast overgrowth (candida infection), food intolerances, gastrointestinal inflammation (gastritis, inflammatory bowel disease) and ulceration (such as gastric or duodenal ulcers).

---

37   "Cardiac arrhythmia".

It is common knowledge that our diet affects our health, but it is also true that the healthy digestion of the food we eat is essential to overall health. Altered gut function has a major influence on the health of the whole organism. It may result, on the one hand, in the disturbed passage of essential nutrients from the gut into the blood stream, and on the other, in the abnormal entry into the blood stream of large, potentially damaging molecules which should normally have been broken down more completely before passing through the intestinal wall. The latter may be responsible for food allergies and intolerances.

Breathing

Bodily changes and their functions

An immediate consequence of acute stress on breathing is the opening of the airways. This is to allow the passage of more air if strenuous activity is required, and in those scenarios it will be accompanied by deeper, faster breathing. Airway dilatation is a temporary phenomenon, which will usually return to normal after the emergency has passed, even in cases of prolonged background stress.

In normal, relaxed breathing, the main muscle working to suck air into the lungs is the diaphragm. However, during strenuous activity, more air must be taken in by the lungs to provide more oxygen for the body's tissues, especially the muscles. To achieve this, accessory muscles of breathing are recruited, including those at the front and sides of the neck. These neck muscles pull the upper chest upwards during inhalation to increase the vertical dimension of the thorax. When we experience anxiety, our stress response leads the body to prepare for action. A part of this involves activation of these accessory muscles of breathing.

Long-term disadvantages

With chronic stress the heightened activation of the accessory breathing muscles at the front and sides of the neck may become a constant habit. Upper chest breathing, when there is no concurrent need for deep breaths (such as in intense physical activity), creates a pattern of shallow, rapid breathing. There are two common consequences: neck and upper back pain, and hyperventilation.

Neck and upper back pain occurs because the muscles at the front of the neck pull the neck and head forward and down, changing the posture, compressing the vertebral joints and limiting mobility.

Hyperventilation occurs when the pattern of breathing results in more oxygen in the blood stream than the body needs. If this happens an imbalance occurs between the different respiratory gases in the blood[38], with the result that the blood and body tissues tend to become very slightly more alkaline than normal. This change in blood chemistry can result in a variety

---

38 Hyperventilation results in an increase in oxygen and a decrease in carbon dioxide in the blood.

of physical symptoms, symptoms which may induce feelings of alarm and anxiety. This feeds an ongoing vicious cycle involving stress, anxiety and hyperventilation.

In certain individuals, predisposed either by their genes, their past experiences or their environment, stress can provoke airway constriction rather than dilatation, producing the laboured breathing characteristic of asthma.

The immune system

Bodily changes and their functions

It has been demonstrated that short-term stress can enhance our immune capabilities and responses. This is a clear advantage in emergency situations where we might suffer a physical injury, putting us at risk of infection.

Long-term disadvantages

But equally, it is fairly well-established that long-term stress can suppress our protective immune responses and exacerbate abnormal ones. As a result, we can be more prone to infections, inflammation and auto-immune diseases[39].

Other effects

The hormone cortisol is released into the blood stream in increased amounts when the individual is chronically stressed. Two fundamental things about the hormonal system of the body are that (a) if we change one component of it, the whole system changes; and (b) it interacts intimately with the body's other major control systems: the nervous system and the immune system. From this we can deduce that the effects of stress must be very wide-ranging. As we have emphasised, these changes are functional if well-adjusted and in the right contexts.

Nevertheless, science strongly indicates that chronic negative stress can increase our susceptibility to disease in general. The effects of chronic stress in the body are like an engine being revved hard. It wears out more quickly, so long-term stress can cause early ageing and greater ill health.

Stress also changes our behaviour. There are beneficial stress behaviours and detrimental ones. This will be explored in later chapters. Suffice here to say that some stress behaviours lead directly or indirectly to ill-health: behaviours such as drinking, smoking or eating excessively, becoming obsessive about work or avoidance of social contact.

---

39 Diseases in which the body's immune system attacks the body's own tissues. Some examples are rheumatoid arthritis, thyroiditis, diabetes, multiple sclerosis, and Crohn's disease.

Loss of libido is a frequent result of chronic stress. Other kinds of sexual problems, such as impotence in men and, in women, pain during intercourse, are thought to be frequently related to stress.

What makes the difference?

Sometimes stress can be enhancing to our lives, other times it can be damaging. So what makes the difference? There may be things that to a greater or lesser extent lie outside our control, like the kinds of events that happen to us. But, there are other important things which we can control. I would say there are two main things in that category. The first is our beliefs and attitudes with regard to our situation in life and with regard to the events which happen to us. The second is with what attitude and by what means we respond to these things. Our beliefs, attitudes and behaviour can not only be protective against the negative consequences of stress, but can also be enhancing in our striving to achieve our goals in life in the face of the inevitable adversity which we will meet. They make the difference between adversity being treated as a threat, a demand, a challenge, or an opportunity. Think about that. You will read about many of the things that can make that difference in this book, things that, crucially, are under your control!

It matters not how strait the gate,

How charged with punishments the scroll,

I am the master of my fate:

I am the captain of my soul.

- William Ernest Henley (1849-1903), *Invictus*

Main points

- Stress can enhance or harm.
- The bodily effects of stress are regulated by our hormones and by the nervous system.
- Bodily and mental responses to stress have biological and evolutionary purpose.
- But ill health can be generated by long-term stress.
- Our beliefs, attitudes and behaviour can make the difference between experiencing the negative effects of stress, and enjoying meaningful, fulfilling lives.

Part 2: Getting to know your stress

6. Getting to know your stress

Stress symptoms, contexts, responses – Describing your stress – Sensations, emotions, thoughts, behaviours – A stress diary

Formidable is that enemy that lies hid in a man's own breast.

- Publilius Syrus (85-43 BC)

Know thyself.

- Delphic maxim

Being under too much stress is a disagreeable experience. Most people associate stress with demands placed upon them, yet demands in themselves are not a bad thing, they are not necessarily "the enemy". They just have to be managed well. Moreover, fundamentally the experience of stress is part and parcel of a series of mental, bodily and behavioural responses intended to protect us. They often have to make the best of a bad job in doing this, because we do not possess or have not learned to use the kinds of responses that would do a better job. So we have to work with our stress responses to find better solutions. Learn from them. Make them our friends, rather than our enemies.

Getting to know your stress is the first essential step towards finding better solutions to manage challenges more effectively. Just as when interacting with another person, it is essential to take into account their character and behaviour patterns, the same is true of managing your stress. Your stress has its character and behaviour patterns, too! Getting to know your stress means:

1. Identifying the things that indicate you are stressed. We could call them your *stress symptoms*. These may be emotions, particular kinds of thoughts, certain behaviour patterns, or bodily sensations.

2. Identifying the kinds of situations in which these symptoms readily occur. We could call these your *stress contexts*: the kinds of situations, the places, and the people which trigger your stress.

3. Identifying the ways in which you consciously or unconsciously try to deal with your stress. These are your *stress responses* or *coping responses*. They are the kinds of responses that you make that are in some way aimed at reducing the impact of the stressful situation or the stress itself.

Talking to your stress

To get to know our stress we face an obstacle which is a bit of a paradox. In order to understand our stress, we have to regard it as a human experience (associated with feelings and habits) rather than just an idea in the abstract. But at the same time we need to distance ourselves from it a little so we can see it at least a little objectively. This is exactly the stance a therapist tries to take when interacting with clients: empathy but distance at the same time. But here you are your own therapist. How are you to manage it? Some people who suffer from depression have called their depression "Black Dog". In doing that they are doing just that personal-but-removed thing I am talking about. They have given it a name which describes its character, but they distance themselves by making it into something outside themselves: a dog. We can do something similar with stress.

So as an interesting exercise, let us imagine that stress is a person. This person has his/her own character, personality and behaviour traits. Let us try to find out about them in order to understand him or her as fully as we can.

Shall we first give him or her a name? Try to choose a name which characterises his or her principle trait. I will call mine "Demanding", because a lot of my stress has come from self-imposed demands. Your stress may have the same name, or another name, you must choose according to the characteristics of *your* stress. He/she may be male or female, as you prefer.

I ask myself: What is Demanding like? What brings him around? How do I know when he is around? What emotions does he feel? What physical sensations does he experience? What does he think? What does he do? When Demanding comes around, I watch him and listen to what he says. I ask him what brought him around. I ask myself: Is he being reasonable or unreasonable? If he is being unreasonable, I challenge him. I ask him why he is behaving like that. What is he feeling? What is he thinking?

I suggest you write it all down. Here is my example:

> *Let me tell you what I found out about Demanding. Demanding hates disorder and unfinished business, and is a stickler for detail. Therefore, he is constantly at me to put things in order and get things done. He nags, he cajoles, he threatens, he blusters, he bullies, he whines. I think he is actually afraid that his life will spin chaotically out of control if he does not attend to these things, NOW. And if there is one thing he cannot tolerate, it is chaos. It gives him an intolerable sense of angst and tension in his upper body. He feels as though his very fibre is being pulled apart with rusty probes. I must admit it has been useful on occasion having Demanding around, the time, for example, when having been lax about my cash flow, any further laxity would have led to serious economic consequences for myself and my family. Demanding got me out of that. Nevertheless, he has gained an*

inflated sense of his importance in my life, and he exaggerates and catastrophises when he fears he might not get his way. Demanding has a lot to do, as by way of circumstance, he associates with a person who has an inordinately creative mind (me), always coming up with some new idea or interest which needs investigating or developing NOW. Demanding doesn't want to allow any idea, interest, or task, to fall by the wayside. He is not very good at seeing that some of them aren't really important. To him, all have equal importance, that is, they must be attended to before the day is done. I remember a time when I had a two-year break from Demanding (after a breakdown and a new love), but he gradually insinuated himself back into my life. He still comes around, but he isn't so troublesome now as before, as I have learned how to deal with him better. Sometimes I persuade him he's wrong, sometimes I come to terms with him, sometimes I show him the door. Also he has become mellower, more understanding, somewhat less demanding. He no longer reduces me to tears of frustration.

When you do this exercise, be sure not to make the mistake of imagining that your stress, the one you are about to give a name, is the thing or person that triggers your stress. Do not give him or her your boss's name, for example. Do not call him or her "Money", referring to your difficult personal finances. What you need to do is take *your* responses - the feelings, sensations, thoughts and behaviour that you associate with your stress - and characterise *them* with a name.

There are situations where we may justifiably find that our stress actually *is* being entirely reasonable. But they are more likely to be situations of acute stress due to recent events. Remember, here we are more concerned with chronic negative stress of the kind that blights our life day by day over a long period. There can be few situations of this kind, if any, where more realistic attitudes and responses to the perceived sources of stress would not improve our life quality.

Remember too, this is only an exercise: "Demanding" isn't really a person separate from my own being, and neither is your stress. But it has been useful to write about your stress in the third person, hasn't it?

Now let's look at a more methodical way to achieve the three points listed above - identifying your stress symptoms, stress contexts, and coping responses. First of all, we have to know what kinds of things we are looking for. What are the physical symptoms commonly associated with stress? What are the emotions? What are the thoughts and behaviour patterns?

Stress sensations

Some of the physical and other sensations you might feel when your stress level rises are:

- Feeling your heart beating strongly or rapidly[40].
- Sweating.
- Tension in the shoulders, neck, head, face, jaw.
- Headache.
- Increased sensitivity to pain.
- Tightness in the chest.
- Abdominal symptoms (bloating, internal discomfort or pain).
- Nausea.
- Feeling a "knot" in the throat.
- Dry mouth.
- Dizziness.
- Feeling hot.
- Pins and needles.
- Difficulty concentrating and poor memory.

Some symptoms[41] of stress may be chronic and always present to some degree, but they may be exacerbated by stressful situations. Others may be largely absent and only occur with increased stress. Typically, your symptoms of stress will always be the same, according to your make up, and each person has their own pattern. In the long term though, your pattern may gradually change, with new symptoms cropping up and staying, and old ones either dying out or worsening. Symptoms of chronic stress may be related to a recognised disease process, like morning headaches in high blood pressure, or abdominal pain in the presence of a stomach ulcer. Clearly symptoms such as these require medical assessment. When you have been under a lot of stress for a long time, symptoms of "exhaustion" may occur such as a feeling of persistent tiredness, depression, continual inflammations in various parts of the body, shifting aches and pains, recurrent infections, general lack of energy and poor health.

---

40 The medical term for feeling your heart beating in your chest is "palpitations".

41 Stress-related sensations are "symptoms" of stress. By definition, a sensation related to a condition is a symptom of it.

Stress emotions

The most common emotional symptoms of stress are those associated with anxiety. Anxiety most frequently manifests itself emotionally as feelings such as tension, fear, irritability, hostility, being "under pressure", being overwhelmed, panic. People who have a tendency to depression may experience exacerbations when under stress, with feelings of sadness, blunting of the emotions and a desire to withdraw.

Stress thoughts

I have written below a rather random list of common thoughts that people think when they are stressed:

- "This is an absolute disaster."
- "I just cannot cope."
- "I just don't know what to do."
- "I must do something to solve this problem."
- "I must not put myself in these situations."
- "I've got to get out of here now."
- "I'm responsible for this."
- "I'm just not going to think about it."
- "There's no point in worrying about it."
- "The world is against me."
- "The world is a bastard."
- "There's no point in trying to do anything about it, it won't do any good."
- "I'm going to get drunk / smoke some weed."
- "I must ask for help."
- "I must find out how I can best respond to this."
- "I have to put my thoughts in order."
- "I've got to get a grip / pull myself together."
- "Please God, help me."
- "We'll see about that... right now!"
- "I'll sleep on it."

Many or all of these thoughts may be appropriate in one situation but inappropriate, unhelpful or counterproductive in another. Context is everything. If you said, "This is an absolute disaster", just because you had lost your wallet, it would in most cases be an exaggeration. If your house fell down during the night, the thought would be more justified. As an exercise, before reading further, look down the list again and see if you can think of different situations in which each thought would or would not be appropriate.

Doing this, it may have occurred to you that these thoughts can also be expressed with different moods. One could say, "This is an absolute disaster", in an exaggerated way in a joking mood or in frustrated exasperation, or in horror at the enormity of a truly devastating event. Look again at the other thoughts and consider how their meanings could change according to the mood in which they are spoken.

Let us take a situation in which you are worried about money in your domestic economy. For as long as you can remember you have had money worries. You have never quite been able to pay for everything you have to pay for on the money you earn. This has led to a slow bleed of your financial resources, taking you gradually but inexorably further and further into debt. Then another large bill comes in which you will not be able to pay. Think about the thoughts in the above list in relation to this situation.

- Which of them might help you feel better in the short term?
- Which of them might help you improve your situation in the longer term?
- Knowing yourself as you do, which of them would *you* think?

Stress behaviours

Behaviour derives from emotions and thoughts. If you feel frightened, you freeze or you run away. That is, unless your thoughts take over and you can see, even in a split second, a better response and are able to act upon it. But behaviour is often "automatic", that is, you produce habitual, stereotypical responses to given kinds of situations.

Some instinctive behaviours powered by sudden emotions can be lifesaving in situations of immediate danger because they happen faster than we can consciously think. However, if similar behaviours are habitually repeated as "knee jerk reactions" to any sudden or unexpected event, they may not actually be appropriate for the contexts in which they are produced. Then they become obstacles to the positive resolution of problem situations. We can say that such behaviours are dysfunctional, that is, detrimental to overall functioning.

Not only habits, but also consciously chosen behaviours, may be dysfunctional. One way in which a consciously chosen behaviour may be dysfunctional is when its goal is to satisfy short term desires instead of providing for long-term needs, when the latter would be more useful. Often the steps necessary to achieve these different goals can be in direct conflict.

You may have realised by now that there are stress-related thoughts and behaviours that are actually useful in managing stress, and others that are not useful, or that may even be counter-productive. These need to be changed, and the first step necessary in order to do that is to recognise them.

How to identify your stress symptoms, emotions, thoughts and behaviours

If you keep aware, after a while of observation, already with the information you have been given you should be able to recognise and describe how stress affects you physically and emotionally, and what kinds of thoughts and behaviour are typical for you when you are stressed.

However, as well as this informal awareness, a highly useful technique is to use a diary for a while to record your responses to stress methodically and systematically. The pages of the diary are best organised into a table with rows and columns. An example of such a diary is shown overleaf. It is quite self-explanatory, except for a note about the last two columns. What you do when you are stressed is usually motivated by a desire to feel less stress. This will give you a clue as to how to fill in the last two columns: What did you do to make yourself feel better? And how did you think those actions would help?

You need to keep this diary for at least a week, recording all the occasions in which your stress level rises above level 1. When you have done this, read through it carefully and see if you can see any patterns in it:

- What physical sensations and emotions did you experience when you were stressed?
- What were the triggers for your stress responses?
- What sorts of thoughts did you think in stressful situations?
- Typically, what actions did you take when you were stressed?
- Why did you take those actions?

With this new knowledge, you are in an excellent position to begin to reduce the impact of stress in your life.

Main Points

- You cannot change your stress without first knowing your stress.
- Knowing your stress means knowing:
  - What triggers it.
  - What you feel when you are stressed.

- What kinds of thoughts you have when you are stressed.
- What things you tend to do when you are stressed.
- This knowledge will allow you to change.

Date	Time	Situation (people, place, context)	Stress level (0 - 5)*	Emotions	Sensations	Thoughts	What did I do about it?	Why?
27th March	8:00 till 13:00	Myself, at home. Have to teach a seminar this afternoon with people I don't know.	3	Anxiety. Regret.	A sort of tension in my chest and upper abdomen.	I don't want to do this. I wish I hadn't taken it on. I'm not going to do it again. I'm not cut out for this. I'm not up to it.	Spent all morning worrying about it. Spent all morning going over my lesson.	I am trying to reassure myself. I am afraid of making a mistake, so I am spending as much time as possible on preparation.

* 0 = No appreciable stress; 1 = Slight stress; 2 = Moderate stress; 3 = A fair degree of stress; 4 = Quite a lot of stress; 5 = Severe stress.

Table 6.1: Example of a stress diary

7. Troubleshooter or worrier?

Troubleshooter or Worrier – Meaning of coping – Ways of coping – Four types – Same methods, different results? - Your world within

Escape from it, ignore it, fall down and cry about it, yield to it, worry about it, blame someone for it, accept it, make friends with it, act upon it. Which costs least and which offers most?

- Anonymous

Are you a Worrier or a Troubleshooter?

The Troubleshooter confronts an issue and uses strategy to overcome it. The Worrier does nothing about it and continues to worry.

The Troubleshooter faces up to fear. The Worrier is controlled by fear.

The Troubleshooter is a problem-solver. The Worrier thinks endlessly about his or her fears.

The Troubleshooter is active and engages his or her problems. The Worrier is passive and avoids proper engagement.

The Troubleshooter foresees a positive outcome and works towards it. The Worrier foresees a negative outcome, but does little to avoid it.

The Troubleshooter works for peace before conflict. The Worrier hopes for peace without work.

The Troubleshooter thinks deeply before acting. The Worrier thinks chaotically, without acting.

The Troubleshooter's master is their head; their adviser is their heart. The Worrier's head is hostage to their heart.

The Troubleshooter says "Yes" and "No" with conviction. The Worrier says "But", "Maybe", "What if?"

The Troubleshooter respects and values himself equally to all other human beings. The Worrier acts as though he or she were lesser than others.

The Troubleshooter never gives up. The Worrier gives up before he/she has met the first hurdle.

Which are you?

There are many ways to deal with challenges, a process psychologists call "coping". This chapter will introduce you to some of them, and encourage you to recognise and appraise the ones you most often use.

Coping with stress

In the last chapter, we looked at some common sensations, emotions, thoughts and behaviours which occur when we are stressed. Some of the thoughts we think and the things we do have the fundamental goal of self-protection. The event or situation that triggers the stress is perceived by our brains as being in some way a threat to our well-being, health and happiness. Protective thoughts and behaviours are an attempt to maintain our equilibrium. Our current equilibrium may not be the best we could achieve – in fact, it most probably isn't, for you, if you are reading this book! – but we have found it satisfactory enough not to risk rocking the boat and changing it. Better the devil you know. The attempt to maintain our equilibrium is called "coping".

There are different ways of coping with stress. For instance, we can stand up to a challenge and try to deal with it directly ("facing the music"), or we can distance ourselves from it and actively avoid it ("running away"). These two options have been termed "fight or flight", which are the most basic animal responses when faced with a threat. But there are other options. Just for example, we could try to see it differently ("looking on the bright side"), we could ignore it or pretend it does not exist ("burying our heads in the sand"), or we could just sit and worry about it, perhaps creating a "storm in a teacup".

Different ways of coping

There are many, many specific kinds of behaviour which people use to cope. Some of them are better than others, although that does depend on the circumstances, one's perception of the situation, and one's goals. I have compiled a list of some of the ways in which people try to cope. It does not pretend to be anything like a complete list. As it is rather long I have put it in Appendix 1. I do suggest you have a look at it now. After looking at it, can you answer this question: Do you recognise your own behaviour in any of the ways of coping in the list?

Coping means things we think or do to reduce stress or its impact upon us. If we think or do any one of these things on a specific occasion, we can say we have used a "coping *strategy*". Most people have a general tendency to use the same kinds of strategies whenever they are faced with a challenge: this is called their "coping *style*". Different people have different styles of coping. Here though, we will simply talk about "ways of coping", which encompasses both strategies and styles.

Psychologists have tried to categorise ways of coping. Here are some of the categories that have been proposed. Ways of coping are either:

- Active or passive.
- Positive or negative.
- Problem-focused or emotion-focused.

- Cognitive or behavioural.
- Impulsive or reflective.
- Functional or dysfunctional.

Active and passive ways of coping

Active coping means positively acting to engage with a problem situation, e.g. trying to solve the problem. Passive coping means not acting, or reducing one's engagement, in response to a problem situation. Thinking about a situation or experiencing negative emotions with regard to it but not acting to try to solve the problem is passive coping, e.g. worrying. In general, active coping is usually more likely to be beneficial in the long term than passive coping.

Positive and negative ways of coping

Positive coping means behaving (thinking or acting) in constructive and uplifting ways, or ways which give you a sense of control, e.g. seeking social support, self-encouragement. Negative coping means behaving (thinking or acting) in counter-productive or destructive ways, ways which devalue you, or ways in which you relinquish control, e.g. avoidance, self-denigration.

Problem-focused and emotion-focused ways of coping

Problem-focused coping involves thinking about practical ways of modifying the problem that is the source of the stress, for instance:

- Seeking advice, information, support.
- Learning new skills.
- Generating and assessing possible solutions.

Emotion-focused coping is to do with one's own emotional response to the problem. It is actually of two kinds, a direct focus on our emotions, and a focus on our interpretations and meanings, which will then feed into our emotional response. They are both "emotion-focused" because their goal is to make us feel better.

Examples of coping that directly focuses on our emotions:

- Expressing our emotions.
- Avoidance of situations which cause us anxiety.
- Engagement in distracting activities.

- Relaxation techniques.
- Self-control.
- Anxiety medicines, alcohol, drugs, chocolate.

Examples of coping that focuses on the meanings we attribute to our situation:

- Denial.
- Humour.
- Changing our goals or values.
- Seeing a positive side to our situation.
- Seeing a deeper meaning in a situation.

Cognitive (thinking) and behavioural (doing) ways of coping

Cognitive coping means thinking about a situation, e.g. rationalisation, changing our expectations, changing our point of view. Behavioural coping means things that we do about a situation, e.g. acting, talking, crying, and laughing. In practice a modification in behaviour usually follows a change in thoughts. Thinking about a situation differently changes the way we behave with regard to that situation. It would be quite difficult to think of a situation in which this were not the case.

Impulsive and reflective ways of coping

Sometimes our response to a situation is spontaneous, impulsive: this may be vital in a situation of imminent and grave physical danger, but detrimental in more everyday situations. In everyday situations, we have to be mindful of the people around us when we act. For instance, in a situation of underlying discord in the extended family which is affecting your marital relations, calm reflection may lead to more positive developments than a heat-of-the moment decision. Many coping behaviours, such as assuming responsibility, seeking social support, humour, blame, can be done impulsively or reflectively. However, when dealing with long-term stress, strategies that are carried out reflectively (e.g. organising resources, problem-solving, giving meaning, rationalisation), are generally more likely to be beneficial in the long term.

Functional and dysfunctional ways of coping

This is what concerns us the most. A way of coping is most functional if it increases the likelihood of beneficial long-term outcomes while avoiding excessively detrimental short-term ones. Active, positive strategies tend to do this more often than passive, negative ones. A way of coping is not functional if it reduces the likelihood of beneficial long-term outcomes, even though it may provide short-term relief or compensations. Favourable long-term outcomes should include the reduction of stress.

This may be achieved in many ways. For example, if the source of your stress is your relationship with your boss or colleagues, clearly suffering in silence is not going to reduce your stress. Crying on a friend's shoulder may make you feel better, but only temporarily. In order to change things in the long term, you might decide to change your job, or learn better communication and inter-personal skills, or talk to your colleagues directly to try to reach an understanding. The first of these might work, but in a sense it is an escape, and if similar problems occur in the next job, nothing will have been solved. After all, working with people is never plain sailing, and without the necessary inter-personal skills, difficulties are bound to crop up sooner or later. The second two, then, might be better long-term options.

However, if to achieve a long-term reduction in stress, the use of a certain kind of strategy risks short-term disaster, it is not the right strategy. For example, a discussion with colleagues about a delicate issue might lead to serious conflict if handled the wrong way, so if your communication skills are poor, it would be better to improve them first, or choose a completely different course of action. A full-blown row with colleagues may give a sense of relief immediately afterwards ("At least I've got it off my chest and told them what I really think"), but may not improve matters in the long term.

What type are you?

As I mentioned above, active, positive ways of coping tend to be functional more often than passive, negative ones. The table below compares some ways of coping according to whether they are active or passive, positive or negative.

The ways of coping in the lightest box are generally more likely to achieve good long-term outcomes. Those in the next lightest box may be functional or dysfunctional depending on the context, while those in the darker two boxes are the least likely to bring long-term benefits. It is important to remember that we have the long term in mind. Benefits may be different if only the short term were considered. For instance, some of the strategies listed may serve an invaluable protective function in the short term, but be mentally and physically draining, or counter-productive, in the long term (e.g. passive distraction, maintaining a heightened state of alert).

Are you a Troubleshooter, a Fugitive, a Philosopher or a Worrier? If you are a Worrier or a Fugitive, you definitely need to change your coping habits!

	Active	Passive
Positive	**The Troubleshooter** • Assuming responsibility to act. • Taking control. • Problem-solving. • Seeking information. • Organising yourself, your life, your resources. • Learning or improving your skills in relation to the problem. • Seeking practical help. • Bodily care. • Active entertainment, e.g. sport. • Seeking appropriate emotional support.	**The Philosopher** • Rationalisation. • Acceptance. • Deciding to be positive. • Looking for positives in a situation. • Finding deeper meaning in the situation. • Changing your expectations, goals or values. • Passive entertainment, e.g. watching a film. • Humour. • Religion. • Self-control. • Self-encouragement.
Negative	**The Fugitive** • Escape and active avoidance. • Intransigence. • Recklessness. • Ritual and superstition. • Active distraction, e.g. working harder.	**The Worrier** • Passive avoidance. • Blame and self-justification. • Self-denigration. • Catastrophising. • Denial or dissociation. • Giving up. • Maintaining a heightened state of alert. • Worrying. • Alcohol, smoking, drugs. • Emotional compensation. • Passive distraction, e.g. watching TV when not really interested.

Table 7.1: Active and passive, positive and negative coping

Same methods, different results?

Do you believe you can expect different results in life by continuing to do the same things in the same ways? Do you think you have just been unlucky in your life so far, and someday soon, your luck must change? Or do you agree with me that that is not a realistic position? Do you agree that the more you take control of your life, the less things in your life will be the result of pure chance? The bare bones of the matter are these: if you are going to manage your stress effectively and deal better with the situations in which you typically feel stressed, you will need to jettison your ineffective ways of coping and replace them with a range of better ones.

Very often when talking to my clients, at this point they will say to me:

"But that's just the way I am."

So I say:

"You can change."

They say:

"But it's difficult to change."

So I say:

"Of course it isn't <u>easy</u>, but it's not <u>impossible</u> either, and if you want to make the effort, you will feel much better in yourself."

I cannot emphasise this point too strongly: you *can* change. And you must. He or she who has no more to learn has stopped living a vital life. He or she is a fossil, petrified and rigid in his or her habits. But in order to change you cannot keep on defining yourself by the way you already are ("That's the way I am"). In order to change you are obliged to throw that old, bankrupt definition away. You need a new, fluid description, and a new self-image, always open to improvement. Only you can give yourself permission for this. When you begin to accept responsibility for the role your current habits play in maintaining your stress, then and only then will you begin to have control over it.

Of course if you do not want to make the effort, you can choose to go on as you are, hoping in the ever receding chance that one day your luck will change. But then, why read this book?

Your world is within

If you have got this far into this book, you have probably already realised that something must change, and you have recognised that sitting around waiting for the world to change for your benefit isn't working. You may also have realised that you cannot change the world at large, at least not unless you change yourself first. But what you *can* do is to change *your* world. What you must now realise is that your world is not "out there", it is within. I do not mean that you must withdraw into yourself, you must not. What I mean is that your entire mental map of the world is a subjective affair, dependent on how you perceive and interpret the world. *That* you can change; and you *must* change it if you want to reduce your propensity to suffer stress.

Main points

- There are many ways of coping with a given situation.
- Habitual ways of coping are often counter-productive and detrimental in the long term.
- Active, positive coping strategies are better than passive, negative ones.
- You can learn to recognise your habitual coping strategies and change them into better ones.
- You must change your world within.

8. An experiment

A 5-step procedure for change – A coping diary - A behaviour experiment

They must often change, who would be constant in happiness or wisdom.

- Confucius (551-479 BC)

Growth is the only evidence of life.

- John Henry Newman (1801-1890)

We have established the need to change and grow as a person, and we have suggested that despite what you might previously have believed, it *is* possible to change. Let us make an experiment to see what it might mean to you to change. You are going to do this with your dysfunctional ways of coping. First you are going to find out how you habitually try to cope, and what kinds of results you get, then you are going to find out what happens if you behave differently.

But before that, I am going to outline the basic procedure you need to adopt to go about changing your habits. It is a 5-step procedure:

1. **Know yourself**, in particular here, know your habits.

2. **Question yourself**: Examine your habitual ways of coping and identify the dysfunctional ones. Identify the cues which trigger them. Think about which better (more functional) strategies you could use instead.

3. **Just stop!** Instruct yourself *not* to react automatically to the cues.

4. **Take control**: Take your time and choose the best strategy under the circumstances.

5. **Review**: Assess how you have coped with difficult circumstances, and what could be modified to get an even better result.

Steps 1 and 2 must be taken in preparation for future threatening events or situations, in order that you may enact steps 3 and 4 at times when you are confronted by a challenge or threat. Let us now look at each step of this procedure in turn, and use it as an experiment.

Know yourself

In Chapter 6, I suggested you keep a diary to record your responses to stress. At this point it would be useful to take it out and look at it again. Pay particular attention to the columns in which you have recorded your thoughts and your actions, for your thoughts and actions in response to stress indicate how you attempted to cope. You may notice patterns, the same kinds of thoughts and actions repeated more often than others. In this case you are adopting a particular style of coping.

Has your coping been active or passive? Positive or negative? Are you a Troubleshooter, a Philosopher, a Fugitive, or a Worrier? Is your coping focused on the problem or on yourself? Do you react impulsively or do you think about the consequences of your actions first?

Now, in order to find out whether your way of coping works for you, you are going to modify your diary to include the outcome of the situation, and a guess as to the long-term consequences of your responses. It will now look something like the one shown on the next page. Keep it for about a week.

Once you have kept this diary for a week, look at how you have responded to situations and whether the outcomes have been positive, negative, or neither one nor the other. Positive outcomes reduce your problems and make you feel better. Negative ones increase your problems and make you feel worse. When you do this, try to be sensitive to the difference between short-term and long-term outcomes. Something that you do or say may leave you feeling temporarily elated, but be likely to increase your problems over the next few weeks or months. Let us try to be more concerned about how things will turn out in one year's time than how they turn out tomorrow. Write in both positive and negative consequences, then you will be able to come to an overall judgement about how beneficial your thoughts and actions were. Coping which is largely beneficial in the long term we call *functional*, and if it is detrimental in the long term, we call it *dysfunctional*.

Question yourself

Hopefully you will have identified some of your dysfunctional ways of coping, that is, the kinds of things you thought and did (or didn't do) which might not produce the best long-term outcomes. Think about whether you have sacrificed long-term benefits (e.g. lasting peace of mind and happiness) for short-term gains (e.g. immediate relief or superficial good cheer). By analysing the "situation" column you will also have gleaned some useful information about the kinds of cues that "set you off".

The next thing you must do is to think about how you could have done better in each of the situations you have identified. Work through them in your mind methodically. For each one go through a range of alternative, more beneficial strategies and try to compare and contrast them. Once you have short-listed a few strategies, decide which one might have been the best overall.

Date and time	Situation (people, place, context)	Stress level (0 - 5)*	Emotions and thoughts	What was the outcome of the situation?	What might be the long-term consequences?	How appropriate or justified were my responses? (0 - 5)**
27th March 8:00 till 13:00	Myself, at home. Have to teach a seminar this afternoon with people I don't know.	3	Anxiety. Regret. A sort of tension in my chest and upper abdomen. I don't want to do this. I wish I hadn't taken it on. I'm not going to do it again. I'm not cut out for this. I'm not up to it.	Spent too much time worrying about it and perfecting a lesson which was already good, and which I already knew by heart. Actually, the lesson was much easier to teach than I had anticipated and I enjoyed it.	If I acted on my exaggerated negative thoughts, I would deny myself these kinds of opportunities in the future. I would avoid the anxiety of the challenge. But I would not learn how to face a challenge with confidence. If I worry unnecessarily about things so much, I'm going to waste a lot of time and energy.	1

* 0 = No appreciable stress; 1 = Slight stress; 2 = Low stress; 3 = A fair degree of stress; 4 = Quite a lot of stress; 5 = Severe stress.

** 0 = Not at all appropriate or justified; 1 = Only slightly appropriate or justified; 2 = A little appropriate or justified; 3 = Fairly appropriate or justified; 4 = Quite appropriate or justified; 5 = Very appropriate or justified.

Table 8.1: Example of a coping diary

You will need to consider both the need to improve the chances of long-term benefits, and the desirability of avoiding excessive negative consequences in the short term. But try to be realistic about this, and avoid exaggerating the potential negatives ("catastrophising"). You will also have come to the realisation that you may need to adopt one kind of coping strategy in the short term (e.g. self-control to avoid impulsive responses) and another in the longer term (e.g. engaging in calm, rational thought).

The exercise you have done is just a start to help you begin to develop an alternative range of responses to try out, which very likely will prove more beneficial than your habitual ones. It is also designed to help you build a habit of awareness. In the long term, effective stress management is enhanced if we develop a habit of awareness of our emotions, thoughts, actions and their consequences.

Just stop!

Habit can be an insidious and obstinate obstacle to self-development. Then, it is an enemy within. But now that you have identified the cues that trigger your habitual behaviour patterns, you are in a position to be able to control them voluntarily. You now have the power of knowledge. Now you can move on to a position of greater control over yourself and therefore over the situations in which you are involved.

You need to begin by *not acting* on cue. We have discussed how impulsive responses are often counter-productive in the long term, even though they sometimes afford short-term benefits. We compared them with reflective responses. Reflective is not the same as *reflexive*. Reflective means considered, while reflexive means "of or like a reflex". Often we talk about "knee-jerk" reactions. The "knee-jerk" is an automatic reflex response that doctors test by tapping the tendon below your kneecap with a rubber hammer. Cues for habitual (reflex) behaviour patterns may include people, the words they say or their body language, places, or particular contexts. When trying to change your strategies for coping with situations of chronic stress, you need to nip in the bud all automatic, reflex and impulsive responses.

To do this is simply stated: whenever you notice a cue for your usual responses, give yourself a mental instruction, such as "Just stop!" or "Don't react now!" For some people a physical signal to do this might help better. A useful trick is to wear an elastic band around your wrist and to "twang" it whenever you feel you are about to act automatically "on cue". Or you could just pinch yourself or take a deep breath.

Simply stated though it may be, it is not so easy to perform every time. However, just as with all skills, while it may not be *easy* to learn, neither is it *impossible,* and practice makes perfect. With practice, it will soon be easy enough for it to start making a positive difference in your life.

Take control

The conscious mind hates a void, and you have just created one by halting your habitual response. You are going to need to find something useful to fill the void. Imagine that you are now feeling the onset of an increase in stress. We may describe it as a rise in inner tension, or anxiety. This tension needs to be dispelled, but you have just flipped the off-switch on your usual method of doing that. What are you going to do?

Take a deep breath. If necessary and possible, excuse yourself and arrange to come back to the problem a little later. Make sure you *do* come back to it soon! Meanwhile, bring out that mental list you have made of a range of better responses than your usual ones, and the kinds of situations they might serve in. Do any situations you have considered match the one you are in now? If not, generate your list of potential responses now. Which short-term actions would be most appropriate in the situation you are in? Which long-term ones?

Until you become adept at doing this quickly, the best short-term strategies may be those which help to diffuse acute tension, such as instructing yourself to maintain your calm, slow breathing, and distancing yourself to somewhere removed from the situation (a "safe zone").

A small word of warning: do not become complacent with your "new" strategies; do not let any of them become lazy, settling into the status of a default response. You must keep flexible, keep widening, refining and updating your range of useful responses, and improving your sensitivity to the nuances of context which might make one response subtly more suitable than another.

Review results

When you begin to do this you may find that while some of the outcomes of your responses have been satisfactory, others have not. You will need to constantly review your interactions to see how they are working, and if certain kinds of responses consistently lead to unsatisfactory results, try to understand why and refine or modify them.

You may do this in an organic, unstructured way. However, it can be helpful to do it methodically by using again the daily diary you kept above (table 8.1). In essence, you will be feeding back the information gained from your experiments, and using it as input for another cycle of the five step procedure just outlined.

If results have been unsatisfactory, you will need to decide whether this is because the strategy you chose was the right one used badly, or whether, on reflection, it has turned out to be an inappropriate strategy after all. In the first case, it only needs some refinement. In the second, it needs changing. If it needs changing, could another strategy from your range have done the job better, or do you need to find a new strategy to add to your range?

This, essentially, is one way in which we learn and develop our behaviour patterns. Usually it is an unconscious process. But if your behaviour patterns have got stuck in an unproductive or counter-productive rut, by bringing the learning process into your conscious mind and making it explicit, you can break negative automatic patterns and develop new, more positive ones over which you have control.

What you have just done is called a behaviour experiment, and you have just made a giant leap forward in having the courage to allow yourself to depart from your habits and experiment with new ways of doing things.

Main points

- Behaviour experiments can help you to learn the benefits of new ways of coping.
- First observe your habitual ways of coping. A coping diary can help you to do this.
- Question yourself about the appropriateness of your responses.
- When you recognise the cues that make you stressed, stop your automatic responses, take your time and choose, review-adapt-improve.

9. Outrageous fortune, goblins and allies

Slings and arrows - A realisation - Stress begins with a thought - Change is possible, slowly but surely - The tipping point - Don't be a robot - Goblins and allies

Oh, I am fortunes fool!

- William Shakespeare, Romeo and Juliet

Staying with Shakespeare (a matchless student of human nature), Hamlet agonised over his response to the "slings and arrows of outrageous fortune". But we may be authors of our own fortune to an important degree. We all want life to go our way. It cannot do so all the time and potentially negative things happen to all of us. What counts is how we respond to them, which can make the difference between a disaster and an opportunity. Do you find that the world punishes you more often than it rewards you? If so it might be that you need to consider whether a change in your attitude to the world would reap greater rewards!

If you go to a job interview and you come across as a pessimistic loner, you will not get the job. The person who gets the job will be the bright, smiling person who came in after you. You may think you are the "realist" and the relentlessly optimistic person may be deluded, but they got the job because they put a positive spin on life. Remember, the world will respond to you in kind and your attitude can often result in the enactment of self-fulfilling prophecies. Is that "realism" really so realist? Or is it just part of another vicious cycle going on between a negative outlook and negative outcomes?

The moment of realisation

Problems are only as big as our attitude to them allows them to be. A lady client of mine understood the sense of this at an intellectual level, but found it very difficult to put into practice. This lady was tortured by unpleasant (though not serious) stomach and intestinal disturbances, aggravated by her anxiety. Her worries and frustrations were related to family conflict, as well as certain difficulties with another person over a property she owned. However, she confessed that as she had grown older, she had developed fears of all sorts of things that previously hadn't bothered her, fears that limited her lifestyle, despite the fact that she was generally fit and healthy. In one conversation we had she told me about the quite mundane and ordinary problems she was having with this property, which seemed to be causing her much anguish. I suggested to her that her thoughts about the situation may be more of a problem than the situation itself. She acknowledged the truth of this, and then went on lamenting her problems in exactly the same fashion as before. This went on for several cycles until she suddenly sat down, silent, on the verge of tears. She had come to the realisation that focusing emotionally on the problem was only causing her more anguish, but she had no other tools in the box. Her habitual behaviour pattern had become so much part of herself that in that moment, without it, she felt lost. It is in these moments that one truly realises the need to change one's mind.

Thoughts underpin behaviour

Consider the simple observation that negative thoughts lead to unpleasant emotions. One negative thought also tends to generate a succession of others. One follows the other. If one gets into the habit, one can go on like that for ever! Negative thoughts, then, could be considered a sort of toxin that damages our emotional health.

The way we feel and the way we act are underpinned by the way we think. So we can only really change our proneness to stress if we change the way we think. While relaxation exercises, for example, can help us maintain our calm in the short term, the task will be all the easier, and the effect more stable and long-lasting, if it is underpinned by more beneficial ways of thinking. When I speak of "ways of thinking", I refer to thoughts, beliefs, and attitudes. Beneficial ways of thinking:

- Foster calm, balanced, appropriate responses to any situation.
- Are unlikely to result in exaggerated or inappropriate responses to any situation.

The most important thing to understand about coping with stress is that...

The way we think is the major factor that can make challenging situations feel stressful (or otherwise).

You can change your thoughts

While the bad news is not the news itself but our bad attitude to the news, the good news is that we can change our attitude.

We have learned that our appraisal of a challenging situation occurs in two basic stages: (1) "Is this a threat?" and (2) "Can I deal with it?" What I would like to suggest to you now is that the way in which we appraise a threat lies within our conscious control. You may remember that each of the two stages of appraising a challenging situation is influenced by a series of factors both from within and without. We have the power to modify a number of these factors to a greater or lesser extent. In particular, we have the power of control over our beliefs, values, attitudes and goals. The answers to the two questions, "Is this a threat?" and, "Can I deal with it?", are powerfully influenced by these things. So the next most important thing to know about coping with stress is that...

You __can__ change your habitual thoughts, and in doing so feel less stressed.

Slowly but surely

One of the things that people often say when confronted with the need to change, is "I can't change, that's the way I'm made". At times this is a convenient excuse to avoid the need for making an effort. At other times, as the example of my lady patient illustrates,

it reflects deep-rooted identification of the self with one's behaviour patterns.

Yes, it may not be easy to change and it will not happen overnight, but neither is it *too* difficult to do. The truth is that one *can* change if there is sufficient motivation to do so and if the right approach is taken. That is certainly not beyond most people. The secret is to take one small step at a time but to keep working at it, without worrying about how much there is to do or how long it will take. Slowly but surely, like a child learning to play a musical instrument. I say a child, because children do not tend to worry about their slow progress, they just practise a little at a time, day by day. *Slowly but surely*.

The tipping point

"Motivation" is a key word. As it is not always so easy to change one's habits, you're going to need a good dose of this. The unfortunate thing about motivation is, people tend to get it only when faced with truly dire consequences. You know the kind of thing: inveterate smokers or drinkers who only acquire the motivation to give up once they've received some dreadful diagnosis or prognosis. Clearly, when considering taking a certain action, we weigh things up. How much do I need to do this? What might be the consequences if I don't? Might I get away with it? What will the benefits be? Will it really work? How difficult is it going to be? Will I be happier going on as I am or will I be happier making the effort to change? Is the answer to that question the same if we are talking about tomorrow, next month, next year or in five or ten years' time? If I go on doing things as I do them now, can I really expect my life to get any better? Can I put up with that? Will it get any worse? How much worse? Can I put up with that? Will a point come when I can't put up with things any longer? Do I want to reach it?

I would ask you now, gentle reader, do you want to reach the tipping point (if you have not already)? If your answer is "No", read on.

More about thoughts

I am using the word "thoughts" to refer both to single thoughts, and to habitual styles of thinking, attitudes, mental models[42], and beliefs.

---

42 A mental model or schema is a set of beliefs about a general subject, such as our place in the cosmos, the way society should be organised, or health and disease.

Styles of thinking are the thought patterns we habitually use. For example, we may habitually think positive thoughts or negative ones. We may habitually make intuitive judgements or rationally weigh up the evidence or the pros and cons. We may make superficial judgements or look for deeper truths. Our thoughts may habitually carry conviction or be riven with uncertainty.

Attitudes are the general stances we adopt with regard to things, people or ideas. They are heavily influenced by our beliefs and experiences, and in turn influence our style of thinking. Optimism, scepticism, benevolence, suspicion, and hostility, for example, are words that describe attitudes.

Mental models are complex sets of notions (thoughts) about specific spheres of knowledge. They are often heavily influenced by our culture. For example, with regard to the human body, the west has developed anatomical and physiological models based upon the physical sciences, whereas traditional Eastern models have viewed the body's workings in terms of energy flow. Mental models that are prevalent in a whole society are called *paradigms*.

Beliefs are thoughts concerned with our fundamental views about things: from the origin of our world to the nature of human life, to ideas about health and disease, to ethics and morality, and so on. Anything, large or small, important or trivial, which we can think about, we may have beliefs about. Beliefs, in fact, are the foundations on which all other thoughts are based.

One essential thing to realise about all of these things - styles of thinking, attitudes, mental models, and beliefs...particularly beliefs - is that they can be limiting. If we are suffering and that is because of the ways in which we think, we must be prepared to question our beliefs. We must even be prepared to ask ourselves whether our deepest held and most cherished beliefs are contributing to our suffering. We must be prepared to try to examine this question as impartially as we can. Because if we honestly find that the answer is "yes", then we are in a position either to modify our limiting belief (it will be weakened by this realisation), or to accept its contribution to our suffering. Either is a valid response, so long as we are fully aware of what we are choosing and why.

Don't be a robot

If we do not choose for ourselves, we are to an extent, like an automaton. Our thoughts are moulded by our past, our culture, our education and upbringing. Habitual thoughts, including prejudices and assumptions, become automatic and self-maintaining. Habitual thoughts are like reflexes. When a doctor taps the tendon below your kneecap you find yourself kicking the air without having willed the action yourself. What happened? Your nervous system perceived the information that your tendon had been suddenly stretched, the information was transmitted to your spinal cord, and an impulse was sent from there to the muscle of your thigh, resulting in a kick. It required no thinking, no information processing in the brain. It was automatic. The same can happen, and often does happen with thoughts. We think certain kinds of thoughts in automatic response to certain kinds of situations. Automatic thoughts can feed our stress in the long term. Our automatic negative thoughts make us feel bad and then we make other people around us feel bad. But humans have evolved big and complex brains so we can make judgements on specific occasions according to the circumstances, rather than, robot-like, regurgitating automatic responses. Don't be a robot! Don't be a prisoner to your past, your culture, your education or your upbringing! Take responsibility and stand on your own two feet!

Thought goblins

Stress begins with a negative thought. When faced with a threat, thoughts may be beneficial or detrimental. (Remember that we are thinking more about long-term benefits than short-term ones. A thought may bring some short-term result that seems positive, but bring us misery in the long run).

We saw just above how thoughts can happen automatically because they have become habits that we reproduce in certain situations. So we have *habitual negative* thoughts. Just for fun we will call these "Thought Goblins"[43].

Thought Goblins are those habits of thinking that cause you to worry, lose your cool or become hostile, fearful, cynical, pessimistic, and so on. Goblins lose you friends because people do not want to be around you. Goblins make you less successful because you do not have the courage or the judgement to take your chances. Goblins attract more goblins, because they create the kind of negative environment that goblins love. While some goblins are easy to recognise, some others are quite subtle. Let me tell you about some thought goblins[44] and what they can do to your mind:

The Black and White Goblin makes you think that things are clear-cut and opposed to each other when the reality is much more complex; also known as the All-or-Nothing Goblin because it makes you think in extremes, with no middle ground. If someone doesn't side with you in an argument and you think, "If she's not with me, then she's against me", you have the Black and White Goblin.

The Sweeping-Generalisation Goblin makes you generalise inappropriately, for example, from insufficient evidence. If you think the whole world is bad because the world contains some bad people, the Sweeping-Generalisation Goblin has been getting at you.

The Selective-Vision Goblin makes you only see the side of things which confirm what you already believe. If you believe you are not well liked, then you see two of your workmates talking together and one of them glances towards you, so you conclude they must have been talking unkindly about you, the Selective-Vision Goblin has been at work.

---

43 Goblin: a mythical, magical, mischievous, grotesque little being in European folklore.

44 Many of the "goblins" in the list are adaptations of the descriptions of "cognitive errors" (thinking errors) developed by the psychiatrists Aaron T. Beck and David D. Burns in their work on depression and anxiety. Such errors are just as important in poor coping with stress as they are in depression.

The Empty Glass Goblin has a couple of tricks. It can make you see only the negative side of any situation ("My glass is half empty"). Or it can make you choose to deny or minimise any positive side even when you do see it. For example, if you concede that you have done better in your sport this week but say that you still weren't any good, you may be infected by the Empty Glass Goblin.

The Catastrophe Goblin makes mountains out of a molehills and creates storms in teacups. Under its influence, you see problems as being very much more important or difficult than they really are.

The Negative Assumption Goblin makes unhappy assumptions about a situation based on prejudice or insufficient evidence. For instance, your partner goes hiking and they are not back by five minutes before they said they would, so you think they must have had an accident or got lost.

The Doomsayer Goblin is a cousin of the Negative Assumption Goblin. It likes to make pessimistic predictions based on your fears. According to this goblin any enterprise is always doomed to failure.

The Musturbator Goblin[45] becomes angry or frustrated if things don't happen as they should by rights or morality. It might, for instance, become all upset and indignant and complain loudly if the service in a restaurant is only average, or if it has to stand in a queue for too long at the post office.

The Pigeon Hole Goblin likes to label other people on a pretty arbitrary basis. It is a close cousin of the Black and White Goblin. The Pigeon Hole Goblin says things like, "There are two kinds of people in the world, etc. etc." But it has prejudices too. Just say you have formed the impression that a colleague is a bad mother just because she has a tattoo on her arm. If so, the Pigeon Hole Goblin is in your head!

The All-About-Me Goblin takes all things personally. It has a double-edged sword which, while it always blames itself, also takes all credit. If your teenage son has started to take drugs and has been caught stealing from a shop, you might think: "Where have I gone wrong?" Or, if you are secretary in a small, busy, understaffed company, you might think, "This company would fall apart if it weren't for me." But actually, it might not be all about you!

The Stone-Throwing Goblin is blameless. It blames all bad things on others: other people, its tools, the government, Murphy (of the eponymous law), God, etc. Never itself.

The Always-Right Goblin is, sensibly enough, always right. It believes it is diminished if it is wrong or makes a mistake. It feels the need to argue until it makes a point the other cannot return, or until the other is blue in the face, or until the other gets fed up and concedes. If it loses, it presents a spurious argument to justify itself.

---

45 "Musturbation" is a term coined by the psychologist Albert Ellis.

The Always-Wrong Goblin makes you believe you will be more highly valued if you accept you are in error. It is always making you apologise for things which are not your fault.

The Perfectionist Goblin is a real slave-driver. It wants you to believe that only perfection is acceptable, and that you are uniquely responsible for correcting the imperfections around you. It makes you believe you will not be valued if you do not achieve and maintain impossibly high standards. It forces you to take an inordinate amount of time over any task in order to correct tiny unimportant details.

The biggest, baddest goblins

You may have noticed that some of the goblins I introduced you to seem quite similar to each other, but are subtly different. That is because they work for the same bosses! You might consider them all the foot soldiers of three big, bad controllers:

The Ingrained Belief Goblin

Nobody gives up their ingrained beliefs easily. But as explained previously in this chapter, faced with overwhelming evidence that they cause us or others harm (which can't be a good thing for a belief to do), we are bound to look at them critically. In order to challenge our beliefs, we need to be flexible mentally. The ingrained belief goblin is not mentally flexible!

The Pessimism Goblin

Pessimism is an attitude that comes from an abiding belief that things in general are likely to turn out badly. Not unsurprisingly, again this tends to be a self-fulfilling prophesy, as it actually generates "bad luck".

Ingrained beliefs and pessimism are nasty partners. For example, during hard times it is easy to believe that somebody or something (God, the world, the universe, etc.) has got it in for us, or that we were "born unlucky". Some people go through life saying to themselves, "I am unlucky". That is an ingrained belief. That particular belief leads to a vicious cycle of self-pity, fatalism, believing it's not worth the effort, not looking for solutions, further failure, and so on. If the person who believes he or she is unlucky does not begin to change that belief, they will go on hexing themselves for the rest of their lives. They will be constantly frustrated, stressed and unhappy.

The Egomaniac Goblin

A lot of stress comes from too much self-importance. Take inter-personal conflict. Much inter-personal conflict comes from placing excessive importance in our own desires relative to those of others. Many arguments go on and on, not because we are both right but because our egos demand that we try to convince ourselves, even against all reason, that we are justified. Or take our self-image, the one we wish to see reflected in other people's eyes. It wastes an awful lot of energy in maintaining the tension we set up in ourselves when the image we wish to project is not what comes naturally to us.

I am sure these are only a few of the goblins which haunt our heads. Have you recognised any of your own? Good, because recognition is the first step to change. I would like you from now on to keep aware of the apparition of these goblins in your mind. Be vigilant, they are sneaky!

Get some thought-allies

Every time you realise there is a goblin at work on your mind, I would like you NOT to think or do as it says. Instead, make an effort to think of other, more helpful, more rational, thoughts you could have had instead. These are your allies!

Allies, in contrast to goblins, are those thoughts that foster calm, balanced, appropriate responses to any situation, rather than exaggerated or inappropriate responses. Of course, whether a response is appropriate depends very much on the context. What might be appropriate behaviour if attacked by a troop of angry baboons might not be quite so appropriate in a situation in which your work had been criticised by a colleague. Nevertheless, in both cases the prior cultivation of a general state of mental calm and poise would favour clarity of thought, purpose and effectiveness in the heat of the moment.

For example, it sometimes happens to me that I have a long list of things to do, and if by evening there are still six things on the list, I regard it as a catastrophe. If I leave six undone things on my list tonight, I think to myself, by tomorrow night there will be twelve undone things. I feel overwhelmed. But, under the influence of my Catastrophe Goblin, I am magnifying the negative. An alternative response would be to think: "*Look* at the list: of the six things three will not mind not being done, even if they never get done, and only one is a real priority. The three things I have to do I can get done in 15 minutes. And not every day is as intense as today. Be reasonable and go easy, relax!" Phew, I don't feel overwhelmed anymore! I have been helped by my ally!

Practise shutting out your goblins and bringing in some allies. Good to cultivate are:

- Calmness.
- Kindness.
- Balance.
- Reasonableness.

- Optimism.
- Proportion.
- Flexibility.

You can rework your thoughts, making them kinder, more realistic and more helpful, and the new way of thinking can slowly but surely become part of you. In a later chapter we will look in more detail about how you can rework your thoughts.

Main Points

- Problems are only as big as our attitude to them allows them to be.
- Beware of goblins!
- You can change the way you think.
- Be prepared to question your beliefs.
- Imbue your mind with allies.

Part 3: From coping to thriving

Introduction to Part 3

Very often in books or articles about stress, we can read about how we can better manage, deal with, handle, cope with, or even think about stress. In fact, there is considerable research that shows that if we manage our thoughts, emotions and behaviour better, we experience the negative effects of stress less or not at all. But really, it is not stress we ought to be learning how to manage/deal with/handle/cope with/think about, it is living itself.

> *It is our imperfect capacity to manage/deal with/handle/cope with/think about living that results in negative stress.*

But I'm not over keen on the word "coping". While it is technically current (i.e. standard in the scientific literature about stress), in lay language it carries somewhat negative connotations;

"How are you doing?"

"Oh... coping."

"Coping" implies a weary effort to ensure mere survival against the odds, whether that be emotional or physical. It implies we are on a long and gruelling desert crossing, does it not? But we want more than that from life - we want to thrive! We want to develop as people and lead happy, fulfilling lives, feeling enthused and energised in our work, relationships and leisure time activities.

To thrive we have to strive to become Masters of the art of living. Mastery of a skill or art implies that we have successfully faced the challenges along the way of learning. Having done so, we are able to carry out our skill or art with inspired ease because we feel at one and at home with it and well able to meet its demands.

Psychologists speak about "positive stress" (aka "eustress"), which is that kind and degree of stress which energises us rather than depletes our energy, leading to development of the self. It is the burden that strengthens. Even a Master must learn. Learning incurs effort to overcome obstacles. But if the path is right, the effort is a pleasure. Then, the more one knows, the more one realises how little one knows. Acquiring knowledge or a skill is like canoeing down a river from its source, observing the ever widening banks on either side the farther one goes, until, arriving at its mouth, the endless ocean opens before us. And finding it wonderful, awe-inspiring, and inspiring. That is thriving.

Now that you know yourself a little better, we must move gradually but surely from coping towards thriving.

10. First things first

Attending to the basics - Diet and hydration - Alcohol, tobacco, and other drugs - Rest and sleep - Activity and exercise

Mens sana in corpore sano.

- Juvenal

In my osteopathic practice, the first thing I do when a client presents with a chronic or complex health problem, problems which usually include a significant stress component, is to assess their general lifestyle:

- Diet and hydration.

- Alcohol intake, smoking, other "recreational" drugs.

- Rest and sleep.

- Activity and exercise.

Sometimes people appear disappointed by this at first, expecting some more technical approach or some esoteric solution. The trouble, I explain, is that if you don't go back to basics and make sure they are healthful, no treatment will bring any long-term benefits. On the positive side, if one does get the basics right, everything else is so much easier.

Stress is greater when the body is not functioning well. It is not just that it *feels* greater, it actually *is* greater. Having read the previous chapters of this book, you will have no trouble understanding this. But just to emphasise once more, stress is not what happens *to* you, it is what happens *with* you, as a result of how you approach and manage life. A healthy, vital, energised body makes the mind healthier, more vital, and more energised. So the whole of your organism can deal with the events and situations of life effectively without making excessive difficulty out of them. So there is less stress.

Diet and hydration

More and more research evidence is pointing at the wide-ranging benefits to physical and mental health to be gained from diets characterised by:

- Whole grains rather than refined ones.

- Abundant vegetables.

- Less animal foods than it is common to eat in modern Western societies.

- Only small amounts, and infrequently, of red meat, if at all.

85

- Fish twice a week.

- Olive oil rather than either animal fats (e.g. butter) or highly polyunsaturated oils (e.g. sunflower).

- Little or no added sugar or salt.

I don't mean this to be taken in black and white terms. For example, we shouldn't stop eating butter or sunflower seed oil, it's just that olive oil is a healthier choice for most culinary purposes.

It is important to drink enough fluid, which is best supplied as water. The caffeine in tea and coffee can make some people produce more urine, so they are not so reliable to keep us well-hydrated. Alcohol dehydrates the body's tissues.

The European Food Safety Authority currently recommends that women should drink about 1.6 litres and men should drink about 2.0 litres of fluid per day. However, people's individual needs vary according to their size and body composition, and factors such as activity level and the weather also make a difference. People who have drunk quantities of water far exceeding their needs have been seriously harmed or even died. So the best advice is, drink the recommended minimum as specified above, plus whatever your thirst tells you, but no more than that.

Do not obsess about food. That does you no good either. Follow a healthy diet steadily for the whole of your life but don't be rigid about "allowed" or "prohibited" foods and don't punish yourself about food. I love a fresh tuna steak occasionally. A nutritionist colleague tells me I will die if I eat tuna. (It contains unhealthy levels of mercury if eaten regularly). I tell him I will surely die if I don't eat it, too (at some stage)! I also tell him, tongue in cheek, that I have a points system of virtue. The mercury in tuna loses me 3 points when I eat it, which isn't very often. However, the enjoyment I gain from it accrues me 5 points, so overall I come out on top. This is nonsense of course, but the serious points are (a) that psychology and emotions are just as important as nutrition in determining our overall health; and (b) that we can make positive choices about our food which are informed not only by nutritional considerations, so long as we *are* informed, and so long as we exercise moderation.

Alcohol intake, smoking, other "recreational" drugs

The recommended maximum alcohol intake is 14 units per week for women and 21 for men. One unit is equivalent to 10 ml of pure alcohol. One small glass of wine is the equivalent of 1.5 units, half a pint of medium strength beer is 1.25 units, a single shot of spirits (25 ml) is 1 unit. If you regularly exceed the recommended maximum, you risk serious damage to your health. If you rarely or never have days without alcohol, you may have a problem of addiction.

Smoking - any amount of smoking - is bad. It is the major cause of lung cancer and an important cause of heart and circulatory disease. It compromises the blood circulation, which is the fundamental giver of life and health to all of the body's tissues.

Many people use alcohol, tobacco, and other recreational drugs when they are under stress, as a short-term means to reduce the stress. This is dangerous as it can quickly lead to addiction. It will not resolve the reasons for the stress, and may become an important source of stress in its own right.

If you believe you have a problem with alcohol, tobacco, or any other drug or addiction, please do seek specialist help.

Rest and sleep

Work can become all-consuming: some people affected like this just love their work; others have an obsessive or perfectionist attitude about it. Then others are business owners who work excessively through fear that if they worked less, their businesses would fold; and employees who work long hours of overtime not only for economic necessity, but because of a sense that they would be judged badly by their employers or peers if they did not do so. In addition, work, activity and general "busy-ness" can take our minds off problems in other domains of our lives. But people in all these situations would gain from the realisation that we perform better, both in our work and in our management of difficulties, when we are well rested.

Rest means passing time engaged in ways which do not exercise the mind or body very intensely or strenuously. It should be a pleasant or pleasurable experience of low-intensity engagement. We all need some of this, every day. Rest includes sleep, but not only. It also includes things such as listening to music, pleasurable reading, watching a good film, going for a picnic in the country, and so on.

The minimum for most people would be 6 hours' continuous rest per day, preferably at night. Normally this minimum would be spent sleeping. But finding time during the day, too, for wakeful rest and relaxation will enhance your life and reduce your stress levels.

Sleep is one of the best medicines for stress, but sometimes stress can result in insomnia. So what to do? This is a vicious cycle: stress... insomnia... lack of sleep... more stress... worse insomnia... greater lack of sleep... and so on. You have to try to break the cycle. In addition to managing more effectively the demands and challenges of life, you could try the following to improve your sleep. Much of this advice is adapted from the website: www.nhs.uk.

1. Make your environment conducive to sleep. It should be dark, quiet, and comfortable. Not too hot or too cold. If your bed, mattress, or pillow are uncomfortable, change them. If your partner snores, cure him/her, move him/her, change him/her, or wear ear plugs! Banish television, computers, tablets and phones from the bedroom.

2. Go to bed and get up at the same time every day. Don't make it less than 6 or more than 9 hours. Stick to the routine. This will train your body to associate these times with

sleep, and thus generate a regular sleep/wake cycle. If you suffer from insomnia at night, don't try to sleep during the day.

3. Reduce or cut down on caffeine, found in coffee, tea and cola drinks; and smoking. Caffeine can have effects lasting many hours, so cutting it out only in the evening may not be enough. Smokers have more sleep problems than non-smokers.

4. Do not over-indulge in food or alcohol, especially in the evening. Both too much food and too much alcohol can disturb your sleep pattern.

5. Regular physical exercise, even if it's just a daily 30-minute walk, will improve your sleep. But don't do vigorous exercise just before bed.

6. Except sex. Sex promotes sleep. Really!

7. Don't do anything requiring intense mental thought too late in the evening. Don't take worries or planning for tomorrow to bed with you. Write down what you have to do tomorrow well before going to bed so you don't lie in bed making mental notes.

8. Allow ample time to wind down before going to bed. Do things to help you relax: gentle yoga, quiet music, imagination and visualisation (see Chapter 12), a warm bath before bed, a few drops of lavender essence on the pillow.

9. In bed, do not fix your mind on any particular thought. Let your mind free-wheel. Let thoughts come and go of their own accord.

10. If you wake up during the night and can't get back to sleep, get up, have a warm herbal tea (something relaxing like chamomile), and do something which will relax you, like reading a chapter of a good book. Don't go on the Internet!

Activity and exercise

Everybody needs to exercise, and I mean everybody. Within that generalisation, however, there are a lot of variables. How you may best do your exercise, when, for how long and how intensely, will all be different according to who you are. A baby does it differently to a 90 year-old, a pregnant woman differently to a middle-aged man, a professional athlete differently to an accountant.

The effects of an exercise deficiency combined with age can be witnessed in people all around us: stiffness, physical deconditioning, pain, anxiety and depression. Don't be one of them!

Most adults should be able to manage 20 minutes of exercise 5 times a week. Unless there are compelling health reasons to the contrary, the exercise should be sufficiently intense to make you break sweat a little, breathe more deeply, and make your heart beat a little faster. This will also release endorphins in the brain (endorphins are "happy

hormones"[46]).

Ideally, some parts of your exercise should stretch the muscles as well as working them. I often see amateur athletes who, through their sporting activities, have toned their muscles but not stretched them. The inevitable result of this is that those muscles become strong, short, hard and inelastic. Short, stiff muscles compress joints and limit their mobility, leading to stiff joints at risk from trauma and wear. You may choose to carry out a planned, general stretching routine alongside your regular activity, or choose an activity like yoga in which stretching is an integral part.

Do not exercise too intensely. "Too" is a relative concept: what is too intense for one person may be not very intense for another. Since this book is about stress, we can look at these things in the same way. Physical exercise places demands on the organism, which require a response. This too is a kind of stress, and you know from your reading so far that different people vary in their ability to manage different kinds of demands. You know also that if the demands exceed your capabilities, there can be negative effects on your mind and body. Furthermore, you know that your ability to manage demands can be improved through training and practice, but that any increments must be slow and gradual. Physical exercise is like this. Don't wear yourself out, but do become steadily fitter. And as with food, do not become obsessive about your sport, about fitness, or about anything. Obsession produces stress.

The best exercise comes with those activities which are functional or which have developed organically over a long time. Some kinds of so-called fitness involve the very specific training of individual muscles. The other day I watched a YouTube video produced by a physical trainer to teach us specifically how to strengthen *obturator internus*[47]. Well, really! You do not need to do things like that. Those are notions deriving from simplistic theories about how the body works, thought up by minds imagining we have the knowledge to be able to micromanage nature. For an activity that has developed organically over a long time, I could give the example of yoga, which exercises the body as a whole rather than as a number of parts bolted together. By activities which are functional, I mean things like swimming or walking, things which one learns to do because they serve practical and natural purposes.

Finally, do things which you enjoy, which raise the spirit as well as conditioning the body, and do them with joy, not sufferance!

---

46 Endorphins: endogenous opioids. Strictly speaking they are not actually considered to be hormones. They are morphine-like chemicals released by cells in the brain and pituitary gland. They inhibit pain and produce mild feelings of euphoria.

47 A muscle in the hip area which helps move and stabilise the hip, and forms part of the pelvic floor.

Main Points

- It is easier to have a healthy mind if your body is healthy.
- First get the basics right.
- Healthy diet and good hydration.
- Manage alcohol intake, cut out smoking and other "recreational" drugs.
- Good rest and sleep.
- Appropriate activity and exercise.

11. In the hot seat

What about right now? - Fright, hostility, anxiety, defensiveness – First response strategies – Catch 22 - Training yourself - Best laid plans - Five "be's"

Here and now, eyes open, one step at a time.

- Anonymous

In Part 2 we looked at changing your ways of coping in order to achieve long-term benefits. The long term is all very well, but what about *right now*?! You still need "first response" strategies, and if you are reading this book, the chances are the ones you are already using are proving unsatisfactory.

What do you do when you feel threatened or challenged? Do you:

- Become frightened and give in to the challenge, escape from it, or freeze?

- Become angry or hostile and speak or act aggressively?

- Become flustered and awkward or clumsy in your words and behaviour?

- Become anxious about exposing your weaknesses and behave defensively?

A large proportion of people do one of these things in response to a sudden challenge. This is because in our early evolution our stress responses developed primarily as a mechanism of survival in a dangerous world, and they are still heavily conditioned by the primitive logic of "fight or flight". So we have a relatively small number of basic responses to draw upon quickly, driven by anxiety, fear and/or aggression.

However, in modern civilised societies we are fortunate that fighting or escaping, in the literal sense, are rarely vital responses in everyday life. Moreover, they can be inappropriate in various ways:

- If fear determines your words and actions, it will be very easy for people to take advantage of you, and the less you will get out of life. The more you yield, the more demands will be placed upon you. The more you escape, the less satisfaction you will have in life and the lower your self-esteem and confidence levels will sink. Yielding or escaping will bring an immediate relief of tension, but then resentment will build up. Furthermore, each time you yield or escape, you will miss opportunities to develop your coping skills and to prove to yourself that you are in fact capable. Instead, you will reinforce your fundamental lack of self-confidence.

- If aggression determines your words and actions, one of two things will happen. You may enter into an unpleasant conflict which will raise your stress levels in the immediate aftermath, as well as giving rise to distrust and hostility directed against you in the long term. Alternatively, if you are dealing with somebody who reacts with fear, there may be no immediate conflict, but you will still be regarded with distrust and fear/hostility in future dealings, by that person and by the other people around you.

- If anxiety, hesitancy and confusion determine your words and actions, you will be unsatisfied with yourself (thus raising your immediate levels of tension), you will not achieve your goals, and you will not be taken seriously in the future.

First response strategies

So, what more appropriate things might you do instead? Clearly, stressful situations are of many kinds. However, a great many involve other people, for instance at home, at work, driving your car, in government offices, talking to customer services on the phone. In personal interactions, you might, for example:

- Exert self-control, refusing to act impulsively or to get upset.
- Count to five before responding.
- Take a slow breath or two.
- Focus. Really listen to what the person talking to you is saying.
- Try to look at what is happening to you from the outside.
- Go out of the room for a minute.
- Close the immediate interaction and agree to talk later.

I have noted above how our immediate responses are heavily influenced by primitive mechanisms which, in the complexity of modern society, are often inadequate or inappropriate. Nevertheless, we still want to enact them. How can we change them?

Simply by employing the same five-step procedure introduced in Part 2. Let us briefly recap:

1 Know yourself.
1. Question yourself.
2. Just stop!
3. Take control.
4. Review results.

If you have forgotten what these steps involve, go back to Chapter 8 and review them.

Steps 1 and 2 must be taken *in preparation* for future threatening events or situations, in order that you may enact steps 3 and 4 at times when you are confronted by a challenge or threat.

Catch 22

Since you are reading this book, you are probably suffering from chronic stress. Remember that chronic stress comes about not only because of the situations in which we find ourselves, but also because of our habitual responses to them. Indeed, those responses often help to maintain the situation which we believe is the source of our stress.

We certainly need to change responses that favour short-term relief over long-term benefits, but we also need to ensure that adequate emergency responses are in place. The only way to do this is through practice and experience, and here we come up against a classic "Catch 22" situation. You need to develop new skills to manage your stress, but the experiences needed in order to develop them will cause you a little more stress until such time as you are sufficiently proficient.

Learning is never easy at the beginning. On the one hand though, we must reflect that a lifetime of increased peace of mind will be well worth the small cost. On the other hand, there is a way to ease the learning experience. It is to enact typical situations of stress in role-playing games with the help of friends.

Training for the hot seat

Role-play with friends is a safe and entertaining way of practising your responses. Keep the situations simple and the role-plays short. Do not make things over-elaborate or over-long. You do not want to rehearse what you would say and do in a long and complex interaction. You are not a fortune teller; you cannot know how a situation will evolve. Instead, you need to develop a range of basic responses which protect you but which are also fair to the other people involved, and which diffuse tensions rather than escalating them. Concern yourself only with basic responses to simple situational cues of the kind that "press your buttons". For example, if you know you react badly to sudden and unexpected demands made on you when your day has already been planned, imagine and role-play a *simple* situation of this kind and your *immediate* responses to it.

If you don't feel happy about asking friends to help you, you can enact the situations in your imagination, although this is less effective. Also, a word of caution: If you are role-playing in your imagination, the activity has to be dosed carefully, because by overdoing it you risk actually raising your anxiety levels through the constant reliving of stressful situations in your mind. For this reason, it is advisable only to do this kind of imaginary enactment during short periods which you specifically assign to it, like you would when practising any other skill, such as playing a musical instrument or a sport. Do it for no more than a few minutes at a time, then stop. Avoid doing imaginary role-play if you have an obsessive-compulsive tendency or disorder.

This does not apply when role-playing with friends, because the activity is more like a game and will have a beginning and an end. In both cases (either with friends or in your imagination), do not let your creative fantasy run away with you: make sure the situations you enact are realistic, typical of the ones you are likely to meet in everyday life. And introduce some humour - have fun with it!

Instructions to yourself

Another thing you need to do in preparation of typical or anticipated situations of stress is to build and retain a short mental list of instructions to give yourself[48] when you find yourself in the hot-seat. An example list in a situation of anticipated inter-personal conflict might be:

- "Just stop!"
- "Two slow breaths."
- "This is difficult but I can do it."
- "Steady...!"
- "Be in control of yourself!"
- "Listen to what (s)he is saying, then answer calmly."
- "Tell her/him I need to think about what he has said, and agree to meet later in the morning to talk about it."

Best laid plans

As Robert Burns wrote, *"The best laid schemes o' mice an' men gang aft a-gley"*, by which I am told he meant they "often go awry". This is because you can be as sure as you can be sure of anything that your encounter with your situation will not happen exactly as you rehearsed it in your role-play. That is why you should keep your role-plays basic and simple. But in any case, there will always be unforeseen turns or events to deal with. Some of them might be welcome, so prior to the event don't indulge in negative "fortune telling" about how things will go. But some turns of events might be unwelcome. So what can you do to deal effectively with negative events that might not happen as you have foreseen? I will give you five instructions that should help you to do this. You can turn them into instructions to tell yourself.

1. Be aware.
2. Be calm.

---

48 "Self-instructions".

3. Be flexible.

4. Be brave.

5. Be fair.

You will notice that I have chosen to use the word "be" rather than a verb for "doing" something. This is in keeping with your admonishment to "just stop" i.e. stop your habitual "doings". Concentrate on *being* for a moment, rather than *doing*. Assuming this is not a situation in which you or anybody else is in grave danger, you do not, right here, right now, *need* to *do* anything. You may take your leisure to act when you choose to act: that *might* be now, if you feel sufficiently calm and capable of doing so, but it *does not have* to be.

Being aware

It will be useful to you, when you find yourself in the hot-seat, to have developed the habit of awareness: of the situation, of what is going on around you, of the people present, in particular yourself and the other key players in any interaction. Take them in for a moment while suspending any judgement or reaction.

With regard to yourself, focus for a moment on those responses which we have seen are part of your stress response: your sensations, your emotions, your thoughts and your behaviour (for example facial expressions and body language). If, for example, you feel the nervous rush of adrenaline coursing through your body, take a second to appreciate the sensation. Do not judge it ("this is bad") or try to change it, just observe it. If you feel angry, look upon the feeling with interest. Imagine you are a normally emotionless alien like Mr Spock of Star Trek, feeling this emotion for the first time. How does it feel, to feel "angry"? Again do not judge it or try to make it pass, just observe it. If you find yourself thinking, "I wish I were anywhere else but here right now", let the thought come and observe it for a moment, then let it go... like a feather carried on the breeze. Do not let your ego interfere: the more say it has, the less you will see yourself objectively!

If you are talking to somebody, observe them, their expressions, behaviour, tone of voice, again with interest and, again, suspending judgement. Listen to their words, take in their meaning, that is, without your own prior judgements projected onto them.

All this is done in a few moments. It is amazing how much ingoing and outgoing information the brain can handle and process in a very short time. The ability to multi-task helps, and multi-tasking, like any skill, improves with practice.

Why is this kind of passive, detached awareness helpful?

1. It helps to keep you calm.

2. It helps you not to misunderstand other people because of your own preconceptions.

95

3. It helps you avoid committing yourself to impulsive and inappropriate action, keeping your options open, and thus maintaining your flexibility.

Being calm

Another way of saying it would be to stay "grounded". The utility of this should be obvious. But how to achieve it? You will already have a great advantage if you have remained aware. Further, there are three concrete techniques you can employ to help you.

1. Control your breathing. Slow, abdominal breathing engenders calm. In the next chapter I will introduce you to a breathing exercise which will help you to reduce your anxiety levels. By practising the exercise every day, you will gain a level of control over your breathing, which can be applied immediately in any stressful situation.

2. Control your heart beat. People can learn to exert voluntary control over the activity of their internal organs and indeed there are mind-body techniques that are used to achieve this. One is called "biofeedback", for which technological apparatus is usually required, as without such apparatus we are unable to perceive the workings of many of our internal functions. The heart however, is relatively simple to work with because we can feel its beat. If it is beating fast or powerfully, we can often feel it in our chest, but if not, we can put the index or middle finger of one hand on the pulse at the other wrist. Fundamentally, the technique of control is not complicated. In fact, it is easier than you might think: we simply focus our attention on our heart beat and use our will or intention to make it calm. With a little practice, you will be amazed at how easy this is. Taking a few slow, abdominal breaths will also help. Practice this technique so that you can use it when needed. (Obviously, you are not going to be taking your own pulse at the moment you are confronted by a difficult situation - that was only for practice!)

3. Mentally lower your centre of gravity. Or rather "lower your mental (emotional) centre of gravity". (You will not literally be lowering your physical centre of gravity, but it will feel as if you have done so, giving you greater stability and poise). In the Japanese martial art of Aikido, it is taught that we have a "one-point" within our abdomen, a few centimetres below our navel. (Interestingly, this is very close to where the physical centre of gravity of the average human body is supposed to be). In order to maintain perfect coordination between the mind, the body and the whole universe, one must keep one's "one-point" low in the abdomen. Fright, anxiety and anger are said to make it rise up into the chest, and so in these states it helps mentally to "lower" it again to below the navel. This is a form visualisation technique and a brief act of meditation rolled into one. See the little locus of energy dancing in your chest, take it with your mind's eye, surround it by a pool of serenity, and take it gently down to where it should be calmly residing. Its serene stability must be down there to help you stay grounded, it should not be jumping up making you feel flustered and confused!

Being flexible

You have to be flexible because you do not know what is going to happen next. If you have committed yourself to a course of action beforehand, it is difficult to produce appropriate behaviour if things do not turn out as you had planned. If you have followed my advice to "just stop", it will be easier to keep flexible.

Of course it is not always so easily done as said. The unpredictable can raise anxiety levels. You might become flustered, or you might "just stop" but then "freeze" right there! How can we remain calm in the face of the unpredictable? How do we retain a degree of command in uncertain waters? It requires a certain amount of belief and faith – belief in oneself and one's own abilities, and faith that in the normal course of things everything will be all right, as true disasters are rare. It also requires a certain tolerance of uncertainty, which like all attitudes, can be learned. A lot of the things we have been talking about to favour the positive resolution of stressful situations – attributes, skills, behaviours – build upon each other in a network of virtuous cycles, in which the development of one aspect will favour the others. This will begin to happen for you if you read and digest the material in this book and begin using it by the simple expedient of facing life with a calm and positive attitude.

Being brave

Being brave means facing our own anxieties and fears. It means having the courage to do the right things despite our fears, because they have to be done. This is really the only way to overcome our anxieties. Being aware and calm, knowing ourselves and developing as people (I will say more about the latter two things later), all help us to be brave.

Being fair

The object of all the above is to help you remain calm, rational and balanced in a stressful situation. Reflect upon that word, "balanced". Many stressful situations involve minor or major conflict with other people, who may be feeling as much stress and sense of indignation or injustice as ourselves. This advice and these procedures are not suggested in order to allow you to win a battle against the other person, they are to help you *win the battle with yourself*. The best solution is a fair solution, which keeps positive personal relations intact and healthy.

Main points

- You can prepare yourself for stressful situations by:
  - Practising basic positive responses in a safe environment.
  - Learning some positive self-instructions.
- You can negotiate stressful situations successfully by:
  - Stopping your automatic responses.
  - Taking your time and choosing an appropriate response.
  - Being aware, calm, flexible, brave and fair.

12. Body techniques

Stress and breathing - Increased muscle tone - Blood chemistry - Chickens and eggs - Breathing practice - Stretching - Imagination and visualisation

Tension is who you think you should be. Relaxation is who you are.

- Chinese proverb

In this chapter we are going to look at some simple techniques to promote relaxation: slow abdominal breathing, mind-body relaxation, and voluntary muscle relaxation. Practised regularly, they will promote a more relaxed state through a reduction in the body's level of nervous activation. Regular practice means at least 10 minutes five days a week. Should you decide to use any of these techniques, they are really useful only if their practice becomes a habit, just as well-established as cleaning your teeth, washing your face, or combing/brushing your hair. I suggest that you begin by learning the breathing exercise. Only once you are well familiar and comfortable with this, proceed to the muscle relaxation exercise. At that stage you could do the breathing exercise on one day, the muscle relaxation the next, and carry on doing the two exercises on alternate days. Most people could manage that.

Stress and breathing

Our breathing mechanism and rhythm are modified in stressful situations, and when stress becomes chronic, our breathing may become chronically distorted, i.e. the altered breathing pattern becomes a habit in its own right. In the long term this leads to bodily changes that actually induce increased levels of anxiety, making us more and more prone to stress.

In a situation of urgent stress, the organism does not distinguish between situations of danger to life and limb and situations involving less drastic possibilities: our biological responses are the same. One of these responses is to prime for activity the muscles at the front of the neck. These muscles have little role in breathing when we are inactive and relaxed but an important role in it during strenuous activity. Their origins are at the vertebrae of the neck. From there the muscles run down to attach to the upper ribs behind and just below the collar bone. Their role in breathing is to pull the upper rib cage upwards at the front in order to expand the upper part of the thorax. Expansion of the thorax is the means by which air is sucked into the lungs. The thorax can expand in various ways and directions. In normal, relaxed, quiet breathing, much of this work is done by the diaphragm, but when we need more air to come into our lungs in order to provide oxygen for strenuous or energetic activity, other muscles have to be used, among them the muscles at the front of the neck. When these muscles are primed for action, two things happen. Firstly, their tone increases, causing the muscles to contract and shorten a little.

Secondly, their threshold for activation is lowered. That means that it requires fewer nerve impulses to make the muscles contract further; in effect, they become more sensitive.

Increased muscle tone

All this is well and good in temporary situations of stress, and the muscles at the front of the neck should return to normal when the stress subsides. However, in chronic stress the over-activity of these muscles may become a habit, and then the muscles remain tense even in moments when you are not feeling stressed. The upper chest remains raised, so when you breathe in you are starting from a position of partial chest expansion already. This means your breathing is shallow, and it may become fast to compensate for this. Thus, a habit of upper chest breathing becomes established. Furthermore, in situations of long-term stress and the consequent habit of breathing using the upper chest, physiological changes occur which make it difficult to reverse the habit.

Firstly, keeping the muscles tense becomes a new setting in the brain and nervous system. The brain, nerves and muscles are very close in terms of evolutionary development. Because of this, they possess important properties in common: excitability, the capacity to transmit information, and a certain kind of memory. The neuromuscular circuits involved in establishing muscle tone (or tension) can memorise and maintain the same baseline level of activity. When we are stressed or anxious over a long period the baseline tone becomes up-regulated. Increased muscle tension also becomes a habit because of primitive behavioural responses: raising the shoulders and sinking the head into them is a common response to danger, a response that can become a habit even when not required.

Another reason why these muscle changes can take on a more permanent characteristic is that muscle tissue itself changes in accordance with the demands placed upon it. Muscle tissue under constant tension becomes infiltrated with tough fibres[49], increasing its tensile strength but reducing its elasticity and extensibility. This is a long-term change, but one that may be reversed. In fact, the good news is that since muscle tissue adapts to demands, it can slowly adapt to a more normal situation by returning to its normal state.

A further complication is that tense shoulder and neck muscles are not only the *result* of stress and anxiety; *they also generate them*. How is that? Well, our minds become used to associating muscle tension with anxiety. So, when we perceive muscle tension, we feel anxious. (This is called "conditioning".) Then, if the muscle tension is also ultimately responsible for neck pain, this adds to our overall burden of stress in its own right. Thus a vicious cycle is set up.

Altered blood chemistry and anxiety

Upper chest breathing is generally shallower but faster than normal breathing. Under these circumstances too much oxygen enters the blood stream from the lungs and, critically, too much

---

49 Collagen fibres.

carbon dioxide leaves the blood to be expelled by the lungs. This is called "hyperventilation". But oxygen is good, right? Well, it's not as simple as that: oxygen is good for the body only in the right proportion to carbon dioxide. When there is too little carbon dioxide in the blood, the blood becomes slightly more alkaline. It is thought that the changes in the proportions of these gases in the blood may play a role in maintaining states of anxiety. One reason for this might be that blood chemistry influences the tone and control of nerves and muscles. If this affects the muscles of the internal organs (heart, stomach, intestines, and bronchi) or the blood vessels themselves, it can produce unpleasant symptoms, which in turn may trigger anxiety. In turn, anxiety favours upper chest breathing, so we have another vicious cycle. You will have read quite a lot about vicious cycles by now. Vicious cycles involve various elements which feed on each other, and they are generally bad for us!

The chicken and the egg

When we are in the presence of a vicious cycle like this, one can ask, which part of it happened first? For example, did anxiety cause the upper chest breathing or did the upper chest breathing cause the anxiety? So often paradoxes of this kind are generated by faulty logic. This particular one overlooks two possibilities:

1. There could be more elements involved than the chicken and the egg.

2. That chicken-egg is not static and timeless, but evolved over a very long period of time.

In our problem of upper chest breathing and anxiety, a third element involved is stress. Stress is a process involving on the one hand anxiety, and on the other upper chest breathing. Neither "came before" the other, they developed together, each new development in one leading to a further development in the other, and both responding to greater or lesser degrees to ongoing variations in stress.

You might appreciate now that stress involves a network of factors. What we need to do is not to focus only on one element of the network, but to train ourselves to produce new and better responses to challenging situations in various spheres: mental, physiological, and behavioural. This chapter is concerned the physiological sphere, of which breathing is an important part.

Slow abdominal breathing

Now let us begin to learn how to retrain our breathing. The aims of this exercise are three-fold:

1. To make you more relaxed.

2. To retrain your breathing pattern in the long term.

3. To provide you with a technique to control your anxiety levels as needed in the short term.

This exercise should be done for five to ten minutes daily. You should assign a time for it when your mind is not going to be filled impatiently with the things you have to do; a place which is warm, quiet, and pleasant; and rules around it which establish that you are not going to be disturbed (family cooperation, mobile phone silenced and Skype turned off, etc.).

The exercise is done initially lying on your back on your bed, or on a rug, carpet or exercise mat on the floor. Your legs can be stretched out flat, but it is sometimes more comfortable to have your knees bent, resting inwards against each other, feet placed slightly apart on the surface you are lying on. Otherwise, put your knees over two pillows. The exercise is best done with your eyes closed.

Stage 1: Practise every day for one week

You will need to memorise these simple instructions before you begin:

1 Begin to breathe calmly with your abdomen.

1. Make your breathing just a little slower than normal.

2. As you breathe out do not blow the air out forcefully, just let it flow out naturally.

In fact, you will be breathing with your diaphragm, it just feels like the abdomen. You need to learn to use your diaphragm more and your chest less. Rest one hand lightly on your tummy. Relax your tummy muscles and feel your tummy expand as you take an in-breath. Take a few in-breaths like that to get the feeling. What are your chest and shoulders doing? Are they rising on your in-breath? They shouldn't be moving very much. If your chest and shoulders are rising when you breathe in, mentally relax them, and mentally inhibit them on your in-breath. After the first few sessions you will no longer need to rest one hand on your tummy, but you will need to check up on your chest and shoulders from time to time.

Do not focus on making your breathing deeper, or you will make it too deep, which is counter-productive. Focus on making it slower. Then it will also get just a little deeper naturally, but in the right measure. Don't make it *very* slow, just a little slower than normal.

In normal quiet breathing, no effort is required to expel air from the lungs (in contrast to inhalation, which depends on muscular action to suck air in). The thoracic cage is elastic, and this elasticity provides the rebound energy to expel the air without any muscular effort.

By following these three initial steps you will be:

a. Beginning to train the upper chest muscles not to be constantly active and excitable.

b. Restoring normal blood and tissue chemistry.

c. Restoring a normal cycle of activation and relaxation of the autonomic nervous system[50].

d. Beginning to down-regulate the general level of activation of the sympathetic nervous system[51].

e. Engaging in a basic form of meditation, which favours mental and bodily relaxation.

Stage 2: Practise every day for one week

In addition to 1, 2 and 3 above:

4. Make your out-breath slightly longer than your in-breath. During your in-breath, count in seconds: "One, two, three", then breathe out: "...four, five, six, seven".

5. At the end of your out-breath pause for a fraction of a second before beginning your next in-breath.

By making your out-breath slightly longer than your in-breath, you will favour a better balance between carbon dioxide and oxygen in the blood. The slight pause at the end of the out-breath will have the same effect, as well as reinforcing the habit of not activating your breathing muscles too rapidly.

Stage 3: Practise every day... for as long as you need to!

Further instructions:

6. Don't count the seconds any more, see if you can maintain the rhythm without having to count.

7. Now on your out-breath, mentally (not vocally) say to yourself "Relax...".

---

50 The part of the nervous system that controls involuntary bodily functions like the heart beat and the digestion (see Chapter 5).

51 The branch of the nervous system that tends to set us up for "fight or flight" mode: e.g. increased heart rate, reduced digestive function (see Chapter 5).

Stretching as an aid to breathing practice

One of the objectives of learning to breathe normally is to help to relax the muscles at the front of the neck so that they can return to their normal state. Stretching will help to meet this objective, too, and I recommend a brief routine involving not only these muscles but also those with which they have close relations: those of the upper back, chest, shoulders and the rest of the neck. It takes about 10 minutes. It will enhance your breathing practice if you carry out this routine just before the breathing exercise. Details of the routine can be found in Appendix 2.

Practice in other positions

Although it may take you a few weeks of daily practice to become proficient at this kind of breathing, you will quickly begin to feel more generally relaxed before then. However, practising breathing only while lying down will train you in the use of your breathing muscles *while lying down*. It is not necessarily a skill transferable to the seated or standing positions, or to simple, non-strenuous activities like slow walking. The best possible outcome would be to be able to reshape your breathing generally, not just while lying down. Therefore, after a month or two of practise lying down, I suggest you do the following:

1. Every second time you practise your breathing, practise in the seated position instead of lying down. Sit on an ordinary chair, not a sofa or an armchair. Use a cushion if the chair is hard. Place your feet squarely on the ground, feet and knees 6 to 10 inches apart. Do not rest your back on the back of the chair, sit erect but not stiff. Check that your shoulders are not raised, but relaxed. Let your head drop slightly forwards and close your eyes. The rest of the exercise is the same as when lying down.

2. After a further month, begin to try to adopt and maintain the same kind of breathing pattern while you are standing up and going about your normal activities. You can start to do this a few times a day for short periods, until you find it becomes easier. Then you can begin to do it more frequently and for longer. After a while, you will probably find yourself doing it spontaneously. Keep going!

Use of breathing when you are in the hot seat

In the last chapter, I suggested that when you are faced with an imminent stressful situation, you relax and gather yourself by taking a few slow, abdominal breaths. This will immediately take the edge off your agitation, make you feel more relaxed and grounded, give you a few moments to reflect, and make you better able to deal with the situation appropriately. Now that you have begun your breathing practice, you will be increasingly able to employ this emergency measure effectively.

Mind-body relaxation

Slow abdominal breathing is the perfect prelude to other kinds of relaxation exercises. There are many of these. Two kinds which I have found particularly simple and useful, are the use of imagination, and an exercise in body perception.

Imagination and visualisation

Once you can easily practise slow abdominal breathing while lying down, you can begin to experiment with imagination and visualisation. I am using these two words in slightly different ways. By "imagination" I mean creating a scene in your mind and experiencing it in all its details. You will be imagining relaxing, uplifting, energising scenes. With the word "visualisation" I am referring to something more specific: a focusing of your attention on something real but which you are not looking at and cannot actually see. We can do this with parts of our body: for example, a painful hip or tense shoulder muscles.

Imagination

Here is an example of an imagination exercise. First you would lie down with your eyes closed, breathing naturally from the abdomen. Then you would imagine a situation such as the following one.

> *Imagine you are sitting in a sunny glade in a mountain pine forest. The ground is soft with moss, dry and warm in the sun. You feel its soft, warm springiness with your hands. Above you the sky is bright blue and the sunshine beams through the openings in the trees to flood the glade with warmth. See the vivid green of the pine branches swaying gently against the cobalt blue of the sky. Feel the warmth of the sun on your back. The air around you is pleasantly warm. The gentle breeze carries the scent of mountain pine and wild thyme. You can smell them. Breathe them in, slow and deep. Just below the glade a clear stream tumbles joyfully over its rocky bed, forming small waterfalls and deeper pools along its way. You can hear the sound of it tumbling among the rocks. The water is clear and pure and cool. You can cup your hands and take some to drink. Feel it against your lips and in your mouth. Taste its purity and feel it in your throat as you swallow it. When you have drunk, you go and lie in the mossy glade in the sun. Feel the soft moss under your body. The warm breeze is caressing your face and the sun is warming your chest, your tummy, your arms, your legs. Breathe in the pure air, and breathe it in again. You can stay here as long as you want.*

This is an example of a picture story you can tell yourself in your imagination. This story is mine. If you like it, you can use it, but later it will be better if you conjure up your own, one just for you. You might not be drawn to the mountains; you may find other kinds of scenes more relaxing or uplifting. The point is to go somewhere in your imagination that makes you feel happy and relaxed. If the mountains make you feel sad and anxious, don't go there, go to a tropical beach or go somewhere else instead! Go somewhere you feel a deep affinity with.

When you are there you have to fill your senses with what is around you, all your senses: sight, hearing, smell, touch, and taste. Imagine all the aspects of the scene, which create a beautiful picture for your eyes, music to your ears, sweet perfume to your nose; which are pleasing to the touch and delicious to the tongue. In this way you will make the experience whole, all-encompassing and all-consuming.

It is unlikely that you will become distracted if you do this. If you do, it may be because you have been disturbed by someone or something, you are not comfortable, the scene you have chosen is not sufficiently captivating, or you are overwhelmed by troubling thoughts. The first three reasons have simple remedies (arrange things so you cannot be disturbed, make yourself more comfortable, choose a better scene). The fourth is trickier. But you have to tell yourself that ten minutes out of your life is not going to make your situation worse, and these ten minutes could well help you feel better about things and more in control. Just like when the world seems a better place after a good night's sleep. Do your best, that is all you can do. Then, while imagining your scene, if distracting thoughts come into your mind, try to observe them in a slightly detached way, as if from afar, watch them as they pass by and away, and bring your mind calmly back to observing the details of your special scene.

When do you stop? That will come naturally. If I am taking a rest from a real walk in a beautiful, sunny forest glade, a time will come when I have experienced the delights around me to my satisfaction, and I will get up and walk on. It is the same in the imagination. Enough is the right dose. You can always come back. You should leave *wanting* to come back, not having over-indulged so you do not want to.

When you decide to stop, open your eyes and slowly sit up. After a few more seconds, stand up and move your limbs vigorously. Stamp your feet, shake your arms and hands. Use both hands to scratch your scalp lightly but vigorously. This will bring you back to proper alertness, so you can go about your daily life energised and not in a daze!

Visualisation

You may use visualisation to *will* or to *intend* changes in your body. For example, if you feel that a part of your back is tense and painful, you can create an image in your mind to represent the unpleasant sensation. Then what you do is to change the image gradually into a pleasant, soothing, relaxing one.

This can take many forms. If you have some idea of anatomy and some notion of the structures that are causing your discomfort, you could picture them (and it does not matter if your notions are vague or even completely inaccurate!) Picture the state they are in, and then gradually mould them mentally into a normal state. For example, stiff, tough, knotted, taut, dark, tired muscle melts into pliable, elastic, smooth, bright, vital muscle.

You could just as well use abstract images. That is, you do not have to have a picture in your mind of a particular muscle, a bone, an organ or any concrete object. You can just imagine, for instance, colours, textures and sensations. These can form an abstract picture in your mind, which you can morph into something pleasant. Red bogginess might be the image you get from a part which feels swollen and inflamed. You could change it into light pink silkiness, for example.

These are just examples, you must use your imagination: the possibilities are limitless. This is an area where experimentation is key. What are the benefits?

a   The mind really *is* able to change what happens in the body. Research has demonstrated this.

a.   The act of focusing the mind is very conducive to improved regulation of the nervous system.

b.   It is therapeutic to focus on things or qualities that make you feel good.

Body perception

Lie on a mat or rug on the floor, relaxed, practising slow abdominal breathing. For several seconds feel and focus on the weight of your right leg and the sensation of its contact with the ground. Feel the heaviness of your leg. Feel its points or areas of contact with the ground. Feel your leg and the ground gradually melding, merging, as if they were becoming one. Feel them as one. It is a curious sensation but a pleasant one. Take time to focus on it, avoiding trying to interpret what it means. Now do the same with your left leg. Do not hurry. Next, take time to do the same with your buttocks, back, shoulders, arms and head.

Voluntary muscle relaxation

When we become tense, our muscles become tense. The ones that do so the most are those of the shoulders, neck and jaw. This is because these muscles receive more impulses from the nerves of the sympathetic nervous system than the other muscles of the body. For this reason, they are affected by our emotions more than the other muscles. It is a primitive protective response. Long ago in our evolutionary past when stress might commonly mean having to fight "tooth and nail" for one's life, the shoulder, neck and jaw muscles were tensed to prime them for threatening or violent action. You can see this happening in dogs when, confronted with a threat, they raise their hackles and bare their teeth.

As we have discussed before, in chronic stress, a state of excessive tension in these muscles may become a habit. This in itself also *feeds* our stress, by various mechanisms:

1. We learn to associate muscle tension with stress, so that muscle tension then reproduces the emotions, thoughts, sensations and behaviours of stress.

2. Tension and over-activity of the muscles at the front of the neck changes our breathing, leading to the upper-chest pattern typical of anxiety, and changing our blood chemistry in a way that favours anxiety. Anxiety increases our vulnerability to stress. Anxiety and stress go hand-in-hand.

3. Chronic muscle tension is uncomfortable, and can cause further pain by causing spinal disorders. Discomfort and pain add to our overall stress.

The aims of muscular relaxation are to train yourself to be able to recognise when your muscles are tense and to be able to relax them voluntarily. As a practice that concentrates the mind on a non-emotional task, progressive muscular relaxation is also a form of meditation. It is therapeutic for this effect as well as the training it gives you to relax the muscles at will.

How to practise voluntary muscle relaxation

This exercise will take anything from 5 minutes to half an hour, depending how many muscle groups you include. If possible you should always include the muscles of the shoulders, neck, jaw, and face. Add to this any areas that you feel to be tense, and once a week carry out the whole body procedure.

As with the breathing exercise, you should assign a time for it when you are not going to be impatient to get away and onto other tasks, and a warm, quiet, comfortable place where you are not going to be disturbed. The exercise is done lying on your back on a mat, rug or carpet on the floor (not on your bed) with your legs stretched out straight. You may use a small pillow if necessary to make your neck and head comfortable. Your eyes should be closed. You can do these exercises daily but that is not essential. However, anything less than twice a week is likely to be ineffective.

Before you start to do the exercise, just lie relaxed for five minutes practising slow abdominal breathing and body perception. Are there any parts or areas which feel tense or unable to relax? These should be included in the exercise.

The exercise is very simple. It consists in voluntarily contracting different muscles for a few seconds, then voluntarily releasing them as completely as you can. You do this three times, then move onto the next part of the body. The contraction should not be extreme, because that could cause the muscle to go into spasm. However, it should be quite strong, so that after a few seconds you feel mild discomfort. You should not hold your breath, but keep breathing normally throughout the exercise. Here are some instructions for the fists:

Clench both fists. Do this quite strongly so you feel mild discomfort, but not with maximum effort. Do not hold your breath. Keep your fists clenched for about five seconds. Now stop clenching, open your fingers, and let them, your hands and your arms relax. Mentally form the word "relax". Focus on the feeling in your hands and forearms. Imagine that your breathing is coming from your forearms. Each time you breathe out, they relax a little more. Feel them relax more and more, reducing the tension gradually to zero. They may begin to feel heavy and warm. Focus on that feeling. It is a pleasant feeling.

These instructions are easily adapted to any muscle group. The following table is a list of the actions you can make to involve most of the major muscle groups. They are listed in the order I suggest you follow. Before doing the exercises, look at the contra-indications and precautions in the section below.

For most of these muscle groups, when you relax the muscles, all that is required is that you release the contraction and passively "will" them to release all their tension. However, there are two muscle groups which will not return naturally to their most relaxed position when you are lying on the floor, so you will need to gently stretch them out a little. The first are the muscles you use to curl your fingers up when you clench your fists. You need to help them by opening your fingers to their normal resting position before relaxing all muscle activity. The second are the muscles used to raise the shoulders when you shrug. The pressure of the floor will stop your shoulders descending again when you relax these muscles, so you will need to gently lower them to their normal resting position.

Order	Muscle groups	Action
1	Front of hands and forearms.	Clench both fists.
2	Back of hands and forearms.	Open your fingers and pull back your hands.
3	Shoulders.	Bring both shoulders towards your ears in a shrug.
4	Front of neck.	Tilt your head down to bring your chin nearer your chest (without raising your head from the floor).
5	Back of neck and upper back.	Push the back of your head against the floor.
6	Jaw.	Clench your teeth.
7	Forehead and face.	Frown and screw up your face.
8	Shoulders and middle of back.	Push both your arms and shoulders backwards (into the floor).
9	Low back, buttock and hamstrings.	Keeping your knee straight, push your right leg and heel against the floor. Repeat with the left. (Don't do both together!)
11	Calves, soles of feet and toes.	Push your right forefoot down (point your foot) and curl your toes. Repeat with the left. (Don't do both together!)
12	Top of feet, front of legs and thigh.	Bend your right foot upwards and flatten your knee against the floor. Repeat with the left. (Don't do both together!)
13	Tummy.	Make your tummy muscles hard, while continuing to breathe normally.

Table 12.1: How to contract the various muscle groups for the muscle relaxation exercise.

Contraindications and precautions

- If you have poor teeth, do not do the jaw-clenching exercise.

- If you suffer from frequent cramps of any muscle or muscles, do not do the exercises involving those muscles.

- If you have any kind of muscle problem, do not do the exercise involving that muscle unless you have discussed it with a health-care practitioner expert in muscle and joint problems.

- If you have any kind of joint problem, do not do any exercise which works muscles around that joint unless you have discussed it with a health-care practitioner expert in muscle and joint problems.

- If you suffer from any ill effects after doing the exercises, do not do them again until you have consulted a competent health-care practitioner.

Integrating breathing, imagination and relaxation exercises

I once read a book introducing Western readers to self-care practices based on the ancient Indian medical art of *ayurveda*. The number of practices recommended to start the day was quite overwhelming. Clearly in a busy life we cannot do everything, as the hours in a day are limited. We also need to work, attend to our daily tasks, and live a little! Here are some suggestions to allow you to carry out the practices recommended in this chapter without having to sign off work every day.

1. At the beginning, practise slow abdominal breathing for ten minutes every day. As soon as you feel you are able to do it without effort, you may use the imagination and visualisation exercises while you are breathing slowly with the abdomen. You shouldn't attempt to do this until you are entirely at ease with the breathing, probably not before the end of the fourth week.

1. At the same time, you may begin to practise voluntary muscular relaxation on alternate days to slow abdominal breathing. That is, one day you do slow abdominal breathing, the next you do muscular relaxation, and so on.

2. After month 2, begin to practise the breathing activity in the seated position instead of lying down. You can do this every second time you practise it.

3. After a month 3, begin to try to adopt and maintain the same kind of breathing pattern while you are standing up and going about your normal activities, as described above.

These exercises will work if you do them regularly. Better little and often than an occasional long session. (The former is extremely useful, the latter next to useless.) However, don't become obsessed with them. If you find that a rigid self-imposed obligation to carry out your routine every day is adding to your stress levels rather than alleviating them, it is time to vary it, reduce it or even stop it for a while.

Main points

- You can promote relaxation by practising:
  - Slow abdominal breathing.
  - Imagination and visualisation.
  - Voluntary muscle relaxation.
- This will:
  - Relax you if you feel stressed.
  - Relax tight muscles.
  - Promote more general, long-term relaxation, by a number of mechanisms.
- Exercises only work if you do them! (And that means regularly.)

13. How to change your mind

Lead into gold - Learning - Meta-thinking - Five steps to swap goblins for allies - Be brave, experiment! - A sense of proportion - An example

In order to carry a positive action we must develop here a positive vision.

- The 14th Dalai Lama, Tenzin Gyatso

In the last chapter we looked at body techniques. Body techniques focus on the workings of the body, and how you can change them to promote relaxation rather than a state of alarm. With body techniques you are working on an aspect of your behaviour: your body's response to stress. Behaviour though is the most superficial level of the stress response. Below this lie our thoughts and emotions. If behaviour is like a view of the surface of the sea, thoughts and emotions are what lie out of view below the surface.

There are movements and currents, too, that run deeper than our thoughts and immediate emotions. These shape and move what goes on in our thoughts: they are our underlying attitudes and deeper emotional tendencies. When we go down really deep, it is dark and we cannot see as we can see nearer the surface. This is the world of our subconscious. We shall not be going there in this book. This is a practical manual and a toolbox for everyday life, so we will stay near the surface waters. In this chapter we shall deal mostly with how to change thoughts and attitudes.

We have already spoken (in Part 2) about the need to change our mindset, above all our negative or unhelpful attitudes and habitual negative thoughts (goblins!), for example:

- You think everything is bad or will turn out badly.
- You get unreasonably angry over trifles.
- You are worried or fearful all the time.
- You are over-critical of yourself or other people.
- You think you are not as good as other people.
- You would like to appear better than other people.
- You see problems rather than solutions.

These are just a few examples of conditioned thoughts and attitudes which are bad for you and the people around you. If you have them, you need to change your mind!

"But that's the way I'm made", you might object. How many times have I heard this?! No, that is the way you have become accustomed to being. It is a habit. Habits can change: it is called "learning". An infestation of goblins? Goblins can be thrown out. Evict them and fill your mind with allies!

Now you might say, "But it's difficult to change". And I would reply, "Yes, and nobody said it was easy. But neither is it so difficult you cannot manage it!"

Maybe I hear you ask, "How can I change?" Now we're talking! Above all, slowly but surely. In this chapter you will find some practical suggestions on how to begin to exchange your dark, anxious, angry, fearful, hostile, anguished or pessimistic thoughts for bright, calm, gentle, untroubled, friendly, accepting and optimistic ones. Like the alchemists of old, you are going to turn lead into gold!

Keep learning

Life is about learning, and learning is for life. If we stop learning we stop adapting, we wither and die in spirit, we fossilize, we become spiritual dinosaurs. Habits, of mind or action, are thoughts or behaviours which have become rigid. Note that stiffness, whether of mind or body, is a characteristic of ageing and decline. Have you noticed how some people, when they age, become like caricatures of themselves, all their idiosyncrasies becoming exaggerated and stubbornly fixed? This is not inevitable. You will have noticed others who buck the trend. The difference is in an open enjoyment of life and a willingness to learn. If our unbending habits are causing us stress, we have to soften them up and then change them. This means learning new thoughts and behaviours. So it may help if we know a little bit about how learning happens.

- Firstly, many habits are what we call "conditioned responses". For example, you may jump whenever the telephone rings. Why? The telephone ringing does not pose any danger to you. It may be because, due to past experience, a sudden sound has become associated in your mind with an unpleasant or dangerous situation. This is called conditioning. Simply recognising your conditioned responses and thinking about them can help you to tame them, so that they cause you less stress.

- Secondly, thinking or behaving in a certain way is more likely to become a habit if you receive some kind of reward quite soon afterwards. If your bad habit is rewarded in the short term, you will probably keep doing it regardless of any long-term disadvantages. An everyday example is smoking a cigarette because it gives you a buzz or relieves your anxiety or somehow makes you feel better right now, even though you know that smoking may give you lung cancer or heart disease in the long term. Rewards can be quite subtle. For example, you may feel "rewarded" for your behaviour by:

    ◦ The immediate kick of eating a double portion of trifle for which, if you are struggling with overweight, tomorrow you will berate yourself.

    ◦ The relief of getting something off your chest in an argument, which nevertheless you may regret tomorrow.

- Feeling righteous after resigning from your job in a fit of indignation, an action which you may be sorry about tomorrow.

- Receiving sympathy for bodily symptoms such as pain arising from your stress.

- You need to begin to recognise your "rewards" and weigh them against their long-term consequences. Remember, you said before that you didn't want to reach the tipping point (or you have already reached it and you don't like it). So however difficult it is going to be to give up your addiction to short-term rewards, you have to do it.

- But let's turn it around: if your good thought or action, your ally, is rewarded in the short term, you will probably keep on doing it. So, every time you choose a less damaging response to stress than the urge to light a cigarette, that good response should also bring a swift reward, either in itself or because you reward yourself for it in some other way. You could, for example, put the price of that cigarette in a special piggy bank to go towards a special treat for yourself. The more you don't smoke, the sooner you'll get the prize! Or you could arrange with a friend who also wishes to give up smoking to congratulate each other every time you each make a healthy decision. Learning is easier if it involves other people.

- Thinking or behaving in a certain way is more likely to become a habit if any fear of negative effects is removed or neutralised soon afterwards. For example, I know people with chronic health problems who are unwilling to take any time off work during acute exacerbations because they are proud of their work record and know they would feel guilty about taking time off. Or they are self-employed and they would lose out economically. Such fears may be neutralised by the realisation that contrary to their belief, it is the more responsible thing to manage their health and their work rationally. By taking sick leave when they need it, they will avoid the risk of driving themselves until the illness takes a more dramatic turn, at which stage they may be forced to take a much longer period off work.[52]

- Bad habits are likely to occur less if they are punished. The problem is we are talking about stress, and punishing yourself would add to your stress - I don't recommend it! But what you can do instead is to administer small joke punishments. A fun technique is to put an elastic band around your wrist and twang it every time you submit to a goblin or give in to a bad habit. Make it light hearted. For goodness' sake don't get mired in guilt if you slip up. Just get up again and get on again!

---

52 Sometimes this too might actually be an unconscious or partly conscious motivation: the socially sanctioned release from responsibility, and the sympathy that serious illness or breakdown would bring. However, that would be a lie. We are still responsible for the outcome, one with potentially serious consequences, because we did nothing to avoid it. In the situation described, if we are aware of this feeling and acknowledge it, we can manage it.

115

- Bad habits are likely to occur less and less if the incentive to carry them out is removed. So, remove from your life anything which may make you want to behave in a way that isn't helping your stress. That may mean anything from not keeping chocolate anywhere near you, to not keeping your tablet glued to your body, to reassessing your friendships.

- Changing habits is much easier if:

  ○ You have clear and realistic goals. You cannot become a perfect person by tomorrow morning. In fact, you cannot become a perfect person. But, you can have made a small but significant step towards being happier by tomorrow morning. Slowly is not a problem. Surely is a must.

  ○ You keep tabs on your behaviour. Observe yourself, praise and constructively criticise yourself. Watch out for Goblins. Tread lightly though, not obsessively, you really don't need to breathe down your own neck from morning to night!

  ○ You involve other people. The right people. Surround yourself with optimistic, supportive people. They are your allies. Shun negative, complaining, selfish people who go around spreading goblins.

Meta-thinking: seeing beneath your thoughts

Many people much of the time say things or do things while completely oblivious to the underlying meanings or motivations attached to what they have said or done. But you cannot learn to change your thoughts without digging a little into what lies beneath them.

Meta-thinking[53] is a deeper and broader mode of thinking, which thinks about what you think, about the hidden meanings and motivations beneath your thoughts, and about the thoughts behind your actions. Meta-thinking requires and trains deeper awareness of your thoughts, words and actions. It is a useful skill to have because it enables you to understand more completely your own thought processes, the ideas, needs and emotions behind them, as well as your interactions with others.

In order to reduce your stress, you need to change your thought processes, and you can only do that if you are fully aware of them. The more you can engage in meta-thinking, the more easily will you be able to change the thoughts that are generating or maintaining your stress.

Next time you recognise a troublesome goblin in one of your thoughts, ask yourself:

- Why did I think/say that?
- What emotions propelled that thought / those words?

---

53 Meta- is a Greek prefix meaning "beyond".

- What needs am I expressing by that thought / those words?

- Have I ever thought or said anything like that before? When and in what situations?

- What other situations have made me feel the way I did when I thought / felt that?

You may not get any instant answers, but it's the habit of questioning that counts. If you keep questioning, answers will start arriving.

Keep replacing goblins with allies

Do you remember the steps for changing that I introduced in Chapter 8?

- **Know yourself.**

- **Question yourself.**

- **Just stop!**

- **Take control.**

- **Review results.**

In Part 2 we looked at your coping strategies and suggested that it was possible for you to change them. The above 5 steps can be applied to that end. In Chapter 11 we saw that they can be applied in the short term when you find yourself in the hot seat. But they can also be used to change your habitual, background patterns of thought.

Here's how:

Knowing yourself means being self-aware, particularly of your automatic thoughts and your attitudes. Meta-thinking helps you to be more self-aware. Most people think things and do things without consciously observing themselves. If you want to change the thoughts and actions which are causing you problems, you have to become used to observing them. When you feel an increase in your stress level, ask yourself: What did I think that brought with it that feeling? What happened to trigger that thought? What did I think and do then, as a result of feeling stressed? We have talked about methods to do this systematically in previous chapters, but once you get the hang of it, you will start to do it spontaneously.

Questioning yourself means thinking about the appropriateness of your thoughts. Ask yourself, was that thought rational? Was it realistic? Was it fair? Was it balanced? How far am I being biased by my ego? What evidence do I have to tell me it was valid? How reliable is that evidence? Am I looking at things objectively? Is there a goblin behind that thought? Try also to think of ways of thinking that would have been less stressful for you and produced a better outcome. In this exercise in rational thinking and introspection, don't be unfair (to others or yourself!) or selfish. If there are other people involved, try to put yourself in their positions, and try to be respectful to them. Being kind is not a weakness, it makes you feel good and that in itself is a stress buster.

Just stop! You need to "stop" your habitual thoughts. Your habitual thoughts represent a sort of explanation of the world. You need to stop it. I stole this idea from Carlos Castaneda. Castaneda wrote a series of books about his apprenticeship in sorcery, under the supervision and mentorship of a Mexican Indian he called Don Juan, his "benefactor". Don Juan repeatedly exhorts his pupil to "stop the world", without which he would never truly be able to take ownership of the "sorcerer's explanation". One of the means used to achieve "stopping the world" was "not doing", that is, by not doing or thinking one's habitual actions or thoughts. If you are reading this book I doubt you are in training to be a sorcerer, and the transformation we are talking about is nothing in scope or degree to the one required by Don Juan of his apprentice, but we can still make use of the basic idea.

The idea is that your world is constructed by you. One could debate this philosophically until we all get a headache, but the fact is that the way you perceive and understand the world is very much your own. You made it! If that is holding you back or causing you stress, and if you wish to move forward and be free of stress, you are going to have to change it. A vital step in this is to stop making the world in the same mould you have been using until now! "Not doing", in our case, means not taking for granted that our point of view is the right one or the best one, putting our assumptions on hold, and reining in our automatic responses. Only once we have weakened the grip of our old "world" can we begin to fashion it into a new and better one.

How do you even begin to do this? It is easier said than done, of course, but you have to do it. When you feel the amber button pressed and that familiar feeling of stress coming on, with all its attendant thoughts, you have to nip them in the bud. Stop them forming, developing, materialising, acting upon you. This may begin with something as simple as letting your shoulders down, or refusing to become angry or flustered as you usually do, or choosing only to observe rather than interpret. Then you must remove yourself (metaphorically rather than physically) to a place of stillness. A useful set of thoughts is this: breathe a little more slowly from the abdomen, lower your centre of emotional gravity to a point within you below your navel, mentally form a whisper to yourself of the words "Just stop", and create a quiet stillness around yourself, within which you will dwell for a short while... seconds or minutes, depending on the needs and possibilities of the circumstances, and your own abilities.

Taking control is to use the window of opportunity you have just created by stopping your world to choose to think something more positive. When you choose to think a certain thought, rather than thinking automatically, you are swiping away a goblin and reclaiming your sovereign will. You are taking control and with this you are taking responsibility for your thoughts. Well done! This is how it should be. You are an adult person, bound to act with a sense of responsibility for your own life, and worthy of that responsibility, too. Remember, you are responsible for your happiness, nobody else is. Once you realise this, you must take up the reins, sit in the driving seat, and assume control.

Reviewing results means observing the effects of your new way of thinking. This is like having conducted an experiment, a behaviour experiment. If the outcome was satisfactory, you will be more likely to think in a similar way the next time you are in a similar situation. If it was less than satisfactory you will try something else. That is how we learn.

Better the devil you know?

In Part 2, you made a behaviour experiment. You want evidence that a different way of thinking will improve your life? Quite right. So make an experiment. Try it for a while and see what happens! It may be a risk, but it is a risk worth taking.

Some people don't like taking risks because they are afraid of the consequences. They act as though any chance of negative consequences were always more important than the chance of positive ones. Behind that behaviour lie some unsound assumptions:

- If I do something different, negative consequences are likely. This is wrong. Serious negative consequences can happen in life. Most of us have experienced them, sometimes on account of our own actions. But, *a priori*, they are no more likely than extraordinarily positive ones. The truth is that extremes of bad and good are rather rare compared with middling degrees of both. However, our skill at managing the world can only improve with experience and thought, and that can only happen through continued trial, error and success.

- Any risk is unacceptable. This is wrong, too. I am hard pressed to think of anything you can do or not do to avoid any risk. The acceptability of a risk depends on its gravity, its likelihood and the importance of the opportunity associated with it. If the risk, reasonably considered, were simply to expend a little effort and have friends temporarily raise their eyebrows, but the opportunity is lifelong peace of mind, the risk is worthwhile.

- If I do nothing, there is no risk involved. Wrong again. If you are under chronic stress, the risks of just going on as you are very important: anxiety, depression, burn-out, ill-health, unhappiness. It is unreasonable to go on doing the same things and expect different results.

The bottom line is that if you do not start to experiment, you will not change, and if you do not change, you will remain stressed. Is that what you want? NO! Wonderful! Let's go then and see what happens if we think more positively and do things differently!

The concept of behaviour experiments is to challenge your ingrained beliefs about the consequences of your behaviour. I have a lady client who told me she hated having days off, weekends away or going on holiday, because all the time she would be worrying whether something awful would happen to her son. On normal working days she didn't worry because her mind was otherwise occupied. There was no particular reason for her worry: her son is grown up, healthy and happy, and is not engaged in any hazardous work or pastimes. I proposed she make an experiment. It was a national holiday the next day and she was going on a day trip with her husband to such and such a place. Just for one day, I asked her to forbid herself to think about her son. If he came into her mind, she was to let him pass on through, and bring her mind back to the here and now. She did this, no disaster befell her son, and the sky stayed in its place in the heavens. That experiment was just a small step towards learning. But if she carries out this experiment repeatedly, it will gradually begin not to be an experiment any more: it will become her natural behaviour to focus less on fears about her son.

Words, words, words

Sometimes people tell me on the phone that they are in "agony" with back pain, and then I see them walk quite happily and sprightly through my door a few hours later.

How often do you hear people (or yourself) describing things as "terrible" or "dreadful" or "an absolute disaster" or "a complete nightmare" or "horrific", when they are nothing of the kind? A war is a disaster. Having forgotten to buy an ingredient for the dish you are now making is not.

Of course, we sometimes use exaggerated words for comical effect. There is no harm in that. But sometimes we can get into the habit of using them to draw attention to ourselves and our unhappiness. This is called "catastrophising", and it means we are under the influence of the Catastrophe Goblin!

If we get into this habit, we risk two undesirable side-effects. Firstly, the words will become devalued, people will realise this and pay them less attention. (This is, in effect, what is said to happen if you "cry wolf" too often.) You will have to think of ever-more catastrophic language to produce the same effect. It is a sort of linguistic inflation. Secondly, every time we use an exaggerated word or expression, we reinforce our own belief about how bad our life is. In short, the catastrophic use of words helps to maintain a negative attitude to the world.

If this is you I am talking about, you need to be aware of the words you use, catch yourself before uttering a disproportionately negative one, and replace it with something more measured. And read the next section.

A sense of proportion

Resetting one's sense of proportion can quickly mitigate stress. The Sunday Times of 1st March 2015 carried an article about an RAF nurse and paramedic called Charlotte Thompson-Edgar. Squadron Leader Thompson-Edgar was awarded a Victoria Cross in recognition not only of her "exceptional performance" in six tours to Afghanistan, but also the "great skill, courage and determination" she showed in saving a badly injured soldier in difficult circumstances. She had used a pioneering medical technique in an ingenious and unconventional way to save the soldier, who had lost 75% of his blood. Thompson-Edgar said of her experiences in Afghanistan: "You see injuries like that and then you come home and you hear people in Tesco whingeing about this, that and the other. You just want to say, 'Oh my God, have you any idea?'" Her observation, I feel, needs no further comment.

Chucking out the Perfectionist Goblin

Let us, by way of example, consider a person infected by the devilish little goblin inside her head that tells her she must do everything perfectly. Perfectionism, an enormous stressor, derives from a complex set of beliefs about personal responsibility and personal value. Unconsciously, the perfectionist believes that only perfect performance will bring the regard that he or she desires. Perfectionism is often related to narcissism (excessive self-regard) and is stop number one on the main line to obsession/compulsion. It is a tiresome burden because it throws a spanner in the works of setting out reasonable priorities based on urgency and importance, and reasonable expectations based on necessity. No, every task, even the most banal, becomes demanding of all the time, attention and care required for perfection to be achieved. Zen is well and good, but this is ridiculous. At its extreme, it is immensely frustrating, time-consuming, fatiguing, and distressing.

Let us call our subject Miss Perfect. The Perfectionist Goblin tells Miss Perfect she is not quite good enough. She may be good, but she is not good enough. The goblin tells her that if she wants to be valued by those around her, and if she wants to value *herself*, she must do better. Only the best is good enough for her. This is not true, it is a lie, but that is what the goblin tells her. Further, the goblin makes Miss Perfect believe that she personally is responsible for anything around her which is not perfect. This is another lie. We shall not concern ourselves with how Miss Perfect got the Perfectionist Goblin, just with what it tells her and how she can get rid of it. So, how can Miss Perfect get rid of her goblin?

1. **Know herself.** She must look at the deep needs she expresses in her attitude and behaviour. If she looks hard and honestly enough she will recognise in herself an excessive desire for the esteem of others, low self-esteem, but exaggerated self-importance.

2. **Question herself.** She must ask herself:

   a. Does every task *really* have to be performed to Olympic standard to be fit for purpose?

   b. Isn't it possible that beyond a certain point, the returns are not worth the expenditure of time and energy?

   c. Couldn't I be spending that time better in some other way, like relaxing, talking to my friends or engaging in a hobby?

   d. Is it *really* so important what everybody else thinks about me?

   e. Aren't there many good things within me *as a person,* beyond my wish to live up to expectations?

   f. Are my efforts really so important in the greater scheme of things?

   g. Might I not be important for my *human qualities* instead of my abilities and my work ethic?

3. **Just stop!** Every time she realises that she is being perfectionist, she must stop. She may have to be firm with herself that she is not going to behave as usual. Then she must create a quiet stillness around her and stay within it for a little while. She must refrain from doing, and stop her train of thoughts, for that time. She could breathe as she has practised and mentally form the words to herself, "Just stop", until her mind is soothed.

4. **Take control.** Then, quietened, she must choose a response. On the one hand, she has her habitual ones, on the other, some alternatives. If she chose one of her habitual responses, how realistic, reasonable and balanced would they be? Can she find a more realistic, reasonable, balanced response than her habitual ones? I am sure that she can. Then she must *choose,* rather than acting automatically.

5. **Review results**. She must regard this as a behaviour experiment and observe the results. If she has acted differently than normal, she should ask herself first: Did the sky fall in? Have I become an outcast? I expect the answers to both questions will be "no". In fact, I would expect the contrary: the clouds will have cleared from the sky, and she will begin to be appreciated more as a more balanced person who is a pleasure to deal with. Then she should ask: Has my work or family life suffered? My guess is that it will improve, because she will stop wasting time on useless details, be more aware of broader needs, be less wrapped up in herself, and less tense to be around. But the principle viewpoint

from which to view results is that of peace of mind and happiness. She should ask: How do I feel within myself? I would expect her to be able to answer: "Better, more relaxed, more at ease".

Nine things for Miss Perfect to think about while she is "not doing":

1. There is no perfect thing, act or person.

2. The law of diminishing returns. After a certain point, any further degree of improvement requires an ever greater input of effort. There comes a time when the further effort is not worth the further improvement. Maybe I have a distorted idea of how far along the road to infinity that point is.

3. Perfectionism is an extreme position and a distortion of the mind. Surely balance is a better goal than any extremism.

4. *"The better is the enemy of the good"* (Voltaire). You might redo the same task infinitely, and find new imperfections each time. How far do you want to take it? You might scrap something that is very good because you cannot attain perfection. Learn to say, "It's not perfect, but it will do fine."

5. Learn to distinguish between the important and the unimportant, the urgent and the non-urgent. While important tasks require more care, unimportant ones require much less or none at all! Urgent tasks require speed, not perfection, which would slow them down. Not all tasks are urgent. Some can be left till another day. Some can be safely forgotten. Doing things which are not important or urgent just because they exist takes time away from my true priorities: the people and things I love.

6. I see imperfections entirely imperceptible to most other people. I will not be judged on these.

7. Perfectionism is a goblin. Do I want to be its slave?

8. The longer I remain a perfectionist, the longer I will remain stressed and the more my perfectionism will become ingrained.

9. Humility. I am small and the world is large. I am not so important. I don't have to be the best at whatever it is I am trying to be the best at. I am already the best at being me. Value that. In being myself, I am no more nor less worthy than any other person.

Main points

- You can apply the principles of learning in order to change your thought patterns.

- Get used to asking yourself why you thought a certain thought (meta-thinking).

- You can swap goblins for allies by knowing yourself, questioning yourself, stopping your habitual responses, taking control, reviewing results.

- Behaviour experiments will set you on your way. See what happens if you approach things differently for a while.

14. How to solve problems

Problems and stress - A clever snake - Ten steps to problem-solving - Emotional problems – Intuition

Most people spend more time and energy going around problems than in trying to solve them.

- Henry Ford

What's it got to do with stress?

Problems and stress are inextricably linked. So, to have less stress it is good to be able to solve problems. But as Henry Ford observed, many people don't do this very effectively. The ability to solve problems is an enormous advantage if you wish to reduce your stress. The reason for this is three-fold:

1. A lot of stress is related to practical problems which seem too great or too many to deal with. So the better your ability to solve the problems in your life, the less stress you will suffer.

2. In the face of a problem, the simple knowledge that you are responding to it to the best of your ability itself reduces your stress. A difficulty can escalate into a major catastrophe or diminish to nothingness. The same problem may trigger a great deal of stress or very little stress at all. The difference is often in whether you engage with the problem constructively or do other things like ignoring it or running around it tearing at your hair.

3. At another level, stress is itself a problem. So you can apply problem-solving skills to the problem of stress, too.

So let's learn how to solve problems rather than spending time and energy "going around" them.

A clever snake

My son and I were on a hike in the mountains in north-eastern Italy. We were walking along a mountain stream, looking for pools to fish or bathe in. We came to a beautiful pool by a low waterfall. In the pool we spotted a grass snake swimming on the surface of the water by the near bank, and at the same moment the snake spotted us. It turned and fled, swimming gracefully across the pool straight towards the far side of the waterfall. It seemed to know where it wanted to go. The bank on the far side of the pool was high, rocky and nearly vertical but the snake was clearly taking a habitual route. It began to slither up the narrow ledges in the rock over which water was tumbling. The water washed it back down into the pool. It tried again in the same way and the same thing happened. It tried once more, twice more, but it couldn't get up the waterfall. Lying back in the pool, it raised its head and looked around. Trailing in the water to its left were the branches of a willow. It swam to the nearest one and, winding its body up and around the slender hanging branch, it climbed up, through the tree and over to the top of the bank above the waterfall – the point it had been trying unsuccessfully to reach a few moments before! This was no mean feat, as the animal was under stress and yet it still managed to think clearly.

I tell this story here because it is a lesson in problem-solving from an unlikely source. The snake wanted to get from where it was in the pool to a point above the waterfall on the far bank, but it found that it could not achieve that by its first choice of route. What did the snake do to solve its problem? It stopped. It analysed the situation. It looked for and found a potential alternative method. It tried the alternative method. It succeeded! Snakes are not supposed to be possessed of intelligence and they have tiny brains, so much tinier than ours. If a grass snake can so ably solve problems, we surely can!

Ten steps to problem-solving

What the snake did – analysis, search for ideas, trying a new idea – was, in a rudimentary way, the procedure I outline below as a method of problem-solving. I have expanded it just a little for human use because, as I have said, our brains are slightly bigger!

To do your best at solving any practical problem, this is what to do:

1. Decide if the problem is solvable and if so, whether you can and want to solve it.

   a. *Is the problem solvable?* If it seems impossible to you now, don't take that as your final answer. You may be feeling particularly weak and vulnerable right now and you haven't got the energy or the creative space to work it out. See how it looks when your energy levels are higher. Then, don't rely only on your own perspective, ask other people, as many as possible who you think will take an interest and give you a sensible answer. Then think about it again.

   b. *If the problem is solvable, can _you_ solve it?* Given that the problem is solvable in theory, have you got or can you get the necessary resources (knowledge, skills, equipment, money, and help) to solve it?

   c. *If the problem is solvable and you can solve it, do you _want_ to solve it?* I don't mean ideally, I mean realistically, considering the outlay in terms of time, effort and money. Sometimes, having weighed this up, you may consider that, actually, it is not worth your while to solve the problem.

If the answer to any of these three questions is "no", the answer to your problem is 100% clear: you are going to have to follow a different strategy, that of acceptance of and/or adaptation to the situation. If the answer to all three is "yes", great, let's go and solve your problem.

2. Analyse your problem.

   a. *What are its root causes?* If you know the cause, you are half way to a solution. However, remember that causes are often not so clear cut. Frequently there is no one distinct cause, but a network of factors which feed into and off each other. Try to see some of its salient elements. Also, try to be a little objective about this. It usually isn't going to help much to blame everybody else. Try to consider whether your own actions, too, are part of the problem.

   b. *Can it be broken down into several smaller problems?* What seems too great a problem to handle can often be made manageable by breaking it down into smaller parts. These can then be dealt with in order of urgency and importance.

   c. *What is the one thing that, more than any other, you could do to make things better?* Once you have a picture of the causes, or have broken down the problem into smaller parts, you will usually find that you do not have to deal with each and every element. There may be a key element which, if dealt with, will make everything better. Start with this!

3. Brainstorm your problem.

   You need to generate some ideas about solutions to your problem. Brainstorming means letting your mind create as many ideas as it can without worrying for the moment about being realistic or practical. You can do this on your own, but you will get a better "storm" of ideas if you have some other trusted people to do it with you. It is a relatively chaotic process. You must free your mind to think laterally, allowing it territory to be creative. Write down *all of* the ideas which are generated, no matter how absurd they may seem at first sight. Even the most absurd idea might produce some insight into the problem that you would not otherwise have thought of. And the exercise can be quite entertaining, generating some humorous banter as well as serious ideas! (But that is secondary: do not turn it into an exercise in generating absurd ideas just for laughs!)

4. Consider each idea seriously and reduce them to a short-list of five. Whereas step 3 was chaotic, this is where you put order into the chaos. First exclude any ideas that are clearly and obviously impossible to achieve for whatever reason. Be open minded and give each some thought: an idea might seem impossible at first but achievable on deeper examination. Do not exclude ideas which seem absurd but are possible to achieve, only those that are clearly impossible after adequate reflection, no matter whether they are otherwise sensible or absurd. For each of the remaining ideas, write down in an orderly

fashion (see the table below) their advantages and disadvantages. Once you have done this you will be in a position to select the five best ideas.

Idea	Advantages	Disadvantages
1	1. 2. 3. etc.	1. 2. 3. etc.
2		
3		
4		
5		
6		
7		
8		
9		

Table 14.1: Assessing and comparing problem-solving ideas.

5. Once you have selected the five best potential solutions, put them in order of "goodness". What is goodness? Chiefly, insofar as concerns problem-solving, it comprises:

a. Likelihood of success.

b. Simplicity.

c. Economy (not only in terms of money, but also effort, time, peace of mind, specialist help, etc.).

The simplest plan is the one with the least component parts, and hence the easiest to set up and with least potential to go wrong. Combine this with low expense and you get a measure of which is the easiest to achieve. And if you combine that with "likelihood of success" you have your measure of "goodness".

I suggest you assign points out of 5 for each of these attributes – likelihood of success, simplicity, and economy – to obtain a potential total out of 15 for each idea on your short-list. The best idea – the one you are going to work on – is the one with the most points.

Now you have a good idea, you are already at a good point on your path to solving your problem!

6. Sleep on it. Try to get a good night's sleep. Make sure you have not been working on your plan late into the night, otherwise you may not be able to stop thinking about it during the night, and you won't be able to sleep.

   Sleeping on it serves two purposes. Firstly, the next day you can review your thoughts and decisions of the previous day with a fresh mind. You may see opportunities, or pitfalls, which you missed the first time around.

   Secondly, during sleep the creative side of your mind is freed and comes to the fore. Many are the instances of intuitive solutions to seemingly intractable problems coming in dreams. Elias Hunt took out the first patent on a sewing machine with a needle with an eye in its point. Hunt claimed he had this idea in a dream, after a fruitless day trying to work out a key technical solution for his machine. In the dream he was chased by African cannibals who caught him and put him in a large pot. He kept trying to get out but they kept forcing him back in with spears. When he awoke in a fright, he realised that the tips of the cannibals' spears each had a hole in it. This was the solution he had been looking for!

   Needless to say, this step of sleeping on it doesn't have to come at this precise point in the process – it can be done any time, and you should do it as often as you need to.

7. Make your plans and gather your resources. Now is the time to draw up a detailed plan of action. What things need to be done? In what order? At what time? With what resources? This isn't a plan that is going to be set in stone. You will change it if the circumstances require it to change. Pay particular attention to the resources: What people, things and money are you going to need and how are you going to get them? To a certain extent we all have to work with what is available, we cannot hope for a perfect set of tools, people and limitless funds. However, we also need to be mindful of the old adage that you need to use the right tools for the job.

8. Act and persist. Don't give up. This quote has been attributed to Albert Einstein:

   "It's not that I'm so smart, it's just that I stay with problems longer."

Many a good plan has not succeeded for want of persistence. I have friends who throw in the towel at the first difficulty. The first difficulty does not mean that what you are trying to achieve is impossible or even too difficult for you. In fact, a first lack of success bears no relationship whatsoever with the chance of eventual success. This has been observed time and time again in the world of business and entrepreneurship. Make your mind up that you are going to succeed and don't stop till you find a way!

9. Take a rest. If you get tired, if you reach a plateau, if you find yourself banging your head against the wall, take a rest. In all probability you will find that things take off again when you start again refreshed, when the stars have shifted slightly in the sky, or whatnot.

10. Review and modify/change. At all stages stay flexible. Review your progress regularly and assess the adequacy of your plan. You will probably find along the way that it needs a tweak here, a shift in focus there, a wholesale change of course in another place. Don't be afraid to change your course as the wind and the tides dictate! Forging on stubbornly in the same direction regardless of prevailing conditions is not a recipe for success.

The whole process of problem-solving is summarised in the table below.

How to solve problems
1. Decide if the problem is solvable, and is worth the effort.
2. Analyse your problem.
3. Brainstorm your problem.
4. Consider each idea seriously and reduce the list to a short-list of 5 approaches.
5. Put your five potential solutions in order of goodness.
6. Sleep on it.
7. Make your plans and gather your resources.
8. Act and persist. Don't give up.
9. Take a rest.
10. Review and modify/change.

Table 14.2: A ten-step procedure for solving problems

But what about emotional problems?

The ten step procedure outlined above will work brilliantly for most practical problems. But some kinds of problems are emotional rather than practical. They require other approaches, including seeking emotional support from friends, trying to see things from a different point of view, and counselling. However, even emotional problems have a practical element. If your relationship is in trouble, if you are estranged from your children, if you have been tricked out of all your savings, if there is serious illness in the family, if a friend has treated you badly... you are certainly going to feel bad, and you are going to need to address your feelings and your emotional needs. But even while doing so, you will still need to work out what action to take and by what means. The analysis proposed above might seem a little cold and distant for emotional troubles, but sometimes that is just the perspective you need in order for you to see clearly the options and opportunities open to you. We will discuss emotions more fully in the next chapter.

What about intuition?

This practical, rational approach is not in any way to diminish the utility of intuition. I have mentioned above how solutions may sometimes pop into one's head in dreams, and equally frequently, a strong gut feeling is sometimes worth following. I am a great believer in intuition and what I propose above does not supplant it, but it is certainly a powerful string in your bow to use alongside it. In fact, the two should complement each other.

Intuitive dreams

Amongst other things, I am also an acupuncturist. One day I had been reading up about the particular approach to acupuncture that has developed in Japan. That night I had a strange dream.

> *I was standing in a room with a table to my left. Behind me at the back of the room two Japanese men were engaged in quiet conversation. I knew they were teachers who were there to examine a student. The door opened and a young Japanese man walked into the room. He was blind and had some sort of disability which affected his gait and movements. He walked over and stood in front of the table to my left, facing me. After a quiet pause, he came closer and took my left wrist in his hand. Then he took a small needle from the table behind him and inserted it into my upper lip in the middle just where the skin of the face meets the darker skin of the lip.*

The dream ended soon afterwards. It was such a clear dream and had a definite sense of "purpose" about it, that it created an impression on me. I was not familiar with the acupuncture point the young student had needled in my dream. In truth, I could not have sworn that it existed at all, although from my general knowledge of acupuncture theory, it seemed probable that it did. The next morning, I looked it up. It turned out that one of the uses of this particular point is to treat tongue ulcers, an affection that has troubled me regularly since early adulthood.

From this and other dream experiences, I have observed and identified two characteristics of the dreams that have in some way provided me with answers or true insights. Firstly, they have heightened clarity. Secondly, they emanate a feeling of "purpose". I would suggest that if you have a problem and you have a dream with these characteristics, take close notice of it.

Main points

- A better ability to solve problems will reduce your stress.
- Problem-solving is a skill you can learn.
- Problem-solving requires method.
- Intuitions and strong gut feelings can provide valuable answers or insights.

15. What about emotions?

Emotions and thoughts - Wealth of emotional experience - "Negative" emotions - Adaptive and maladaptive emotions - Emotional awareness - Emotional management - Stress and emotion - Sensation and emotion - Dealing with intense emotions - Dealing with intrusive emotions

This too will pass.

- Attributed to King Solomon, among others

A piece of bread, some fresh water,
the shadow of a tree and your eyes, my beloved.
No sultan is happier than me,
no beggar more sad.

- Omar Khayyam (1048-1141)

Another egg, another chicken

It has been said that negative emotions derive from negative thoughts. Let us question this. Could it not also be that a thought may derive from an emotion? Of course it could. So which came first, the chicken or the egg? In evolutionary terms, emotions are much more primitive than distinct, conscious thoughts. The brain machinery and processes that produce thoughts evolved later than those used to produce emotions. In practical terms, I think it is safe to say that both happen: thoughts may generate emotions and emotions may generate thoughts.

But while it is true that emotions will almost always generate thoughts, it is not true that thoughts will almost always generate emotions. Moreover, not every emotion is the result of a conscious thought, and not every thought is the result of an emotion. Emotions can arise in response to situations without the intermediary of a conscious thought. For example, you may suddenly be frightened by a loud noise just behind you. Some thoughts are quite dry, emotionless ones. A thought can arise, unencumbered by emotion, from a previous train of thoughts, for example, when discussing some practical issue.

A wealth of emotional experience

A rich emotional life is a form of wealth. Chronic stress impoverishes our emotional experience. To use a metaphor, the world becomes grey rather than full of colour. Absorbed in our situation and our stress, we fail to take pleasure in the small things in life. I sometimes watch small children and take pleasure in seeing the joy which they find in simple, small pleasures. I would like to look again at the world through their eyes and sometimes I manage to do so. It is tremendously liberating. Of course, small children also experience intense sadness at

133

things that adults may consider trivial annoyances or minor disappointments. But you have to take the rough with the smooth, and on balance, I think it is more beneficial to experience emotions (unpleasant along with pleasant) than to be numb to them. Furthermore, luckily as adults we have the advantage of a mature ability to choose: we can *choose* to delight in small things, and we can *choose* not to be overly affected by trivial disturbances.

Being alive to emotion:

- Allows us to experience joy and love.
- Is energising and enthusing.
- Enhances relationships.
- Reduces stress.
- Protects us from danger.
- Inspires and motivates us.
- Informs our judgement.

Negative emotions

What is a "negative" emotion? Is an emotion to be judged "negative" simply on the basis that it makes us feel unhappy rather than happy? Might not such emotions as fear, anger, sadness, sorrow, and grief actually have healthy functional roles? Of course they do! If we did not feel fear in the face of danger, we might act with indifference or recklessness, thus putting ourselves at greater risk. If we did not get angry at routine injustice, we would never act to change the behaviour of the perpetrators, for example by voting in an election. If we did not grieve for our loved ones lost, we might value family, friends, relationships and life less than we do. These emotions have positive roles. They are "negative", though, when their relationship with reality becomes distorted, when we feel them when they are unwarranted, when their intensity or duration are excessive, or when they are wildly unstable and erratic. That is when they no longer enhance our functioning as human beings, but hinder it. That is when they become "problems", "the burden that harms".

Adaptive emotions

The ability to experience emotional states, including unpleasant emotions, is innate in healthy human beings. But such experiences can be adaptive or maladaptive. What does it mean for an emotion to be maladaptive? Can you answer these questions?

- Are your emotional responses conducive to your thriving?
- Are your emotional responses harming others?

134

If the answer to the first question is "yes" and the answer to the second is "no", your emotions are well-adaptive.

Adaptive emotions are part of our ability to cope with change. We need fluidly responsive emotions that shift in nuanced ways according to changes in the context, not fixed emotional states that are poorly related to them.

Maladaptive emotions are those that are experienced as a general state or stereotypical response, or those that are too intense, prolonged or wildly erratic; or on the other hand, when emotions are deadened. In these cases, the emotions are no longer regulated well according to the environment and circumstances.

The suppression of emotions is not well-adaptive. It sets up inner tensions which manifest themselves as feelings of vague unease, anxiety, physical symptoms, or periodic explosions of uncontrolled emotion. These things will not be resolved unless the emotions are acknowledged and their sources understood and accepted.

Awareness of emotions

Emotions are an essential part of well-being, both personally and in our social relations. Moreover, awareness of our emotions is an essential part of awareness of ourselves, the route to self-knowledge. Emotions are the deeper substrate from which we can gain an understanding of ourselves from past to present.

Emotions help us recognise our affinities, those things, places and people which are good for us. When we understand what makes us truly happy, we are in a position to set true priorities and goals, giving us a compass and a set of landmarks for our unique journey through life. Thus, emotions are the ultimate motive force of our decisions and actions, because in life, we want to be happy, we don't want to be sad. In this, they can motivate us, guide us, and inform our judgement.

They inform our judgement in making decisions because an attuned awareness and response to emotions add an understanding of our true priorities to the equation when thinking about benefits, costs, risks and ethics/morals. While strong emotions should not cloud our judgement, an awareness of our emotional needs should inform it.

Emotional awareness is also directly linked to communication and relationship skills, because it helps us to understand other people's feelings and motivations. It is also important for problem-solving as many problems have an emotional aspect in the form of emotional sources and emotional impacts.

You will have noticed from the above that emotional awareness enhances several skills that we have already discussed in relation to coping with stress. In order that our emotions remain balanced and healthy, we need to be aware of them, so that we can manage our responses to them.

Management of emotions

What is management of emotions? Is not controlling them the same as suppressing them? There is constructive and destructive management of emotions. Constructive management of emotions makes us healthier and happier. Destructive management of emotions makes us unhappier and less healthy. Management of emotions means being aware of emotions to the right degree, not only of one's own but also others' emotions. It means expressing and responding to them not excessively, not insufficiently, but appropriately. Suppression of emotions is an automatic, indiscriminate response. It is not a good way to manage emotions. Constructive management of emotions is a fine and fluid balance, and it is a skill to be able to achieve such balance. Some people have this skill more naturally than others, but it can also be learnt, like any other skill.

Examples of unhealthy emotional behaviour and management are:

   2. Wild and/or extreme emotional swings.

- Dwelling on unpleasant emotions.
- Endlessly analysing one's emotions.
- Fear/Avoidance of emotions or their expression.
- Distraction of our attention or that of others to avoid emotions or their expression.
- Making decisions based entirely on one's emotions.

Emotional reasoning

Emotional reasoning is to interpret things, form judgements and make decisions based entirely or almost entirely on one's emotions. This is unbalanced. Emotions should inform our judgement and that is healthy, but they should not take over it entirely. The tyranny of emotion is just as one-sided as the tyranny of reason. Consider the words of William Gladstone[54]:

> *Men are apt to mistake the strength of their feelings for the strength of their argument. The heated mind resents the chill touch and relentless scrutiny of logic.*

But logic too, has its limits in dealing with human problems. To achieve balance, we need to cool down heated emotions and warm up cold reasoning.

---

54 William Ewart Gladstone (1809-1898): British Liberal politician and four times Prime Minister.

Stress and emotions

Chronic stress interferes with emotional awareness. Remember that when we are chronically stressed we have entered resistance mode. Our bodies and minds have been

primed for the long, hard slog. We must grit our teeth and carry on. Emotional instability would be a distraction to us, so instead, the mind blots out strong emotions. In fact, outbursts of strong emotions are a sign that resistance is failing, that we are entering exhaustion mode[55]. Resistance mode is a long-term compensation for the "desert crossing". But in the human being evolution has not yet produced the perfect article, and compensations have their costs. They can wear us out. Like all the other compensations involved, suppression of emotions is energetically expensive.

Furthermore, compensations tend to become more and more uncompromising the longer they exist. In resistance mode vicious cycles of compensatory responses are set up, one of which is de-prioritisation of / inattention to emotions. The compensatory pattern gradually accentuates and fossilises, until very little flexibility is left. This makes it ill prepared for change - one of its disadvantages. So resistance mode keeps us going only until it tires us out: it is not healthy in the long run. Sometimes we can be unaware of what is happening to us, as we can get used to persistent low levels of stress, to the extent that we consider everything quite normal and healthy. Until something happens.

Of course, emotions do come to the fore when our stress levels suddenly rise over and above their baseline (i.e. we re-enter the alarm mode of stress). Typical emotional responses are anger and fear (fight or flight). Anger may give rise to outward hostility or aggression. Fear may lead to distancing oneself from the source of stress (escaping) or freezing. Depression is another common reaction to stress.

If we tend to feel agitation, irritation or anger when stressed, we may need to engage in calming stress-relief strategies like meditation, massage or listening to tranquil music. Yet physical activity, too, can help discharge our aggression. We should choose activities which are not aggressive or competitive, as these would risk reinforcing our aggressive tendencies.

If we become depressed when we are stressed, we may need to engage in enjoyable, energising activities like a sport or some form of physical activity. However, we must also be mindful that sometimes depression may be nature's way of making us slow down to conserve our resources, so activities should not be too intense, strenuous or prolonged. If we feel depressed, it is much better, too, if we include other people in our stress-relieving activities. If we feel fear when we are stressed, we need to do these activities in an environment where we feel safe and supported.

---

55   For the three stages/modes of the General Adaptation Syndrome: see Chapter 4.

Sensations and emotion

Sensations are on the main line to emotional experience. One can awaken deadened feelings by using the senses, by focussing on what we see, hear, smell, taste, feel with our skin, or the feeling of our movements. What does it mean to focus on our sensations? It means to give them our full attention for a while. When we do this, although we may find them pleasant or unpleasant, we should not judge them "good" or "bad", or any other way. "Pleasant" is an impression, "good" is a value judgement. When you focus on your sensations, avoid making value judgements about them. Rather, you should simply observe them with an open curiosity.

This is an excellent way to de-stress. The other day I went for my evening swim in the sea. I was able to focus on the feeling from my muscles and joints as they moved and stretched. I was able to focus on the effect the cool water had on my skin and body, and on the feeling of the water passing over my skin. I was able to focus on the sound made by my movement through the water. I was able to focus on the salty taste of the small quantities of sea water that entered my mouth, and upon its smell in my nostrils. And I was able to focus on the interesting effect of the evening sunlight through the bubbles before my face as I pushed through the water semi-submerged. You do not have to go for a swim to do this. You can do it anywhere, any time, in any situation, for a few seconds or an hour. It is a great technique to reduce stress and diminish pain. Moreover, since the impressions of the senses are closely connected to our emotions, it helps you to connect with your emotional world again. This helps break the vicious cycle of chronic stress and numbing of the emotions.

Focusing on your sensations can be done as an exercise, as a useful recourse when your stress levels rise, or as a frequent habit. Hopefully, it will move gradually from the former to the latter.

Intense emotions

As we have seen, unpleasant emotions can have useful functions. Anger can stir us to action. Fear can save us from danger. But uncontrolled emotions, whether pleasant or unpleasant, risk bringing negative consequences. Uncontrolled anger is a threat to ourselves and the people around us. Intense and uncontrolled happiness (manic euphoria) can lead to reckless action and an equally intense, uncontrolled descent into sadness.

Fear or avoidance of emotions does not lead to whole health and well-being, and neither does indulgence in them. In my career as a health professional I have met many people who do one or other of these things. I do not wish to be sexist, I merely report this as an observation. Those people I have met who avoid their emotions have more often been men, and those who dwell on them have more often been women. I note also that emotional avoidance relates to limited self-knowledge, while emotional indulgence goes with a greater focus on the self. Thirdly, I see that people who avoid emotions are more often affected by sudden, serious illnesses, while those who dwell on themselves and their emotions suffer from a succession of minor but distressing complaints. These are not scientific observations, merely my own subjective ones, and I report them as such for your consideration. The important point is, neither avoidance nor over-indulgence are healthy strategies in the long run.

We need to feel our emotions and we need to express them in a balanced and fluid way. If the emotion we are experiencing is unpleasant, we should know that intense emotions do not last long. They subside and wane. This one, too, will pass. But they will last longer if we dwell upon them, think or talk about them endlessly, judge them, dissect them, discuss them at length or at every opportunity, even value them for their worth in secondary benefits, such as ongoing sympathy.

One of the best things anybody can do to cope with intense unpleasant emotions is to open up to somebody they can trust to listen to them and support them without judging them, and without telling them their opinion and what they should do. Remember, different people have different motivations, beliefs, ideals, priorities and goals, which won't match yours, so well-meaning advice from somebody else's point of view is often misguided. But being able to open up unconditionally to another trusted human being is immensely therapeutic in itself.

These are my suggestions about how to deal with intense emotions:

- Acknowledge but do not judge.
- Feel but do not dwell.
- Observe but do not act impulsively.
- Respect but do not fear.
- Share but do not indulge.
- Master but do not suppress.

Intrusive emotions

Negative emotions can be persistently intrusive. Intrusive emotions are those that come upon you seemingly of their own accord, and are persistent, difficult to dispel. Among them are fear, anger, sorrow, guilt, shame, envy, jealousy, and hostility. They tend to be the same ones each time, each to his own, and follow their own pattern depending on the person who has them. They may even be a more or less constant presence. They intrude into one's mind from deeper currents below. Those currents are the substrate which has nourished the growth and development of one's personality. They are the long tides arising from past experience, particularly the social, cultural and emotional context of one's early life and formative years, especially traumatic experiences. There may also be a genetic influence, more or less important according to the individual. There are a few pieces of advice which I would offer to help manage intrusive emotions.

First, do not act impulsively upon them. Stop! Take time. Take control of your actions but allow yourself to experience the emotion. Feel it but do not dwell upon it. It will pass, let it do so. Like leaves of different shapes and colours blown on the wind, emotions come and they go. Like the shadows of a clouds that move across the landscape. Like the moon which rises and falls. Do not allow the emotion to blow you away on its wind. Observe and experience but do

139

not act. See how you feel tomorrow. Wait till the edge of the emotion has softened before deciding whether or not to act, and if so, what steps to take.

Second, do not place great significance in them or fear them. Remember that although they may have great meaning in your past, they do not necessarily have any significance in the present. That is, the events or situations that gave rise to them in the past hold no danger for you here and now. Don't let them control you.

Third, although you are feeling them, do not dwell on them. Do not create a prolonged internal dialogue with yourself about them. Think of a pet dog sitting looking at you while you are eating, expecting food from your plate. It will only go on sitting there expectantly if you indulge it by constantly looking at it, talking to it or giving it food from your plate. Being aware of its presence is one thing, indulging it is another. If you do not indulge it, it will go and lie down somewhere else instead of sitting expectantly. The same is true with intrusive emotions.

Fourth, some emotions derive from thoughts, even though the thought may be an unconscious one. Thoughts can be intrusive too. Do not let intrusive negative thoughts upset you, no matter how disturbing you might find them. Everybody has disturbing thoughts, but they are only thoughts. Let them come and let them go. Do not attach any great significance to them.

Fifth, in the longer term, work on your attitudes and thought patterns, as explained in previous chapters. If your attitudes and thoughts are generally more positive, your intrusive negative emotions will be less frequent and bothersome.

Sixth, if intrusive negative emotions or thoughts are particularly troubling, intense or persistent, you may need to see a professional therapist.

Main Points

- Chronic stress deadens emotional experience.

- Emotions have useful functions and enrich our lives.

- It is not healthy to suppress emotions nor to allow them unbridled free rein.

- Allow yourself to experience emotions without interpreting them or attaching value judgements to them.

- It is normal for intense emotions to pass quite quickly. They do so if you do not dwell on them.

- All head or all heart are not healthy, they need to be balanced.

16. The art of communication

Good communication lessens conflict - Control of responses - Body language - Meanings -
How to listen - Empathy - Clarity - Tact - Negotiating - Assertiveness - Managing the ego

The brow, the eyes, the countenance very often deceive us; but most often of all the
speech.

- Cicero (79-51 BC)

Thus he speaks, and by his word he quickly pacifies the raging waters.

- Virgil (17-19 BC)

The bottom line is that a lot of stress is caused by conflict between people and a lot of conflict could be avoided or lessened by better communication. Good communication includes such things as:

- Being in control of your responses.
- Being aware of body language.
- Being aware of meta-meanings.
- Listening.
- Empathy.
- Seeking clarity.
- Being tactful.
- Negotiation.
- The ability to be assertive when necessary.
- Managing your ego.

Being in control of your responses

In the preceding chapters I have placed much emphasis on taking control of our thoughts and behaviour. This control should include how we communicate with other people. The rest of this chapter looks briefly at various aspects of being in control of the way we communicate with people.

141

Body language

Body language means the signals we give out through our expressions, posture and gestures. It is a part of what we call "non-verbal communication". Usually people are not aware they're doing it. It helps to make communication more effective if we are aware of body language and its significance. People instinctively respond to other people's body language because of the messages it carries. This usually remains at a subconscious level. But our goal is to be in conscious control of our behaviour, so we have to bring our reading of body language into our conscious minds. The only way to do that is to observe it and reflect upon it.

A lot of words have been spent in entrepreneurial manuals and other guides to wealth and success about how to use body language to give a certain impression and, to a certain extent, gain an advantage over you are interacting with. Do you know the kind of thing? Turn your palm downwards over the other's hand during a handshake to indicate status, who will call the shots, etc. I view this kind of advice much as I would view rat droppings in the larder. If you are attempting to tell lies with body language you will be found out. If you are using it coercively you will eventually get your comeuppance. In both cases you will create stress for yourself, in the first case because falsity goes hand in hand with anxiety (of being found out), in the second because conflict and resentment reside in the coercive situation.

Our objective is not to give a false impression, nor is it to gain unfair advantage. It is to understand the feelings and wishes of the people interacting with us, and to express our own feelings and wishes clearly and kindly, while maintaining mutual respect and keeping the temperature down. This is the best way to achieve acceptable and sustainable goals without trampling on the needs or feelings of others.

Your body language will naturally reflect the calm and confident state of mind you will have achieved by following all the other advice in this book! What you now need to do though is to be *aware* of body language, so that you can read other people, and so that you can avoid adopting postures or using gestures that might contribute to increased tension or conflict. The table on the next page gives some examples of these.

Reason for increased tension	Postures or gestures
It looks like (s)he's stressed, anxious, or ill at ease.	• Shoulders raised. • Head drawn down into shoulders. • A lot of blinking.
It looks like (s)he doesn't want to communicate freely with me.	• Closed eyes when speaking. • Arms crossed.
It looks like (s)he's afraid, lying, being evasive, on the defensive.	• Not making eye contact. • Fidgeting. • Constantly shifting position. • Arms crossed over stomach.
It looks like (s)he's being aggressive, hostile, and confrontational.	• Jutted chin. • Standing with hands on hips.
It looks like (s)he's trying to portray or take advantage of a superior status.	• Seated with legs open (men). • Seated behind a desk or on a higher chair. • Relaxed informal postures when the other is bound to observe more formality.
It looks like (s)he's being disrespectful.	• Not looking at the other, turning away, or attending to other tasks while the other is speaking.

Table 16.1: Postures or gestures that might increase conflict.

Being aware of meta-meanings

In Chapter 13 we looked at meta-thinking as a way to decipher the hidden meanings behind your thoughts and behaviour. These hidden meanings we will call meta-meanings. They are what is "written between the lines", or what is left unsaid, lying behind the spoken words. Let's take an example: the word "yes". Try saying the word "yes" in different ways, for example to mean:

- I strongly agree.
- I'm not sure.
- I don't believe you.
- Oh, all right then.

- Well?
- Really?
- Really?!!

You see that saying just one word in different ways can change its meaning. Those are its meta-meanings. It is not only the way you say things that changes their meanings but also the context in which they are said.

Effective communication requires that you get the hang of interpreting the unspoken feelings or thoughts behind the words. To achieve this, you must start with yourself. The next time you are in a discussion with someone, be alert for any moments when you feel a little uneasy (anxious, fearful, angry, uncomfortable, etc.) and be aware of the words that you say that are associated with those moments. Note your choice of words and the tone, inflection, stress and volume you put on the words. Try to think how they have been influenced by the context.

Ask yourself, why did I say that the way I did? What was motivating me? What was I hoping to gain? What emotions, attitudes or thoughts were associated with my words which I did not openly express? What thought did I have which I could not speak?

Once you get a hang of being conscious of your own meta-meanings, you will also be able to read others more accurately and consciously.

Listening

A client of mine comes into the consulting room asking me rapid fire questions about my health, my family, and my life, without once stopping to hear the answers before she starts telling me about her own. Good, I want to hear about her life. However, if I ask her a specific question, her long tangential answer doesn't necessarily relate very well to the question. This can be a problem if I am trying to solve the problem she came with. Imagine the problems in other spheres of her life where a more equal social exchange might be appreciated. If you talk too much or too loudly you won't hear what the other person is trying to say, and you might give the impression that you aren't interested or, at most, only superficially interested.

We live in a society so we have to get along with other people. But people want different things and some of those things are going to conflict with what you ideally want. The resultant conflict results in tension i.e. stress. At the same time, you who are reading this book are looking to reduce your stress levels. The only possible resolution is that people, including you, have to say to themselves, "I cannot have it all my own way, I am going to have to negotiate and compromise".

Having come to that realisation, the next thought is that you cannot possibly negotiate your respective needs and desires if you do not know what the other person's are. This might sound reasonable and even obvious, but many people do not behave as though they have realised these things. That is one important reason why so many people are always so stressed!

The art of listening is that of hearing and understanding what the other has to say, in a way which lets the other know you have heard and understood. Some common flaws are talking too much yourself, seeming uninterested, interrupting, jumping to conclusions, taking people too literally, taking things too personally, and not making an effort.

In order to listen effectively you must:

- Not talk too much or too loudly yourself! And don't interrupt!

- If you are listening, listen! Pay attention to the other person. Don't be thinking what you want to say next when you should be listening to them!

- Don't jump to premature conclusions or make automatic assumptions about what a person means, *listen to their words!* One sort of jumping to conclusions is taking comments personally. Don't assume that negative comments about the world are about you personally just because they touch a raw nerve.

- But don't assume either that spoken words tell the whole story, or nothing but the story. Listen to what hovers behind the words (meta-meanings) and be aware of body language.

- Be interested. You can show your interest in various ways. You can nod or say "Yes, I see..." or "I know what you mean..." to show that you've appreciated a point. Of course, you can also do these things on automatic pilot, but it can pretty obvious to the other person if you do this. Equally, if you are interested, that will be obvious, too. Another way of showing interest is to encourage the other party to express their thoughts and feelings. To do this you can say things like, "Please do go on...", "Tell me more!", or "I'm listening...".

- Show goodwill and really try to understand others:

  - What is their need?

  - What are their desires?

  - What is their motivation?

  - What do they propose?

  - What is their leeway?

If you truly listen, are aware of body language and meta-meanings, and aware of but not prey to your own automatic thoughts and emotions, you will be able to understand the other person accurately.

Empathy

Good communication is more than just an expression of literal meaning, as this quote from Nelson Mandela suggests:

> *"If you talk to a man in a language he understands, that goes to his head. If you talk to him in his language, that goes to his heart."*

Mandela is talking about empathy. You cannot understand another person well without feeling a dose of empathy. Empathy is the capacity to feel or appreciate to some degree what the other person must be feeling like. Some psychiatric disorders, such as psychopathy, schizophrenia, and extreme narcissism, are characterised by a lack of empathy. Most people are able to feel empathy, but to varying degrees. Some people are naturally very empathetic, others less so. Less empathetic people tend to come across as being a little cold or detached when confronted with situations or scenes which would be expected to trigger emotion.

For example, imagine that you saw a television report about a soldier who had been at war, and suffered severe post-traumatic stress disorder after returning to civilian life. He and his wife tearfully discuss the devastating effect it had had on him and his family.

- Would a lump come to your throat?

- Would you feel that it was interesting but not your problem?

- Would you rationalise that this were the inevitable cost of war but feel little for the people you have just seen?

In the latter two cases you are less empathetic than in the first. If you feel you lack empathy, in order to improve your communication skills, you may need to get some more of it! In situations that you witness involving tension, conflict, stress or trauma, begin to ask yourself explicitly what you imagine the people involved must be feeling. Try to imagine yourself in the same situation. If you witness somebody who is clearly angry, afraid, sad, in despair, feeling hopeless, try to imagine what kind of situation would make you feel the same way. Unless it would be too upsetting for you to do so, try to "live" in that situation for a few moments.

The other side of the coin is that some people keep their emotional responses under lock and key because they have suffered a great deal in the past. If that is you, remember that you do need, gently and gradually, to bring more balance into your life by allowing your emotions more freedom.

146

Seeking clarity

Be aware that while too few words can detract from clarity, too many obscure it.

Be aware that words can have more than one meaning, or may be interpreted differently by different people.

Be aware that unconsciously making biased assumptions based on insufficient information and selected key phrases is an important flaw in most human beings. (Goblins do this!)

Be aware that "a misunderstanding" is the collective noun for human beings: a herd of cattle, a pride of lions, a pod of dolphins, a flock of geese, a misunderstanding of humans, etc.!

These things mean that you have to be concise but not too concise, choose unambiguous language so far as possible, check the other's understanding of what you meant, check your own understanding of the other's point of view, and verbally summarise the main points that have been made.

To check the other's understanding, you could say things like:

- "Do you understand what I want to say?"
- "Do you see what I mean?"
- "Do you see what I'm getting at?"
- "Do you get my point?"
- "I hope I've explained myself clearly."

To check your own understanding, you could say:

- Could you clarify that please?
- Could you give me an example?
- Do you mean that...? (Here you can paraphrase what was said).
- If I understand you, you are saying that... (Here you can paraphrase what was said).

To summarise you could say:

- So, to sum up...
- So, in a nutshell...
- So, can we say/conclude that......?

Being tactful

If you are a teacher and you have to inform a hard-working and sensitive teenage pupil of a poor result in an important exam, you soften the blow. You don't say: "You failed". You say something like: "Unfortunately it didn't go as we hoped it would at this session". In doing so you have:

- Shifted the focus from the pupil's performance ("you") to unfortunate circumstance ("Unfortunately", "it").
- Indicated that you are in it with the pupil ("we").
- Indicated that this is not final and there will be another chance ("at this session").

Depending on the context and whom you are dealing with, the level of tact required may vary from being as direct as possible without seeming outright rude, to ultimate velvet-tongued diplomacy. Usually it will be within a range well short of these extremes. Some situations and some people, and some people in some situations, need treating with great tact. Other situations require plain speaking, and other people appreciate it. Clearly in a situation of tension and potential conflict, it pays to be tactful.

Being tactful means:

- Showing empathy and respect.
- Not being too blunt.
- Choosing *le mot juste*, the right language.
- Using tone of voice, expression and body language in keeping with one's choice of words.

Some people are tactful with natural ease. Others have to learn it. It is an excellent idea to observe and learn from the people you meet who have natural tact. Your ability to be tactful, to choose the right words, grows the more your self-esteem, awareness, sense of control and confidence develop. These things constitute one of the main planks of this book: that of reinforcing your inner resources to deal with difficulties.

Assertiveness

Sometimes you have to be able to say a firm "No". To do this you need to:

- Be strong and calm, a lion-burger not a mouse-burger!
- Be decisive and firm, no shilly-shallying, no beating around the bush, and do not waver!
- But be respectful.
- Use the level of tact which the situation requires.
- Use humour, if that will help.

Assertiveness is another of those useful qualities which grow along with self-esteem and self-confidence, but equally, every time you are assertive, you become a little more able to assert yourself the next time, because you are a little more confident in your ability to do so, and you have a little more self-esteem. And on it goes.

Negotiation

The purpose of negotiation is to arrive at a mutually acceptable resolution to differing positions. It is not to get as much out of it for yourself as possible regardless of the other person's feelings, needs and wishes. That would lead to resentment. If you have to have continued contact with that person, the resentment would simmer and lead to increasing tension between you, and hence stress. One may be clever and say, "Yes, but what if I will never see him/her again?" Perhaps, but if that were your habitual way of dealing with people, you would have a life full of stress anyway. Selfishness doesn't pay if you want a stress-free life. Generosity of spirit leads to a stress-free life!

So, what does this arriving at a mutually acceptable resolution involve? Firstly, it involves some of the things we have already discussed: listening to and understanding the person or the people you are interacting with, being clear yourself, using tact.

Secondly, it involves give and take. Concessions require counter-concessions. Often this may involve an offered benefit which was not involved in the main discussion, and may not even have been thought of by the other person (something you "throw into" the deal).

Thirdly, it involves good will and respect.

Effective negotiation:

1. Is not rushed.

2. States at the outset the purpose of the negotiation.

3. Clearly sets out the different positions.

4. Clearly sets out any non-negotiable aspects.

5. Seeks out common ground.

6. Always looks for ways to move forward.

7. Clearly and concisely states the outcome.

Occasions do occur of course when one must defend one's non-negotiable interests ("lines in the sand"), or defend oneself against aggressive or unfair positions on the part of the other party. This requires assertiveness and tact.

Role-play

A really good way of developing these skills is through role-play with friends. Set up situations in which:

- You have to tell somebody something that is probably going to upset them.

- You are approached by someone who wants to talk to you about some conflict of interest between you.

- You have to approach somebody who you feel has treated you unfairly or wrongly.

- You have to assert yourself against majority opposition.

Try to make the situation and the behaviour as realistic as possible. Doing this with friends will enable you to develop and practise a range of responses in a non-threatening environment. It is a little trickier in a real situation because there is an emotional load, but at least you will have practised your repertoire of responses. And you will manage the emotional load very well using the techniques presented in Chapter 11 ("In the hot seat")!

Be kind!

Negative feelings, attitudes and acts sour our lives just as much as they sour those of others. In our dealings with others, it is not good for ourselves or anybody else if we act in selfish, spiteful, vengeful or mean-spirited ways.

Manage your ego

In a way this book is about strengthening your ego, but not in a bad way. A strong ego is self-assured. It knows its strengths and how to manage them. A strong ego is well placed to effectively manage stressful situations. But a strong and balanced ego does not feel diminished by acknowledging its weaknesses or by not winning an argument. It can laugh at itself. It does not attempt to gain unfair advantage. It realises that you are neither better nor worse than anybody else on the planet.

Main points

- Good communication helps avoid tension and conflict between people.

- Good communication involves a number of skills which can be learned, and perfected through practice.

- A strong and balanced ego is an asset in good communication.

17. A little help from humanity

A problem shared - Kinds of help - Problems with access to help - Solutions

When we honestly ask ourselves which person in our lives means the most to us, we often find that it is those who, instead of giving advice, solutions, or cures, have chosen rather to share our pain and touch our wounds with a warm and tender hand.[56]

- Henri Nouwen

This is a short chapter, because the fundamental messages are simple:

A problem shared is a problem halved. Sharing a load makes the load easier to bear. The last straw will not break the camel's back if the other camels carry some of the first camel's straw. Help from other people (sometimes called "social support") is a major buffer against stress. A lot of studies have been done on social support and, taken as a whole, they show that:

- Its availability reduces stress.

- More especially, the *perception* of its availability reduces stress.

That means that if you feel the presence of support, or you can easily access it, you feel that your difficult situation becomes easier.

What kind of help from other people makes the difference? Any kind and all kinds, depending on your needs:

- Emotional e.g. a shoulder to cry on, getting things off your chest.

- Practical help e.g. a helping hand.

- Material e.g. money.

Who from? Anybody who has your interests at heart:

- Family.

- Friends.

- Support groups.

- Charities.

- Government organisations.

Everyone has access to social support of some kind but sometimes they may not *feel* that they have. Why should it be that you feel that help from other people is not available?

- The people closest to you are *the source* of the stress.

---

56 Excerpted from *Out of Solitude* by Henri J. M. Nouwen. Copyright © 1974, 2004 by Ave Maria Press®, Inc., P.O. Box 428, Notre Dame, IN 46556, USA, www.avemariapress.com. Used with permission of the publisher.

The family is the nearest potential source of help, but what if you are having family problems? You need to seek your support outside the family. At the same time, you will need to find some kind of positive evolution of your family situation. If you are having marital problems but you cannot improve matters by yourselves, and you want to avoid either going on as you are or a break up, you will have to seek professional help in the form of marriage guidance.

- You are depressed.

People suffering from depression become withdrawn and so separate themselves from sources of help. But depressed people *need* social support. This is a perfect example of the kind of vicious cycle that helps maintain problems. Research shows that making an effort to maintain social activities helps recovery from depression. You would do well to consider seeking help from your doctor and a psychologist or psychotherapist who is expert in cognitive-behavioural therapy.

- You are a hermit, a loner, or just plain shy.

If you are a hermit and still stressed, being a hermit isn't the life for you!

If you are a loner, great! The world is so full of people who huddle in a flock or follow the pack. You can appreciate things that they cannot. It does limit your access to social support somewhat, but if you are a loner, the chances are you have less need. But when you do? Even loners have *some* friends, perhaps much better friends than gregarious people, and often loners underestimate how much other people love them.

If you are crippled by shyness, you need to do something about it. Hang out with outgoing people and copy them. Exposure to your fear is good medicine to help you get over it. I used to be very shy and this worked with me. It had to as I loved a woman who loved people! If you can't get over it on your own, or with the help of good friends, seek professional help.

- You do not know where to turn.

Look around and ask. There is a lot more out there than you might think. Ask the council. Ask in the library. Ask a search engine. Ask anyone! Look for charities, organisations and departments that might be able to help. Join a support group. The Internet is a great resource. You can search for organisations whose very reason for existence is to provide information and advice to people in your situation. There are online support groups / forums for just about anything, in which members share experiences, advice, information and encouragement. One of their major advantages is that they connect people who are experiencing similar difficulties and can therefore understand each other's emotional and practical needs.

- You have an appearance to keep up.

If you believe your personal, public or professional worth depends on the appearance of being totally independent and self-reliant, and that that is more important than your health, I think you should question those beliefs. I do not doubt that if you questioned them objectively and rationally, you would find them wanting. That appearance of independence you so cherish is a façade. Nobody is totally independent and totally self-reliant. No man is an island. Moreover, if you are chronically stressed, you are deceiving yourself. You *do need* support. Stubbornly guarding your appearance of self-sufficiency is not a mature thing to do.

In conclusion, if you are suffering from chronic stress, don't suffer alone or in silence. Spread the load. Talk to people who are empathetic with you, and find out where you can get any practical and material help you need. Build and maintain a solid and dependable social network that is as extensive as possible. The load will seem much lighter for you!

Main points

- Help and support from other people is a major buffer against stress.
- Help and support may be emotional, practical or material.
- Help and support are available to everyone.
- It can come from family, friends, support groups, charities, or government organisations.
- The Internet is a great resource.

18. A stress toolbox

Basic options - A two-dimensional model - Practical and emotional challenges - From within or without - Shadows from the past - Chronic illness - Some scenarios - The toolbox - A note on priorities

> *You can never be sure exactly what collection of problems you're going to face,...*
> *That's why you need your whole toolbox in front of you.*[57]

- Donald F. Kettl

To handle stress effectively you need to have at hand a range of strategies that are adaptable to different situations – your "stress toolbox". Just as with a real toolbox, using the wrong tool for the job will produce botched results. Have you ever tried to knock a nail in with the head of a screwdriver? I have and I can tell you that it doesn't work very well. Here I present some simple ways of understanding stress and to select the right tools for the job of managing it.

Your basic options

You have basically four options for your attitude to a challenge:

What to do about the situation	**Alter it** 1 Good organisation. 2 Good communication. 3 Problem-solving.	**Avoid it** 1 Saying "no". 2 Avoiding negative people. 3 Avoiding subjects of conversation likely to result in disagreement. 4 Avoiding stressful activities. 5 Reducing the number of tasks you do.
What to do about yourself	**Accept it** 1 Tolerance of uncertainty. 2 Acceptance of things you cannot change. 3 Forgiveness.	**Adapt to it** 1 Emphasising the positive. 2 Reassessing your standards and goals. 3 Learning new skills.

Table 18.1: Basic options

---

57 Excerpted from *System Under Stress: Homeland Security and American Politics* by Donald F. Kettl. Copyright 2006 by CQ Press/SAGE Publications. Used with permission of the publisher.

Two of these options concern what to do about the situation, two of them what to do about yourself. Happily, they all begin with the letter 'A'. The bullet points in Table 18.1 give just a few examples for each option.

I do not wish to suggest that these are all inherently "good" responses. Clearly avoiding a challenge may potentially have positive and negative effects. Whether it is "good" or "bad" overall will depend on your judgement of the situation. How do you make that judgement? Read on!

A two-dimensional model of stress

I once heard of a fellow who claimed there were 18 dimensions. I wondered why not 17 or 19, but I probably wouldn't understand the answer. In any case 18 is too complicated for us, so we will make do with just 2 dimensions!

The dimensions of the model I wish to present relate to the challenges which you associate with your stress, and each one refers to a different aspect of those challenges:

1. Whether the challenges you are facing are mostly practical ones or mostly emotional ones.

2. Whether you are challenged mostly because of factors inherent in the situation itself, or mostly because of factors within yourself.

These dimensions should not be seen in black/white, either/or terms, but as gradients. Most stress has both aspects of each dimension, but in varying proportions, so that often one aspect can be seen to predominate over the other.

First dimension: practical challenges vs emotional challenges

Practical challenges are things you have to do. Emotional challenges are events or situations that impact upon you emotionally. Moving house is a large practical challenge although it may also be an emotional one, for instance if you are very attached to your old home. The death of a much-loved pet is mostly an emotional challenge, but also has practical implications.

Practical challenges require practical solutions. They require you to manage the problem at a practical level. Your strategies, essentially, will be to analyse the problem and organise to respond effectively to it. Emotional challenges require that you manage your emotional needs: self-expression, seeking support, seeing positives.

All of your coping skills and strategies have the fundamental goals of *reducing, simplifying, and/or sharing the* challenges you face. This can be done in different ways, and these ways will vary according to the extent to which your challenge is practical or emotional, and also whether your stress is concerned with too many competing demands or one overwhelming demand.

- Practical tasks can be *reduced* in number by assessing their real importance and priority, and setting realistic goals.

- Seemingly overwhelming problems can be *simplified* by separating them into their component parts and dealing with each one in turn.

- Other complex problems can be *simplified* by deciding what one simple action would reduce the whole problem the most.

- Practical tasks or problems can be *shared* by delegating or seeking help from friends or professionals.

- Emotional problems can be *reduced* by learning to see things in a different light, from a different point of view, or by attaching some higher meaning to them.

- Emotional issues can be *reduced* or clarified (*simplified*) by rest, relaxation, entertainment, laughter, and sleep.

- Emotional problems can be *reduced* by expressing your feelings and *sharing* them with others.

Second dimension: a challenge from without or from within

Stress arises from the interaction between events and our own capacity to face those events. That is, it arises from both without and within. However, it will often be possible for us to identify whether *the key* to reducing our stress lies more in the events and situations that surround us, or within ourselves. What we are looking for is the difference between, on the one hand, an *unusually demanding* outside situation affecting a *normally* healthy, balanced and capable person, and a *normal situation* affecting a *weakened person* who lacks balance and adequate coping skills. In the first case, the key "problem" or challenge is from without, in the situation surrounding us; in the second it is within ourselves.

Another way to think about this is to ask: Is it more reasonable for me to attempt to change the outside pressures affecting me, or to change myself so that I can face them more easily? In other words, do you have greater leverage by facing the challenge from without, or the challenge within? The common adage "learn to accept the things you cannot change" is a reflection of this question: if you cannot change the outside situation, you must change yourself by regarding the situation more positively or by being more accepting of it. Changing the situation or changing yourself will change your exposure to stress, favouring lower stress levels.

Let us look at some examples:

- Earning less than you need to pay for essential expenses despite being in a full time job: the key challenge is from without. It would be unreasonable to ask you to accept a

157

situation which is incompatible with normal life. It may well be though, that you can find ways to increase your earnings or reduce your bills.

- Earning less than you need to pay for your expenses because you are too lazy to go to work or because you spend money on inessential things: the key challenge is from within. The situation is entirely attributable to your own behaviour.

- Being harassed at work because you are a member of an ethnic minority: the key challenge is from without, because it is a situation unreasonably caused by the behaviour of other people in a particular environment. You can change the environment by moving to a different one or by demanding that your employer discipline the abusers.

- Thinking you are being picked on at work because you are over-sensitive and highly attuned to potential criticism: the key issue is within you. You cannot expect the world to conform to your hypersensitivity, so you are going to have to work on that.

- Working over and above the call of reasonable duty because, by general recognition, your boss is an unreasonable tyrant: the key issue is without. You will have to come to a mutually acceptable agreement with your boss or change your job.

- Checking your work five or six times because you are a bit obsessive or a bit perfectionist is a demand you place upon yourself: it is a key issue from within. Your best leverage is with the goblin in your head.

Challenges from without require you to *manage the world* (in relation to yourself), for example by thinking of and enact strategies to reduce, change, or remove the source of the stress, or by distancing yourself from the stressful situation.

Challenges from within require you to *manage yourself* (in relation to the world), for instance by changing your habits, learning new skills, eliminating unhelpful thought patterns, improving your health and energy levels.

Many situations will require both kinds of strategies. Often it is a question of perspective. But our perspective has implications for how we can most effectively deal with our stress, so we have to strive to be as objective as we can about our situation.

The table overleaf summarises the two-dimensional model of stress.

If we look at our stressful situation and describe it in terms of these two dimensions, we can see that it imposes upon us a particular set of conditions. For example, if you have a highly demanding job and you find there are not enough hours in the day to do everything that is expected of you, you can consider that you are facing too many *practical demands* from an *external source*. Crucially, this suggests a path to reducing your stress: focus on the problem situation and organise your work more effectively. You could simplify and reduce your work load by planning and delegation. Planning includes such things as prioritising tasks and realistic time-management. If you have to report to a superior, it will also require negotiation.

Dimension	Source of stress	Strategies
1	Practical demands	Manage the problem (analyse and organise).
	Emotional demands	Manage your emotional needs (expression and support).
2	Challenge from without	Manage the world (modify the situation).
	Challenge from within	Manage yourself (develop and nurture yourself).

Table 18.2: Two dimensions of stress management.

In the situation described in the previous paragraph (practical demands, external source), there is a potential pitfall: before setting out your plans for dealing with it, you need to be sure that the demand really is external. If your time is filled up with self-imposed but futile attempts to make a good job even better in your eyes, even though for practical purposes the difference in quality will be negligible, then the demand is not external but internal. You could probably manage the demands of your job quite well, were you not so demanding on yourself! Let us consider that situation. It is still of the "practical" kind, but this time the main source and the challenge are to be found within you. You are going to have to simplify your life by working on yourself. You are going to have to be more realistic about what is a "good" job and about what actually is important to do today. You are going to have to look at Chapter 13 in this book, "How to change your mind"!

Shadows of past events

A particular kind of situation is when we are coping with the present effects of past traumatic events, such as divorce, the death of a child, or life-changing injury. In these cases, the circumstances that triggered our stress cannot now be changed, and we have to live with the consequences. Some of those consequences may be practical ones. For example, a life changing injury may have left us with some permanent physical disability, with obvious practical implications. We will normally have tried to address these fairly early on, by arranging our physical environment to take account of our disability, so far as possible. Nevertheless, the emotional shadow of the event will remain with us. Long after the traumatic event, we may live with the emotional fallout. In the "here and now" this has to be regarded as a challenge from within ourselves. In such circumstances, since we cannot change what happened, the only option open to us is to look internally: to manage our own emotional needs and responses, and to continue to develop and nurture ourselves personally and spiritually.

Chronic illness

Many chronic illnesses, too, are like this to the extent that they will affect the sufferer throughout his or her future life, to a greater or lesser degree. The onset of a chronic illness might be considered an event produced by circumstance, yet in the here and now the illness is part of oneself, and therefore one will have to "manage oneself" in relation to the world. This might include attempts to make one's general lifestyle as healthy as possible, limiting one's energy expenditure to sustainable levels, and modifying one's negative thoughts about one's situation. However, if the same environmental factors still persist that contributed to the onset of disease, and further, might contribute to its maintenance or severity ("external" factors), it is sensible to try to remove or reduce these. That is, working to "manage the world", as well as "managing oneself". This illustrates the point already made above, that many situations will require both kinds of strategies.

Some scenarios

Let us now look at four different situations, the different conditions that can arise from them according to the two dimensions of stress, and the approaches to management that they suggest. Four relatively uncomplicated scenarios are described in the table overleaf.

Unfortunately, many scenarios will not be so easily pigeon-holed. I have considered some more complex ones in Appendix 3. If you look at them, you may notice how mixed these situations are, so that often they cannot be classified as "practical" or "emotional", "without" or "within" in a clear-cut way. Instead, we have to ask: "To what extent is this a practical problem? To what extent an emotional one? To what extent do I have leverage on the challenge without? And the challenge within? Looked at relatively rather than absolutely, the two-dimensional model is a useful template for analysing problems of stress, in that it may help you to understand the best way forward.

Situation	Conditions	Focus	Example responses
You have a highly demanding job and not enough hours in the day.	Practical Challenge from without	Focus on the problem. Manage the world around you.	Effective planning, prioritisation, delegation, time-management, negotiation with bosses.
You are finding that people impose all kinds of things on you because you cannot say no.	Practical Challenge from within	Focus on the problem. Develop and nurture yourself.	Assess your own priorities, goals, motivations, capabilities. Develop assertiveness.
You have been receiving persistent and upsetting nuisance calls or messages on your phone or social media.	Emotional Challenge from without	Focus on your emotional needs. Manage the world around you.	Seek emotional support from family and friends. Go to the police, change your phone number, change your social media privacy settings or don't use social media.
You are beset by self-doubt, and irrational fears and worries about yourself and your family.	Emotional Challenge from within	Focus on your emotional needs. Develop and nurture yourself.	Talk about your doubts and worries. Challenge your own irrational beliefs and fears.

Table 18.3: Different conditions of stress management.

The toolbox

In the preceding paragraphs I have introduced various approaches to facing your challenges according to the nature of the challenge. Essentially, they fall into six categories, listed in the following table. We will look at each of them in turn.

Approach	Strategies or techniques	Benefits
Organisation	Task selection. Prioritisation. Planning. Time management. Self-discipline. Planned avoidance.	Helps you make your world more manageable. Helps you to build a sense of control and personal effectiveness. Essential for rational problem-solving.
Emotional release / expression	Talking to someone. Having a good cry.	Makes the situation seem somehow less unmanageable. Clears the mind and re-energises the spirit.
Modifying responses	Mind and behaviour techniques, including: 1 Gradually increasing your exposure to challenging situations. 2 Learning different thinking habits. 3 Practising your responses through role-playing. 4 Self-control. 5 Relaxation training. 6 Mindfulness training.	Reduces anxiety in the face of a challenge. Makes you more able to respond appropriately to challenges.

Self-nurturing and self-development	Good nutrition. Appropriate physical exercise. Learning new knowledge and skills. Personal and spiritual development.	Reduces the mismatch between demands and your internal coping resources. Makes you more able to respond appropriately to challenges.
Seeking help	Seeking expert knowledge. Seeking practical help. Seeking emotional and social support. Seeking spiritual help.	Increases your available range of resources. Shares the burden.
Rest, relaxation, entertainment	Getting adequate rest. Finding ways to relax. Doing things that make you feel good. Going out with friends.	Allows mind and body to refresh and recharge. Takes your mind off the problem.

Table 18.4: The stress toolbox.

Organisation

Organisation is essential when practical demands are a source of your stress. Organisation involves task selection and prioritisation, planning, management of resources like time, money, and people, and the maintenance of self-discipline. It may involve avoidance of negative situations, so long as this is planned within a long-term strategy. Organisation is necessary for effective, rational problem-solving.

As an example, imagine you feel overwhelmed by the number tasks you "have" to achieve in the near future. You are anxious to get them all done, so you work without rest. But this frantic use of time may be a false economy. If you get a good night's rest, things will seem much easier to do afterwards. You will work more efficiently and perform better. You will achieve much more than you would if you worked so hard today that your night's rest were insufficient and of poor quality. In that situation you would feel tired and lack the energy or mental clarity to work well tomorrow.

You are not Superman. When you have no time to stop, you need to stop.

Good organisation of time will allow you to work more efficiently, leave some tasks till tomorrow, throw out others without feeling guilty, and allow you some essential relaxation time.

Here's what you could do:
1. Write down the things you think you have to achieve today (or this week / this month / this year).
2. Ask yourself if, considered realistically, you going to be able to do all the things on your list properly in the allotted time, while maintaining a healthy mental balance.
3. If the answer is "no", prioritise the things on your list and write numbers next to them according to their priority (number "1" is the highest priority).
4. Now choose only the top things on your list that you can, realistically, achieve in the given time.
5. Sketch out a plan stating roughly which parts of the day / week / month / etc. will be dedicated to working on each of the things on your list.
6. If your plans involve money, other people or other resources, pencil in how they fit in on your time line.
7. If your tasks have been allotted to you by somebody else, show them the plan and explain your thinking. Negotiate.
8. Stick to your plan as far as possible, unless you find out it is unworkable.
9. If you have over-estimated what you can achieve, or if your priorities change, or if more or fewer resources become available, return to the drawing board and rework your plan accordingly.

A note on priorities. A task may be important or it may be urgent or both. Both of these factors contribute to priorities, as shown in the table below.

	Urgent	**Not urgent**
Highly important	Do it now!	Do it later but do it!
Less important	Decide whether to do it now or not at all.	Do it when other things have been done, or not at all.

Table 18.5: Priorities.

How will this help? First, good organisation and planning will help you to solve your practical problem. Second, they will help you to develop a sense of control and a sense of personal effectiveness, that is, the feeling that you are able to achieve what you set out to achieve. And they will take the pressure off because you will be achieving the essential with less effort and confusion, as well as scheduling in some exercise or relaxation time. Organisation takes a bit of effort, but it is well worth it. What's the alternative? To go on as you are?

Emotional expression

Emotional expression is a safety valve, especially if the source of your stress is inherently emotional, or if practical problems are giving rise to intense emotions within you. Even the simple act of talking to a friend or confidant can make you feel much better, just through the act of expression. We all know how a good cry helps, but emotional expression is always more helpful if another person is there to listen, because then we feel we have that person's support in some way: a shoulder to cry on.

A word of caution: while letting it all out helps you feel and function better in the short term, it is not going to solve any underlying problems. Far better to remove the need to cry on your friend's shoulder, than to go on doing it for the rest of your life.

Modifying responses

How you think and behave may be both a result of stress and a cause of further stress. Problems will always crop up in life, some of them big ones, some of them long-term ones. Your attitude and you actions in relation to those problems make a big difference in the degree to which they affect your life, your health and your happiness. This is a major pillar of managing stress effectively, essential for dealing with stress of any kind and from any source. Changing your behaviour and changing your mind have been discussed in previous chapters.

Self-nurturing and self-development

This strategy attends to the weaknesses or vulnerabilities which lay you open to stress, which constitute what I have called the "challenges from within" in the paragraphs above. It involves various aspects:

1. *Acquiring specific knowledge or skills* to give you greater mastery and control over the stressful situations you face: specific work-related knowledge or skills, communication and interpersonal skills, personal skills such as relaxation techniques, assertiveness, and so on.

2. *Personal development*: for example, working towards a more rounded work-life balance, developing hobbies, activities and interests, changing the things about yourself that you feel are holding you back, developing your spirituality. I took up a musical instrument, which I had always wanted to do but never got around to. I had next to no musical education at all, except listening to music, so it was a whole new world to me. It was the best thing I had done for myself for a long time. I look forward to picking up my instrument in the evenings, even if only for a short time. After practising, the worries of

the day no longer seem quite so important and I feel elated, satisfied with myself about my learning, and newly enthused. For you it doesn't have to be a musical instrument, it can be whatever "makes you tick".

3. *Attending to your physical* health: nutrition, water intake, exercise, rest, sleep, fresh air, reducing unhealthy habits like smoking or drinking.

All of these things will help you by restoring the body and refreshing the mind.

Seeking help

Recruiting the support of other people who will help you in your efforts will spread the load and ease the strain on you. Help may come in different forms:

- Expert knowledge.
- Practical help.
- Financial support.
- Emotional support.
- Spiritual support.

The previous chapter, "A little help from humanity" discusses seeking help in more detail.

Rest, relaxation, entertainment

Aspects of this have been mentioned above under "self-nurturing" and "self-development". Adequate rest is clearly regenerative and necessary for good health. Some kinds of self-development, such as new hobbies or interests, can be entertaining as well. Pleasure and entertainment are also good stress-busters in themselves. We have all experienced how taking time off to do something different and enjoyable can make us feel different about our situation. Why?

1. Problems have a habit of seeming bigger and badder the more we think about them. (I'm sure there is a goblin responsible for this!) If we take our mind off things for a while, they shrink again and become more benign in our eyes, less complicated or large or daunting.

2. The old adage that "a change is as good as a rest" is often true in that a change of environment gives our minds an opportunity to "reset" to a more realistic, balanced mode of functioning.

3. Doing something enjoyable, especially in the company of friends, lifts our mood.

Main points

- Coping has the fundamental goals of *reducing, simplifying,* and/or *sharing the challenges* you face.

- Basic options: Alter, Avoid, Accept, Adapt.

- Challenges may be practical and/or emotional, from without and/or from within.

- Ask yourself:
  - Does the challenge require solutions to practical problems or emotional ones?
  - Do I have better leverage acting on the outside situation, or acting within myself?

- The tool box: Organisation, Emotional expression, Modifying responses, Self-nurturing and development, Seeking help, RRE (Rest Relaxation, Entertainment).

- Use the right tools for the job!

19. Inner strength

What is inner strength? - Developing inner strength - Health - Optimism - Positive inspiration - Personal evolution - Affinities - Wise words - An inner sanctum - Something bigger - The power of love

> *It is a strong thing that can knock you to the ground; you are stronger who can lift yourself up.*
>
> - Adapted from a French proverb

Coping techniques and strategies only become really effective if they are backed up by the power of inner strength. Happily, the gradual acquisition of mastery of the techniques is a powerful way to build and empower inner strength. This is a virtuous cycle! It is when coping becomes thriving. Reading this chapter, you will be able to appreciate how much more confident you already feel in your own abilities to tackle stress and control your life now that you have greater knowledge and have put into practice some of the techniques that have been introduced. Now you can turn things around and contemplate how well you will thrive the more you go on to develop further your inner strength.

What is inner strength?

Inner strength is a quiet confidence that you possess the capacities and resources to be able to deal effectively with the situations life confronts you with.

Where does it come from?

One thing that it comes from is mastery. Mastery means abilities acquired and honed through much practice. Mastery in any discipline, from woodwork to rock climbing to flying an aeroplane, can only be gained through lots of practice. Mastery in rock climbing is gained through rock climbing. Mastery in living is gained through living. The following analogy illustrates the utility of the idea of mastery. If you took somebody who had never climbed before, gave him or her the necessary equipment, and deposited them on a thin ledge half way up a high rock face, they would undoubtedly freeze in terror and/or panic. But if they had 5000 hours of rock climbing practice they would calmly and easily climb down to the bottom or up to the top. Of course they wouldn't have been able to face the situation in the same way when they were just beginning to learn; they would have had the normal reaction of a complete novice placed in a terrifying situation. But they have gradually learned mastery through exposure to progressive challenges, each of which used the skills learned in previous challenges, and at the same time provided the means to develop those skills as well as the basis to begin to learn new ones. Ideally, each successive challenge should only occur once you have learned your previous lessons well, and should provide for a small increment in demands rather than a massive leap. Life isn't always quite like that, but one thing is for sure, you will never gain mastery of life unless you accept reasonable challenges.

A spiritual side

I think inner strength also comes from somewhere else, but I cannot say where, because if I am right that there is another source for it, it is a mysterious one. I observe that belief affords inner strength.

It is a truism that "you have to believe in something". Belief might be a belief in God or it might be a belief in oneself. Belief often allows people to succeed where otherwise they would fail. Why? Is it because it confers single-mindedness, purpose, courage? Or is there a spiritual dimension? If by that we mean something supernatural, I do not know.

For myself, I would define the spiritual dimension as all things that lift the spirit. By that I do not mean good cheer or temporary enthusiasms. I mean feelings of deep enthusiasm, energy, joy and love of life. Different people may find these in a cathedral or in a cave, at Lourdes or Mecca or Benares, in the wild wood or by a wild sea, up a mountain or in the desert, in poetry, prayer or dance, in deep attention to the performance of one's craft or in full song, in group worship or in quiet meditation.

How can you develop inner strength?

I think there are a number of ways, including the following:

- Maintain and improve your general health.
- Think positively and be optimistic.
- Be inspired by positive people.
- Seek to evolve as a person.
- Recognise your affinities and be near to them.
- Keep wise words in mind.
- Keep a "sacred zone" inside, an "inner sanctum".
- Believe in something bigger.
- Love.
- Gain a deeper knowledge of yourself.

In this chapter I will say a little about each of these, except the last - self-knowledge - which we will take up again in the next chapter.

General health

There is a school of thought, in line with the classical dictum *mens sana in corpore sano* (*"healthy mind in healthy body"*), that our body, mind and spirit find health or ill health as a whole. That is, for example, one cannot be unhealthy in body and be strong in mind and spirit. I am not of that opinion. History is full of examples of extraordinary people who despite the ravages of illness or age, have shown a strength of character and a determination of spirit that has transcended physical weakness. Nevertheless, these people are exceptional, characterised by their extraordinariness. Their psychological and/or spiritual characteristics are so strong that they can overcome severe physical limitations.

On the other hand, while physical health may not be an absolute requisite for inner strength, it cannot be doubted that for most people, lack of the former may detract from the latter. Good health and feelings of well-being and energy can only enhance our ability to feel effective and confident within ourselves, to think clearly and to persist determinedly in adversity. So that is why attention to healthy living, such as diet, fluid intake, sleep, rest and exercise help to lay down the physical context in which inner strength can develop, as well as the physical energy to carry through our will. Let us never have to reflect that the will is strong but the body weak!

Thinking positively

"Positive thinking" has become a fashionable buzz phrase, which nevertheless is often spoken in an empty way. Seeing the "bright side" of every situation was lampooned in the Monty Python film "The Life of Brian" and indeed there are situations in which optimism is unsustainable or may seem to be absurd, unrealistic, even delusional.

And yet think of these things:

1. It is a demonstrable fact that optimistic people live longer, happier, healthier, and more successful lives.

2. Think about how the world would be if everyone were pessimistic. When the steam locomotive was invented, many "experts" opined that people would die if they travelled at more than 10 miles an hour. What would you say were the most important scientific, technological and medical advancements in the history of mankind? Would they have been achieved by pessimists?

3. Do you know somebody who is relentlessly positive? I do, and I think most people do. They are good to be around because their positive attitude is infectious, and they make us feel good. How wonderful to have that gift! Naturally they tend to have lots of friends, and in general they are successful in what they strive to achieve.

There is a difference between positive thinking and delusion, between blind belief and seeing potential where others see a dead end.

171

If, confronted by new or unexpected circumstances, you always think immediately of all the bad things that could happen, it is because you have built *your* world in that mould. In reality, if your attitude is neutral (neither optimistic or pessimistic), bad things are neither more nor less likely to happen than good ones, and mildly good or bad ones are far more likely than dramatically good or bad ones. But that is only if we do not take into account the fact that your attitude can result in the enactment of self-fulfilling prophecies. In fact, if you have negative attitudes it is more likely that negative things will happen to you.

Bad things happen and Murphy's Law may seem to be a fact of life. But what are we going to do about it? It is our attitude to this general state of affairs and what we do about the difficulties it throws up that makes the difference between a stressed person with a hard life and a happy person with a good one. The right choices in adversity, powered by a positive mindset, give you the greatest chance of a successful outcome.

It is true that the right amount of caution is also a good thing, because unchecked enthusiasm and unrealistic optimism can lead us into disaster. But caution is not pessimism. The difference may be summed up in two words: judgement and reason. You have heard people who have been called pessimists respond: "No, I am a realist". Realism is obviously in the eye of the beholder. True realism requires a certain objectivity in order to consider evidence impartially and make decisions with good judgement. It also requires that we use our reason rather than our emotion to assess evidence. Caution requires that we think about things rather than resorting to ingrained prejudices. It is a fine line. While pessimism holds us back and optimism presents opportunities, caution reduces risk.

So, decide to smile in the face of adversity, turn the other cheek, and walk onwards and upwards. And while you are on your way, don't let anybody try to hold you back by telling you that you are all bad, the world is all bad, and the future is all bad. That may be the world they inhabit, but it is not yours! But tread with forethought, care and attention.

Be inspired by positive people

If you observe the behaviour of other people and try to understand the reasons why they behave as they do, it can give you valuable insights into your own behaviour. (The converse is also true!) As we have said before, understanding ourselves is the precondition to making positive changes. Yet "no man is an island", each of us affects and is affected by society around us. It is instructive to observe the positive (beneficial, constructive, and inspiring) and negative (deleterious, destructive, uninspiring) behaviours of the people around us, so that we can learn to emulate the positive patterns and to avoid the negative ones.

Being in the company of people who emit enthusiasm and positive attitudes helps you to be positive. Firstly, if you make it a habit to spend time with these people, slowly but surely you will spontaneously "pick up" that same attitude. Secondly, if you do what I have suggested above and observe their behaviour and its results, and reflect upon it, you will consciously reinforce what you are picking up spontaneously.

Evolving as a person

Whichever way you look at it, this is the healthiest thing one can do. Human beings are perhaps unique among the species on this Earth in the extent to which our evolution is driven and made possible not only by the process of natural selection, but also by cultural change and personal development. If we are to live the most satisfying of lives, we need to develop personally. That means, in a word, learning. That does not necessarily mean book learning, although that may be a part of it. It means learning by any means, but particularly by experience and by practice, the skills, mindsets, attitudes, awareness, control and mastery which will allow us as fulfilling and useful a life as possible.

Affinities

A marvellous way to lift the spirit is to know your affinities and to spend time in contact with them, under their direct influence, so to speak. This may seem an enigmatic thing to say, but really it is quite simple. Your affinities are the places, people, things, environments, activities which...

..."make you tick".

...bring you home to the true you.

...uplift you.

An acupuncturist once told me the secret to health is to be kind to your meridians[58]. He meant we should favour ourselves by placing ourselves so far as possible in an environment that is right for our nature, with which we have affinity.

I do not know whether those meridians really exist (and as a trained acupuncturist myself, I suspect not), but I do know the tremendous benefits to the spirit of spending time doing things we truly love, in places we truly love, being with people we truly love. For this we need to recognise our deep affinities. I will go into this a little more deeply in the next chapter, which is about self-knowledge.

---

58 "Meridians" is a Western translation for the channels through which in traditional Chinese medicine it is believed that energy flows through the body.

Wise words

I keep a little notebook and write down my favourite quotations. Writing them down helps me memorise them, so I can "carry them like a photograph in the inside pocket of my heart". (That is one of them, by Elliot Paul, from his book "Life and Death of a Spanish Town", 1937).

Let me tell you about some of my absolute favourites.

In the beginning was the Word.

- John the Apostle

I am not religious in the conventional sense. However, these words of John the Apostle make me think of a basic intelligence at work in the world, with which I must work if I wish to lead a happy, tranquil life.

The moonbeam splinters night's skirt with light,
drink wine, there is no better time than this.

- Omar Khayyam

These are two lines from a quatrain attributed to Omar Khayyam. I like them for their message: now is the time, don't waste it in unnecessary, hum-drum routines of the mind, experience the beauty of life while you have the chance.

Quod est ante pedes nemo spectat: coelo Scrutantur plagas.
Nobody looks at what is before their feet: they gaze at the sky.

- Ennius

This reminds me that while dreams and high ideals may inspire me, I cannot solve any problem without attending to the obvious basics, and that sometimes the answers we seek are there right in front of our noses.

Any man's death diminishes me, because I am involved in mankind;
And therefore never send to know for whom the bell tolls; it tolls for thee.

- John Donne

This reminds me of the truth that I cannot hope for a trouble-free life if my relations with wider society are not fulfilling and useful for all.

To learn the age-old lesson day by day:
It is not in the bright arrival planned,

But in the dreams men dream along the way,
They find the Golden Road to Samarkand.

I believe this verse to have been penned by George MacDonald Fraser (in his novel "Flashman at the Charge"[59]), probably inspired by James Elroy Flecker's original poem "The Golden Road to Samarkand". It reminds me to enjoy the journey and not to wish my life away.

I can go without good food, but I can't live without seeing green leaves and beautiful flowers.
Every flower here is a symbol of paradise.

- Mohammad Kabir, Gardener in Kabul, 2014

A report in the Sunday Times on 15 June 2014[60], told the story of Mohammad Kabir, 102, who had spent over 90 years lovingly tending the garden of the now ruined Darul Aman palace in Kabul. In a world obsessed with tin-pot "celebrities" from the world of entertainment, true worth often goes unrecognised and uncelebrated. Here's a person I'd like to spend a while talking with over a few glasses of *chai*.

Heart, mind, and hand.

These words, I believe my own, remind me that balance is achieved through the coordinated and complementary action of the intellect, the emotions and physical application.

Love, work and patience.

These are three virtues of the alchemists of old. Alchemists tried to turn lead into gold, but for the wise ones, "turning lead into gold" was a metaphor for the transformation of the soul. The alchemists knew this wasn't easy, but they had this motto to sustain them. I have always found these words to give me both solace and strength in times of trouble.

You will have different inclinations than mine and anyone else's, so your own collection of inspirational quotes will be uniquely yours. You can use them in times of trouble and uncertainty as a compass pointing out your cardinal points, thus giving you direction and control. Your cardinal points are your core values and beliefs.

Inner sanctum

My inner sanctum is where I keep the values and beliefs that are most important to me. It is an area of calm, delight and tranquillity. It can be real or imaginary or both. Sometimes it is like a

---

59 Excerpted from *Flashman at the Charge* by George MacDonald Fraser. Copyright George MacDonald Fraser 1973, 1982.

60 http://www.thesundaytimes.co.uk/sto/news/world_news/Afghanistan/article1422697.ece (accessed 12/11/2015).

darkened, quiet, airy little chamber, where I can sit cross-legged on the ground and meditate or reflect. The few ornaments, symbols and objects arranged in the chamber represent my core values and beliefs. One or other may form a focus for my meditation. At other times it is a grassy and shady glade in a pine wood, a mountain stream rushes nearby. Here, the physical world is reducible to basic elements, forces and energies; the rock, the wind, the water, the heat of the fiery sun, motion, the grounding effect of the Earth. Little wonder that the Greeks assigned spirits and gods to these things. When life gets complicated, I come here to contemplate the basics. In this delightful place I feel uplifted and energised, and I remember and reaffirm what for me is important in life. This gives me strength. And you? You will create your own inner sanctum, different from mine or anybody else's, because we are different, and the things we treasure are in some way uniquely our own.

Believing in something bigger

For inmates of the Nazi concentration camps, a strongly held belief - a religious faith, an ideological belief, belief in ultimate survival, or simply a belief in the need for hope - countered the bureaucratised brutality of the camps and may have conferred a greater chance of survival. In an essay on how Nazi concentration camp survivors coped with the privations, misery and terrors of camp life, Joel E. Dimsdale wrote:

> *The mobilization of hope was basic to survival; it acted as a kind of kindling to action. Without it coping was limited to actions that would be easily fatigued by the repeated stress of the camps.*[61]

Hope is a sort of belief - a belief that good outcomes are possible. And what is belief in an ultimate good if not a strong mobilisation of hope?

Neither you nor I are the centre of the universe, but each of us resides at the centre of our own universe. From here we can look out on our fellow humans and we can look millions of miles into the universe and see light from stars that started on its journey to us millions of years ago. In all that we see, from the behaviour of our fellows to the behaviour of that ancient light, there is barely-fathomed mystery.

We can react to this mystery in different ways. We can be frightened by it all and avoid thinking about its implications, or we can reflect and come to our own understanding of it. Those who reflect may fall into the persuasion either that there is some meaning and purpose in human life, or that ultimately all that we see is the result of impersonal, chance occurrences.

If you believe that there is meaning and purpose in life, and in human life in particular, implicitly you are appealing to something bigger and more important than yourself. But even if

---

61 Excerpted from *Survivors, Victims and Perpetrators: Essays on the Nazi Holocaust* by J. E. Dimsdale (Chapter 6: The Coping Behavior of Nazi Concentration Camp Survivors). Copyright 1980 by Taylor and Francis Publishers. Reproduced with permission of Taylor and Francis/Hemisphere via Copyright Clearance Center.

you believe only in chance and objective facts, you may have beliefs concerning right-living (ethics), particularly in relation to other human beings. You may adopt a benevolent, empathetic, compassionate and respectful attitude to other people and humanity in general, believing that to be a good way to live. Again, implicit in this is a belief in something greater and more important than yourself: humanity.

In both the examples given – the belief in a greater cosmic design for humankind, or the belief in the inherent freedom and equality of all people – we mentally derive strength from the idea that we are not alone, and from the idea that our lives, actions and values have worth. These are only two examples, possibly two of the most basic ones. Of course there will be many others. But whatever you believe in, so long as it is uplifting, positive, and enthusing, belief affords inner strength.

Love

It is my belief that love is the ultimate source of all inner strength. Everybody is capable of loving and expressing love, given the absence of obstacles; expressing love through attitudes, thoughts, actions, behaviour and words. Love for a person, or for people, or for beautiful or true things, or for your God if you believe in one. So many of the obstacles to feeling and expressing love are within us, in our thought patterns.

Many of the things I have talked about in this chapter can be seen as manifestations of love in some form, and indeed would be impossible without it: a positive and optimistic attitude to life and the world around us, feelings of inspiration, the desire to evolve, the recognition of our affinities, the recognition of value and meaning in realities bigger than ourselves, and our own place within them, a feeling of belonging. At the same time, these things make us more capable of loving and expressing our love.

At the beginning of this book, Chapter 1 begins with a quote from Thornton Wilder's novel *The Bridge of San Luis Rey.* The story is about a priest who tries to prove to himself the existence of God by a flawed scientific method. He looks at the lives of those who perished when a bridge they were crossing over a high gorge collapsed, expecting to find just cause for each of their deaths, and thus prove the case for divine intervention. His quest is a failure. Another character in the book, the Abbess, while giving solace through her words to a roomful of sick and dying people for whom the Abbey is their last earthly refuge, reflects thus on those who were killed in the gorge. She reflects that although for each of us life will come to an end and memories of us will fade, it is enough to have loved:

> *"...the love will have been enough; all those impulses of love return to the love that made them."*

In moments when one is assailed by feelings of doubt, weakness, confusion, emptiness, dissatisfaction, or meaninglessness, the single thought - that love *is the main thing* – has the power to bring renewed strength and rekindle the glow of the spirit.

Main points

- Inner strength is a quiet confidence that you possess the capacities and resources to be able to deal effectively with the situations life confronts you with.

- Inner strength comes from mastery and belief.

- You can develop it by:
  - Keeping good health.
  - Positive thoughts and optimism.
  - Being inspired by positive people.
  - Personal development.
  - Recognising your affinities.
  - Keeping wise words in mind.
  - Keeping an inner sanctum.
  - Believing in something bigger.
  - Loving.

20. Who are you?

An absurd question - Advantages and meaning of self-knowledge - What is the nature of your pain? - What are you like? - What are your affinities? - What are your strengths and limitations? - What are your valued principles?

A human being has so many skins inside, covering the depths of the heart. We know so many things, but we don't know ourselves! Why, thirty or forty skins or hides, as thick and hard as an ox's or bear's, cover the soul. Go into your own ground and learn to know yourself there.

- Eckhart von Hochheim (Meister Eckhart) (c.1260–c.1328)

An absurd question?

In the 2003 comedy film *Anger Management*, Dave Buznik, a mild mannered businessman, through no wrong-doing on his part, is sentenced by a judge to participate in an anger management program. At his first group therapy session, seated with a motley array of unbalanced and intimidating fellow participants, therapist Dr. Buddy Rydell asks Dave to tell the group who he is. Dave starts by saying what his job is, but the answer is not what Rydell wants. Dave tries again, by telling them something about his pastimes. But Rydell doesn't want to know about his hobbies; he insists Dave tell the group "who he is". Dave asks for an example of the kind of answer expected of him, and turns for help to a fellow participant, Lou. Rydell asks Dave sarcastically if he wants Lou to tell him who he is. Group hilarity. Dave tries once more. He talks about some aspects of his character. Rydell indicates that he is not interested in a description of his personality, he just wants to know *who he is*. At this point, frustrated and annoyed, Dave snaps and raises his voice, blurting out that he doesn't know what the Hell he's supposed say. The room falls silent, comical consternation and disapproval written on the other participant's faces. Rydell, sardonic: "I think we get the picture."

How would you answer the question, "Who are you?"

The problem Dave was having with this question is that it may have many everyday meanings, according to the intentions of the questioner: What is your name? Who's relative are you? What is your role? What is your status? What are your connections? What is your business here?

But Dr. Rydell was looking, to absurd lengths, for some deeper meaning. At which point we are led towards ill-defined ideas for which there are no suitable words. In effect, the question, expressed in the words it is expressed in, becomes meaningless.

The advantages of self-knowledge

Yet knowing yourself is just as important for lowering your stress levels in the long term as knowing about stress. Your stress is all wound up with you, so this is hardly surprising. Let me give you just some examples to make this clearer.

- If you know what your own real priorities are in life, you are less likely to waste time, energy and peace of mind stressing over things that are not really important to you, or agendas set by other people rather than yourself.

- Knowing yourself affords you the quiet self-confidence to deal with challenges, in full awareness of your potential and your limitations.

- Knowing yourself makes you less likely to suffer from existential anxieties. Existential anxiety is worry about the deeper matters of life and death: the meaning or purpose of life; what happens after death; moral questions. Frequently people with existential anxieties experience feelings of meaningless, fear, and guilt.

- Knowing yourself gives you inner strength.

The meaning of knowing yourself

So what does knowing yourself *mean*? I take it to mean several things:

That you are aware of your true affinities, for they reflect your nature and determine your needs, wishes, priorities, goals and ultimately, indicate your path to inner peace and joy.

That you are aware of the influences in your past that have not reflected your true nature, but that you took on board, leading you to live in conflicts and falsities small and large. That you are now empowered with the knowledge which will allow you to recognise them, face them and discard them.

That you recognise the influences in your everyday life by which you may be led but which do not reflect your true nature (the discordant "tunes to which you dance"). That, empowered by that knowledge, you are able to let them go. That you have learned to act, in respect of your fellow creatures, according to your nature and not according to petty social expectations and the agendas of others.

That you have acquired an awareness of your connectedness with the world around you: the people, the natural and man-made environment, the cosmos. That you have at least a feeling, or curiosity, or longing, or sense of wonder, or sense of belonging, about the infinity of space and eternity of time around us, and in which we are all participants.

That you have learned to be content with yourself in yourself, without comparing yourself or competing with other people so far as your worth is concerned, and without undue anxiety about how you are judged in the eyes of others.

That you have learned realistically to assess your particular strengths and weaknesses and to manage them wisely: not to abuse of the former, nor to be ashamed or afraid of the latter, but to work steadily and without hurry or anxiety to improve in areas which will take you forward, in accordance with your true nature.

Questions to ask

Instead of trying to answer Dr. Rydell's question, "Who are you?", try to see to what extent you can answer the following ones.

- What is the nature of your pain and what is your deepest need?
- What are you like?
- What are your affinities?
- What are your strengths?
- What are your limitations?
- What are your valued principles of living?

What is the nature of your pain and what is your deepest need?

This may seem like an odd question. You may say: "But I am not in pain!" The question though, is about any emotional injuries you may have suffered, which you may think you have "got over", yet still exert negative or limiting influences in your life. Most people have these. It is not necessary to bring up the situations or events which may have caused your pain, but simply to recognise the main emotion which is the current shadow of those events. For instance, is it:

- Anger?
- Guilt?
- Sorrow?
- Fear?

- Shame?
- Meaninglessness?
- Worthlessness?
- Something else?

If you can answer this, you are closer to identifying your deep needs, such as to forgive, to be forgiven, to let go, to heal, to face your fears, to find meaning, to be valued.

And if you can understand this, you are closer to understanding your habitual responses to people and events, and the forces that distance you from your true, unadulterated nature.

What are you like?

On the face of it this must seem almost as ambiguous a question as "Who am I?" What I mean, is to name things which you identify with in some way, or in which you can see similarities of character or quality. You could do this, for example, with the Classical "elements" of nature, or with features of the natural world.

- Earth, Fire, Air, Water.
- A mountain, the sea, a river, a tree, the wind.

It is perhaps most interesting to do it with animals and plants. Buddhism and Hinduism teach that your actions in this life will determine your situation in your next life. This gives us an element of control over our fate, through the choices we make. The ideal is to progress steadily from life to life, through evolution of the consciousness, from the less advanced to the more advanced forms of life until the attainment of nirvana (bliss) and liberation from the endless cycle of birth and death.

Here is an interesting little exercise in self-knowledge which is based on the idea of karma. (You don't have to believe in karma to do this!) You must decide what you might have been in your previous incarnations, starting as a flower, tree or some other kind of plant, then moving through the animal kingdom from less to more advanced forms of life. You could include some kind of invertebrate animal, a fish, reptile or amphibian, a bird, and as many mammals as you like. Write it down, using the present tense ("I am") for each new "incarnation". Here is mine.

I am a white willow,
with silvery leaves blown swirling in the breeze,
which freshens the valley where I stand,
and the tumbling stream my constant companion.

I am a mayfly,
rising on a sunny evening at the dawn of summer,
to live my life out in a single euphoric day,
before falling again to the water that bore me.

I am a dragon fly,
cobalt blue and shiny,
flying zig and flying zag, beholding the world,

with my strange eyes and strange brain.

I am a salmon from the deep Atlantic,
ascending a clear river with leaps and thrusts of my tail,
driven by primeval urge back to my origin,
and exhausted by my trials, to mate and die.

I am a kingfisher,
and I will dart like a brilliant arrow,
beneath the willows,
you might catch but a glimpse.

I am an eagle,
soaring to the skies,
I will watch the world with my sharp eye,
before I fall like a shard.

I am a bear in the forest,
solitary, powerful and moody,
in winter asleep in my den,
in summer catching salmon up by my friend the willow.

I am an otter,
playing in the water,
fishing or just having fun,
with my playful mate.

When I re-read this after I had written it, I could see several themes. The most striking of all is that most of these forms of life live near or in water. I do love water, I suppose I would say it is "my element". The second is that most of the animals are naturally solitary rather than gregarious, which reflects my own nature. The third is that, even so, there is another, contradictory characteristic, which is joyful: the beauty of nature, the fun-loving character of the otter, the bear enjoying fishing in the company of his "friend", the euphoria of the rise of the mayfly. And lastly, the value placed in all-consuming, higher purpose, like the mayfly, like the salmon.

Try thinking about which forms of life you would like to develop through, and write a few lines about each. It doesn't have to be great literature or poetry – just write it as it comes out of your head. Then try to decipher it to reveal clues about what you are like, what makes you tick.

What are your affinities?

In developing your answers to the previous question, you have also been exploring your affinities. To understand a little better what I mean by "affinities", let me give you an example.

One evening I went for a walk down by the old bridge near my home and was surprised and delighted to find clear water flowing under it and cascading down the rocks beneath it into the pool below. The ducks there were quacking enthusiastically. I walked down to the rocks and checked the pumps the council had installed to bring water up from the brackish creek below in order to create a nice water feature for the tourists. They were turned off. I walked upstream a little to the other side of the newer road bridge - the water really was flowing down from the valley. Our river is usually just a bed of, at best, damp earth amongst the canes and rushes. Now it was a stream. It was strange. It had rained a few nights before but not heavily, but I had never seen the river flowing so well, even after several days of rain. I interpreted it as an auspicious sign. I do not know if I believe in signs, but am prepared to give them the benefit of the doubt. Just to see the river flowing raised my spirits. I love water, especially rivers, and more particularly fast flowing, clear, small rivers. I find a creative urge whenever I am near them, I am enlivened and enthused and I think good thoughts. I gravitate towards them. If I can actually get into them I am in my element! If to experience spiritual feelings means anything at all, to me it means this. This is what I mean by an affinity.

How can we recognise our affinities? In a word, by enduring feelings of enthusiasm and elation brought by the thought or experience of things. The word "enthusiasm" is derived from the ancient Greek word *entheos* (*en* = in, *theos* = god) and originally meant "possessed by God" or "divine inspiration". Today its meaning is broader, and indicates keen participation or the condition of being emotionally or creatively inspired by a certain thing. Feelings of enthusiasm about things that are sustained for a long time are the surest way of knowing what your affinities are. The word "sustained" is important: more temporary, superficial enthusiasms may be entertaining but do not indicate affinities.

Affinities are not quite the same as similarities - things with the same qualities as you possess. We explored similarities when we asked the question: "What am I like?" That is only a part of what affinities are. But they are also things which inspire you, which attract you in a spiritual way, with characteristics or qualities to which you are drawn and to which you aspire.

Somebody mentioned to me after the karma game that in another life she would like to come back as a leopard. I asked her why. She answered because of its beauty and its grace of movement. "Do you see these things in yourself?" I asked. "No", she said, "But I love beauty".

Let me offer you another example. Think for a moment of the adult salmon. It is weary from its long ocean journey and has entered the river of its birth, which it will ascend to its source to mate and produce another generation. It is lying in a pool below a weir, but it is tired, and cannot leap over the sill. It rests in a quiet part of the pool for a day and a night. In the morning it moves out into the faster water and feels the cold fresh water flowing along its skin. It smells a once-known and strangely moving scent in the cold water, and it is moved. The salmon is enthused by a jolt of energy and drive, to make a renewed push for the place of its origin and the origin of its ancestors[62]. I can picture it in its sudden powerful surge and leap up and over the sill of the roaring weir that only the day before had seemed an insurmountable obstacle. I find that image personally energising and enthusing, I feel an affinity with it.

Do you remember an experience that has left you feeling uplifted, enlivened, enthused, energised, joyful, and with a suggestion of a new direction or a new burst of creativity? Now broaden your exploration further and try to think of other things, activities, places, people, elements or experiences in your life that have had such effects on you.

What about places? Have you been to or known a place where, for no good reason at all and despite any negatives about it, you feel an affinity, a ghost in the soul – a feeling that you must in some past lifetime, if that were possible, have lived there as your home and felt well there, some sort of strange, timeless nostalgia?

For me that feeling is brought up by the whole vast area starting at the Balkans and moving across the Caucasus and into Central Asia. From Macedonia, Bulgaria and Greece in the west, across Turkey and the wild, restless, lands between the Black and Caspian seas; over east to Transoxania with its great Amu Darya and Syr Darya rivers and its fabled cities of Bukhara and Samarkand; southwards to what is now Iran. Some of these places I have known, others only read about in books or seen on television. What is the attraction? The landscapes are so varied, but they have in common their wildness and a certain aridity or harshness: the mountains of the Balkans, the great sweeping steppes of Anatolia, the verdant poplar-clad splinters in rocky grey and ochre under cobalt skies that are the valley oases of Persia. Culturally, it is a melting pot of the many ethnicities, religions and languages that have moved like currents and tides across the region down through history, and mixing, have left an indefinable bonding flavour. "Chai" (tea) is a word understood everywhere from the Chinese borderlands to Istanbul and Turkey's western reaches. In much of this vast region the women are found in the bazaar and the men in the chai shops. They are hospitable people, at once calm,

---

62 Imagery like this is beautifully conjured up in my mind by Henry Williamson's delightful novel, "Salar the Salmon" (1935).

philosophical in approach, yet explosive in passion. Scents and flavours are so much intertwined with feelings: in bringing up images of these lands I can taste lamb cooked with cumin and coriander; delicious accompaniments of cooked tomatoes, aubergines and peppers; potent yoghurt and sheep's milk cheese; figs, apricots, melons and pomegranates; almonds, pistachios, sunflower seeds, hazelnuts; and ultimate sweetmeats of thin pastry, walnuts and honey. I do not know if I would like to live there, but I would go there again and again, to explore, imbibe the atmosphere and savour the impressions.

Are there any kinds of experiences which affect you in this way? People, things, ideas, places, landscapes, arts, activities? If there are, make time for them, to do so will be good for you, good for the people around you and, who knows, perhaps also good for humankind.

What are your strengths?

Everybody in the world is a unique individual. Think about that awe-inspiring fact for a few moments: there is nobody else in the whole universe exactly the same as you. You have a unique set of qualities that afford you a unique niche in this world. Nobody else can do it in exactly the same way as you. This knowledge can nourish your sense of self-worth. You have every right to sing in truth, "I did it my way".

Remember that "unique" does not mean intrinsically better or worse than any other unique individual. Fire is of a nature that can evaporate water and water has a nature that will quench fire. Both are essential to life. Neither is better or stronger than the other. In your uniqueness and true to your nature, you should celebrate and hone your strengths. They form your cutting edge.

In answering the previous two questions, you will have approached also an answer to this question. What are the particular strengths of the things you identified as being similar to you, qualities which you see in yourself?

For instance:

- What is it about the element or elements (Earth, Fire, Air, Water) you chose that you see in yourself? What advantages do those qualities confer on you? For instance, I see some of the qualities of water in myself. It is fluid, movement comes naturally to it and its movements are difficult to constrain, it moves ceaselessly and its currents run deep, it hugs the earth but its vapour aspires to the heavens.

- What about things such as a mountain, the ocean, a river, a tree, the wind? Can any of these suggest to you your own qualities? For example, the ocean waves seem first to yield, then come rolling forwards. I see that in myself.

- Think about the animals you chose in the karma game: what are their strengths? I am thinking of the salmon, for its tenacity and its sense of mysterious connection with something deeper than itself. What about you?

186

Can you think of any other positive qualities of yours, other than the ones brought to mind by thinking about your affinities?

What are your limitations?

Your strengths are your cutting edge, but every blade also has a blunt edge. Everybody has characteristics that are limiting to them in their continuing development. Paradoxically, a quality that is a cutting edge in one context may be a blunt instrument in another. For example, my education in science developed in me an innate predilection for logical analysis. I have used it as a cutting edge in my clinical practice. However, the predilection for viewing problems analytically may be an obstacle to more intuitive forms of understanding, as these take second place. I have had to work at restoring the balance ever since I graduated in my early 20s. Just as your strengths may be honed, the weaknesses that are limiting you may be strengthened.

- What limitations within yourself have frustrated you in things you have tried to achieve?
- Are any of these limitations the "blunt edge" of a "cutting edge"?

Speaking of cutting edges, my Aikido teacher once told me this story, which I have always remembered:

In feudal Japan, there was a warrior widely famed for his mastery in swordsmanship. From time to time one proud and arrogant warrior or another wished to challenge him. He had survived numerous such challenges and achieved quite an advanced age, at a time when the average lifetime for a samurai warrior was short. One day a pupil of his asked him what was the secret of his success. The old man replied: "It is simple, I touch his sword with mine. If I feel his weakness in it, I strike fast and finish him, but if I feel a calm strength in it, I put away my sword, concede, and go on my way."

Hopefully you are not going to be engaging in violent activities of this kind. But the moral of this picturesque little story is still valid: life will be happiest if you are a good judge of your strengths and weaknesses.

Knowledge of your weaknesses is important for another reason: it empowers you to move forward. You can gain real satisfaction by developing in areas which hitherto may have limited your potential to achieve personal fulfilment. I am convinced such efforts to further one's personal development should be carried out in an unhurried, steady way, with an eye to the long term. It reportedly took Beethoven 31 years to write his Symphony N°9 from first concept to completion. And you are writing the symphony of your life.

What are your valued principles of living?

How do you want to live your life? Your valued principles of living are values the application of which will help you live your life serenely[63]. If you find yourself frustrated, dissatisfied with your lot, feel the world is against you, or otherwise "in a bad place", reminding yourself of these principles will help you out and move you forwards. They bring you solace and inspiration in times of stagnation or distress, and a compass when you feel lost.

I have mentioned before that three of mine are taken from old alchemical philosophy: Love, Work, and Patience. I find that reminding myself of these is immediately calming and somehow uplifting. What are your most valued principles of living?

On the facing page are just a few ideas to get you going. There is a longer list of suggestions in Appendix 3 at the end of the book.

An incomplete knowledge

Nobody can ever "know themselves" completely, because of the limitations in vision inherent in our nature as human beings, and because of our subjectivity and the biases in our thinking patterns (of which we will never be completely free). These will colour certain facets with a favoured or un-favoured hue, magnify some facets, shrink others, and not see others at all. As such, most people can only ever have inklings of self-knowledge, but luckily, such an inkling can work wonders for our state of mind and enjoyment of living!

---

63 In some religions, cultural groups and currents of psychology, these are known as "virtues", a word I prefer not to use because of its connotations of absoluteness. These principles for living are relative, subjective and personal: one person's "virtue" may not be considered so virtuous by another person in absolute terms. For example, "scepticism" may be considered a healthy, scientific attitude by one person, but "close-minded" by another.

Authenticity	Integrity	Preparedness
Commitment	Joy	Purpose
Contentment	Judgement	Resilience
Courage	Justice	Responsibility
Creativity	Kindness	Self-discipline
Determination	Love	Sincerity
Dignity	Loyalty	Solidarity
Faith	Moderation	Strength
Forgiveness	Open-mindedness	Tolerance
Freedom	Optimism	Trust
Gratitude	Order	Truth
Harmony	Passion	Vision
Humility	Peace	Wisdom

Table 20.1: Valued principles of living.

Main Points

- Self-awareness empowers all your other efforts to live without stress.
- What is the nature of your pain and what is your deepest need?
- What are you like?
- What are your affinities?
- What are your strengths?
- What are your limitations?
- What are your valued principles of living?

Part 4: And finally...

21. Miscellany

Resizing your ego - Stuff: baggage and clutter - Information overload - Uncertainty- Creative expression - Creativity and destructiveness

This chapter is an optional extra. It contains some snippets which are not essential to the main chapters, and it will not detract from your understanding of those chapters if you skip this one. On the other hand, if you have got this far, you might like to expend a modicum of extra time on some material which you might find enhancing to your stress-busting efforts. You will read about:

- Dealing with your ego.
- What to do about stuff.
- What to do about information overload.
- Tolerating uncertainty.
- The stress-busting value of creative expression.
- An allegory on creativity and destructiveness.

Resizing your ego

I knew a lady (sadly no longer with us), a yoga teacher, who went to California to lose her ego. Really. Actually, she went to take part in a course on losing the ego. When she came back I met her in the street and asked her if she had lost her ego. "No", she said simply. While you are alive, it is never possible to lose your ego, and that would be a bad thing. But many of us need to tweak it a little.

What is the ego? "Ego" is Latin for "I". In his model of the psyche (the mind) the famous Austrian psychiatrist Sigmund Freud described the ego in relation to his two other constructs of the mind: the *id* and the *super*-ego. The *id* represents our raw instincts, and the *super*-ego a critical, controlling element which imposes constraints on the *id* based on our moral or ethical principles. The ego, in Freud's model, mediates between the *id* and the *super*-ego, in order to form a rational, realistic compromise that will satisfy both. That would be entirely reasonable, and if it is so, we could not function healthily without our ego. So why does it need managing?

Trouble happens when the compromises our ego brokers are not balanced. If the *id* is favoured and the super-ego loses out, our own base instincts and desires begin to motivate our behaviour more than will turn out to be good for us in the long run. As our desires become more important to us than any other consideration, we become selfish and self-important. We display, what another use of the word "ego" describes, *egotism,* or an inflated opinion of our importance and personal qualities. Colloquially, while not correct according to Freud's definitions, we would speak of someone having a "big ego".

One might object that a lot of successful people have been motivated by greed, which is a base instinct. But we have to question what we mean by "successful". This book is not about how to get rich. It is about how to be less stressed, which can only really happen if you are whole and happy in a deeper and more balanced way than money can buy.

On the other hand, if the *super*-ego gets the upper hand, our desires are repressed, while moral and social mores dictate our behaviour. We sacrifice our desires for conformity with cultural and social expectations. We may begin to suffer from low self-esteem, as unconsciously we take account of the taboo we have imposed upon ourselves about expressions of our "self". This translates as feelings of low worth or value in relation to others. Colloquially, we would say this person has a "weak ego".

From this point on, I will allow myself to depart from Freud and use these two loose, colloquial definitions:

- Big ego: inflated sense of personal worth.
- Weak ego: excessively low sense of personal worth.

The best is to have neither of these. The best is to have a balanced and realistic sense of personal worth. We need an ego which is strong enough to be quietly self-assured, but not so big that it becomes self-centred and overbearing.

But it is not that simple. There are paradoxes. We all know people who are always right no matter what, who cannot be seen to have made a mistake, and who need to save face if they are caught out. Intolerant of dissent or criticism, they are argumentative, sometimes authoritarian. Or there is the caricature of the manly man who likes to practise sports like body building or the more aggressive kinds of martial arts. Who likes to keep a large attack dog rather than a Yorkie or a Scottie. Who likes to drive a large, fast car. LMBC syndrome: little man, big car.

But people who would like to think of themselves as strong and capable, and would like other people to think of them as such, may harbour weaknesses which they are trying to hide and which cause them anxiety. In the terms of my home-spun and simplistic classification system (big ego / weak ego), an apparently large ego can hide important structural weaknesses. A plausible explanation is that deep anxieties relating to self-worth may stimulate the generation of compensatory behaviours that act as a façade designed to look strong and capable.

Then again, what of those people who truly believe themselves to possess undeclared potential, but are afraid to declare it? They have strength of belief in certain facets of themselves, but they do not have the self-assurance to express that belief by their behaviour. Sometimes they may be over-sensitive to criticism because criticism will injure their fragile sense of self-worth. With a degree of narcissism, they may think they are capable of perfection in certain kinds of skill or work or performance, and that anything less than that is not worthy. This person has an unbalanced and fragile ego.

How are we to manage our egos, working away unconsciously as they do? I think the fundamental thing is to observe their presence in our thoughts, words and actions, and to reflect upon what we see. From there, we have to adjust our aim, for a more balanced negotiation between the assertion of our individuality, and our adherence to values which we hold to be important (our core values). Once we have in mind the course we feel we need to negotiate, we will challenge our ego and call it to account when it leads us off that course.

Finally, for all, big ego and weak ego, I would repeat the following piece of advice (which helps to put all of us in our place!):

> *Recognise that, in full respect for the world around you, yet remaining faithful to your true self, you have no more nor less intrinsic worth than any other person in the whole world.*

What to do about stuff

In Chapter 18, among other things, we looked at organisation, one of the tools in your stress toolbox. This brings up the subject of stuff: the things that populate our lives, and what to do about them when they start to weigh us down. We are talking about excess baggage and clutter.

Excess baggage weighs you down and clutter may complicate your life. But they are not the same. Clutter may be a consequence of excess baggage, but even the essentials of life may exist in a state of clutter. Whereas excess baggage is universally draining, clutter is a subjective affair.

First, let us consider excess baggage. Various religious and philosophical disciplines advise us to relinquish unnecessary material attachments and, so far as stress reduction is concerned, this is good advice. Excess baggage is "the burden that harms". It drags us down. Think of a gas balloon. It has sandbags as ballast which keep it firmly planted on the ground. To free it so that it may rise to the heights, the sandbags need to be off-loaded. Just as it would be unwise to off-load all the sandbags of a balloon at once (it may rise too high, too fast, in a dangerous, uncontrolled way), we do need *some* things: a roof over our heads, a shirt on our backs, the tools to gain our daily crust, etc. But most of us accumulate too much stuff during our lives. It drags us down and shackles us.

We keep all this stuff because it might "come in use" one day, or for sentimental reasons, or for no rational reason at all, just because we have got into the habit of storing things away. In my case I am pretty clean of things, but papers do build up, put into files which I never or rarely look at again. "Things" are worse, especially if we have attached some emotional value to them at some stage in our lives but the things are stored away in a box under a bed or in the attic.

Excess baggage drains our energy because:

- If we are in the habit of storing stuff away, it is an extra thought and task in our lives to do so.

- We will find our living space becoming cramped and cluttered.

- If we have attached emotional significance to lots of things at some stage, and these things are inhabiting our living space long after their emotional expiry dates have passed, we become imprisoned by them and our minds can never be free of their subtle influence.

- There will always be the thought in the back of our minds that the stuff is there, that it must be sorted out one day, but not today.

For these reasons it is best to be ruthless about getting rid of things we no longer need or value. This can be done in one fell swoop every few years, but the best way is to cultivate the habit of living lean and travelling light; that is, of not collecting things for superficial reasons, habitually auditing the things around us for their practical or emotional value to us, and throwing out the things which we realise we no longer value.

Spurious or outdated emotional attachments are a bad thing because, as noted above, we become mentally imprisoned by them. Imagine that you are, slowly but surely, becoming entangled in the old cobwebs of emotions once spun among the things in your life, and never dusted down. You need to clear away the cobwebs and the junk they adorn. What was once very valuable to us does not always remain so valuable by default, and we mustn't assume that it does. A useful thing to do is to get into the habit of asking: Would I *really* miss this object if I no longer had it? In order to do this one has to reassess the value of things.

A lady I spoke to just the other day described very well how she was forced to make such a reassessment. She told me that she once took a load of her stuff to the flea market to sell. She had placed a certain monetary value on each item. Many people seemed interested in the things she had on offer, but when they learned the prices she was asking for them, they left her stall without purchasing anything. She went home that evening having sold very little, and thought about it. She realised that the prices she had attached to her things reflected the emotional value that she had once placed on them, but did not reflect their value to potential buyers, nor indeed her current emotional attitude to them. The fact that they had once been important to her could not translate realistically into the monetary value she had selected for them. She had to say to herself that she had decided to rid herself of these items, that being free of them would not upset her, and indeed, would make her life better. She went back to the flea market a week later asking just nominal sums for her items. She sold a lot of her things, and that way everybody, buyer and seller alike, was happy.

Clutter is another matter. Let me tell you another story. I have always travelled light and I have a well-developed sense of order. Clutter and disorder make me a little anxious, as I feel I cannot function effectively with them around me. I like simple, elegant, uncluttered functionality. I see beauty in it. Once upon a time I worked as a laboratory technician in the pharmacology department of a major British university. There were five other workers in the laboratory, including a brilliant young medical graduate doing post-doctoral research. He kept highly erratic hours, often coming into the lab in the middle of the night. Covering the entire surface of his desk was a mountain of jumbled notes, journals, books, bits of lab equipment, bottles of chemicals, notebooks, paper clips, pens, catalogues, old order forms for chemicals or equipment, and so on. One of my duties was to keep order in the lab and this I did diligently, excepting the personal territories of the other lab workers, such as their desks. One morning I went down to the cold room, also my responsibility, and I found on the work bench, among pools of spilled liquids, a chaotic mess of open reagent bottles, glassware, tripods, plastic tubing, and other equipment. In observance of my duties and inclination, I cleared it all up tidily and cleaned off the bench. Later that morning my brilliant colleague accosted me, and demanded to know where his experiment had gone. For the past three days he had been running an experiment in the cold room, and it had disappeared! Naturally enough he was more than a little annoyed.

I tell this story to make the following points:

- Things + disorder = clutter.

- Not everybody is upset by clutter. Some people can thrive on it. It is the sort of environment in which they can express their natural creativity. The researcher in my story may have been as distressed by the tyranny of order as I was by the chaos of clutter.

- Nevertheless, despite his brilliance, it is probable that he could have functioned even better than he did with just a little less clutter, just as I could have functioned in a more rounded way with a little less order.

- Both unbridled chaos and obsessive order are extremes. Such extremes of attitude limit our potential and can cause us stress. If we are extremely intolerant of disorder, we will be frequently anxious, because we will find it everywhere. But if we clutter our lives with stuff and disorder, for many or most of us it will be a source of stress because it will make it difficult for our lives to run smoothly. As always, balance is the answer. We must develop both a reasonable tolerance of disorder, as well as an attitude of care, parsimony and simplicity to the things we own or use.

What to do about information overload

In our increasingly information-hungry world, rapidly increasing demands put a strain upon our mental capabilities. This is a world in which it can feel imperative, often for no good reason, to stay "connected" "24/7". You only have to observe how soon after your plane has landed people whip out their phones, insanely anxious to see who has called or texted them. It's like the fastest draw in the West. I like to place mental bets on who will be quickest. It's the same with emails – people get anxious and/or annoyed if they do not have your reply the same day.

The Sunday Times of 9ᵗʰ September 2012 carried a report by Nate Silver with the title "The deluge of data keeping us in the dark". From this I learned that the **technology** company IBM estimated that we were generating 2.5 quintillion (that's 2.5 with 18 zeros to you) bytes of electronic data each day, a figure that had been rising vertiginously. So steeply in fact that, staggeringly, over 90% of the data (measured in bytes) that existed in 2012 were created in the preceding 2 years. The information we are exposed to each day is vastly outpacing our ability to process it. And most of this is just "noise" from any practical point of view which immediately concerns you and I.

If we feel pressured by our employers, our government, or our peers into trying to deal with more information than we are able to handle, a typical response is to feel anxious because our performance does not meet our or other people's expectations. Our individual anxieties are part of a wider collective **anxiety**, the **anxiety** generally felt about the perceived need to "keep up" with everybody else in material terms, even though we know deep down this is costing us dear in other respects. This concerns everything on a wide scale, from banalities like having to have the latest generation i-Gadget at one level, to the monstrous socio-political paranoia involved in the push for endless "economic progress" at another.

Within that wider story, it is up to each one of us individually, if we want to remain sane, to protect ourselves from the proliferation of data demanding our attention. Below I list some steps to take to do this, which I personally have found useful.

1. Make an ideological decision to slow down the world. Banish expressions like "24/7" from your vocabulary.

2. Engage with electronic media on your own terms, make sure you are in control of it rather than the other way round. If not, cut it out! Ten years ago, one of my patients, a stock market trader, actually said to me, "How did we ever live before the Blackberry?!" I said it made no difference to my life as I didn't have one and didn't want one. (Now only a few years later, the pre-eminence of the Blackberry phone is like ancient history!)

3. Boycott mobile phone ads (or even better, all ads) on TV by temporarily switching channel or turning down the volume. You don't really need the thinnest, lightest, fastest i-Whatsit ever, honestly you don't.

4. Don't check emails continually through the day. Do so at certain set times, according to your needs. Do not let other people set the agenda for this, if you can help it.

5. Do not respond to emails immediately, do it at dedicated moments that you have set aside for that purpose over the next few days, unless they are truly urgent and important.

6. Don't get bogged down in endless to-and-fro texting. Personally, I don't like texting. It is fiddly and time consuming except for very simple, brief and unambiguous exchanges. Call me and we'll talk instead; it's more personal, more efficient, and usually more effective.

7. Know that you will not cease to exist if you are not in constant communication with others. Develop an inner life. Then you will have more valuable things to say for yourself when you do speak to others.

8. Make yourself available and unavailable when you want to be. Be in control of this.

9. Put some homely routine back into life. Certain times and rituals should be sacred and inviolable, except in an emergency.

10. Take time over meals and rest breaks.

11. Talk to the people who are with you. It is an increasingly common sight to see people out to dinner immersed in their phones or tablets, sometimes everybody around the table. Never, ever do this! And don't tolerate it from the people with you. If that's the way they want to be, don't go out with them.

12. Remember you are only any good to anyone if you remain healthy, vital and enthusiastic.

13. Remember that "more" is not "better", sometimes the opposite is true.

Tolerance of uncertainty

It is an unassailable fact that living carries with it an inherent uncertainty. No matter how diligently you plan things out, whether you are planning your life or a day trip, you will never be able to be sure that the unexpected will not happen, whether that be good or bad. Intolerance of life's uncertainty generates anxiety. If you are intolerant of uncertainty, you are always on amber alert in case something happens. But as human beings we have to accept that things can happen. Bad stuff will happen in life as well as good stuff. I think of an old ship sailing in unknown waters, a dangerous enterprise. Experienced sailors, though, knew the general behaviour of the sea and the weather, knew how to navigate from the stars, and knew what to do in times of trouble. They had mastery. Mastery gave them confidence that in a storm they could generally pull through safe and sound. The best way I know of learning tolerance of uncertainty is by learning the skills necessary to deal competently with challenges. Every time one deals successfully with a challenge the more confident one becomes with dealing with further challenges, not only of the same kind but "challenges" in general; and the more one learns to accept uncertainty.

The stress-busting value of creative expression

Self-expression, that is the expression of your thoughts and emotions, is a liberating experience. Not only does it act as an immediate pressure valve, it also aids the unconscious processing of information. Often it is the incomplete or inadequate unconscious processing of information about traumatic experiences which turns those experiences into permanent influences on our minds. They remain with us, shadows of the past which colour our current thoughts, emotions, and act in ways which are limiting for our growth and well-being.

Vocalising emotion by shouting, screaming, crying, or laughing is the most-basic form of self-expression, one utilised in certain schools of psychotherapy. Talking to our friends, family and professionals is another opportunity to express ourselves, which serves useful purposes in "getting things off our chests", feeling understood, and eliciting support of various kinds.

But perhaps the most sophisticated form of self-expression is through some form of artistic activity. Art is a creative channelling of inner tension. Whether it is literature, poetry, painting, sculpture, music, theatre, or flower arranging, there is no art without a motivating tension, and the art is the expression of that tension. Art is able to treat locked up emotions in a much more nuanced way than a primal scream can, and it is able to express things in ways and at a level of depth that spontaneous conversation cannot. At the same time, it is an immensely satisfying experience to create something original.

I thoroughly recommend any stressed person to devote a little regular time to some kind of creative expression.

An allegory on creativity and destructiveness

I wrote the following as a blog post in 2011. It was intended as an allegorical piece on how to deal with the self-destructive impulses generated by strong, unruly emotions, anger in particular. I have decided to include it here because some of the ideas and themes are relevant to those we have introduced in this book.

Where I live in southern Europe, just as winter turns to spring, almond blossom slowly sweeps the landscape from east to west. It marks the flight of a dragon.

Dragons are forces of nature, bringing creation, and at times destruction.

In days long, long ago, people celebrated and feared the dragon. Each year they welcomed the explosion of fertility it brought, yet were always wary of its might and wild, unpredictable nature. In the middle ages the Church hated dragons with a vengeance, attributing evil to what was simply a force of nature, and set their saints upon them. Saint George, Saint Michael, and a host of others were all reputed dragon slayers.

In the West, many are the legends of the slaying of the giant worm which, come to settle near the village, had become a terrifying burden to the populace. In these we can find perhaps a deep, dark fear that humankind's apparent mastery of nature was always superficial and precarious, that its powerful forces might wrench free from control to become a fearsome menace.

As there are dragons without, so there are within. Italian Lucio had a fiery nature. I met him in a cheap hotel in Lahore, where he was staying after his bus trip from Kabul. He was one of the last western travellers to pass through Afghanistan in the wake of the Russian invasion in 1979. Lucio had spent many hours constructing a beautifully elaborate model ship out of thousands of matchsticks. Then one day, the day he had added the final matchstick, in a moment of fury he smashed it all up in his hands. Only Lucio can know what triggered his fit of anger. Destructiveness is the other face of creativity. This is the nature of the dragon within: creative, fickle, and potentially destructive. Impulsive and jealous, if it grows large and controlling, it must live the solitary existence of the outcast.

In China, dragons have been considered essentially benign spirits, fearful only for their occasional carelessness. This is the best attitude to adopt when dealing with them. Nature is impersonal, but as a human being, it is generally more productive to have a positive outlook. I do not think that slaying is a good way to deal with dragons. Would you slay its gifts along with its dangers? In any case, a slain dragon will always come back to life again even after a long sleep.

Here are some guidelines on how to deal with the dragon:

Follow it quietly to its lair. Observe it. Try to understand why it came there and what motivates it. Do not make your presence known immediately - it would fly into an uncontrollable rage - but gradually, softly, as though you were part of the landscape, and not before you have learned how to behave. (Do not touch its gold! The dragon is jealous of it, and besides, you may like the feel of the gold a little too much!)

Learn its language. If you know what to expect, you can be prepared and adapt your actions and responses. You may have seen those television documentaries of reptile experts going into the water with large and dangerous crocodiles. So too can we learn to live with our dragon if we learn its language. With growing confidence in our ability to interact with it benignly, we experience less anxiety about meeting it.

Learn to prevent or quell its destructive excesses. Train it! The film "Avatar" has the hero capturing and taming a wild, ferocious dragon-like creature, which would become his faithful mount for the rest of both their lives. We can all tame our own dragon. Speak to it. Be kind but firm. Reward it if it behaves as you think fit. Pay no notice if it sulks and wines. If you punish it, be compassionate, sparing, fair and predictable, never random. One day, you may only have to whisper gently in its ear.

201

Appreciate it for what it is. Recognise, celebrate, channel and exploit its tremendous creative potential. Your inner dragon can become your ally!

22. Reminders, golden rules and tips

Like the last chapter, this one is optional. It consists of two parts. The first is a brief summary of everything that has gone before. The second is a list of "golden rules". "Golden rules" is a nice snappy phrase but it is a misnomer. They are not rules, they are suggestions to stimulate thought. You do not have to remember them all. But you might like to read through them, or dip into them from time to time, or write down or remember the ones you think are most apt for you.

Reminders: stress in a nutshell

1. Stress is due to a mismatch between the demands on a person and his or her ability to cope with them. Stress is not an external event or situation that happens to you. It is a tension caused by an interaction between you and the outside world. It is what happens *with* you when you attempt to meet a challenge. How things affect you depends on your attitude to them.

2. Often we intuitively know what stress feels like for us. But stress symptoms differ for different people and different kinds of stress. Stress affects our cognition, emotions, physical body and behaviour. Methods have been developed to assess how much stress you have experienced or are experiencing.

3. When you are faced with a challenge, three stages occur in assessing the challenge: (1) you first become aware of a potential threat, (2) you weigh it up, and (3) you weigh up your options. How a challenging event or situation affects you depends upon a variety of perceptions you have about yourself (e.g. your background, personality, experience, beliefs, values and self-belief), about the situation (e.g. its nature, proximity, magnitude and duration), and about your resources (e.g. the material, personal, social and spiritual resources available).

4. Different people's stress is different. The contexts in which stress develops can be daily hassles ("bothers") or major life-changing events ("earthquakes"). Stress may be sudden and intense ("acute") or long and drawn out but less intense ("chronic"). There are three modes of adaptation to stress: alarm, resistance and exhaustion. Stress involves mental, physical and behavioural changes. Your own experience of stress is unique.

5. Prolonged stress has many effects on the mind and body. The bodily effects are triggered by the activities of the nervous system and the hormonal system, which undergo long-term changes. Much ill health can be generated by stress, as well as early ageing and early death.

6. You cannot change your stress without first knowing your stress. Knowing your stress means knowing what triggers it, what you feel when you are stressed, what kinds of thoughts you have when you are stressed, what things you tend to do when you are stressed. This knowledge will empower you to change.

7. There are many ways of coping with a stressful situation. Many habitual ways of coping can be counter-productive and detrimental in the long term. You can learn to recognise your habitual coping strategies and change them into better ones. You must change your world within.

8. Behaviour experiments can help you to learn the benefits of new ways of coping. First observe your habitual ways of coping. A coping diary can help you to do this. Question yourself about the appropriateness of your responses. When you recognise the cues that make you stressed, stop your automatic responses, take your time and choose, review-adapt-improve.

9. Whether a problem is large or small, or a problem at all, is very dependent on your attitude to it. This is something over which you have control. You can change the way you think, if you are prepared to question your beliefs. You need to develop the habit of forming helpful thoughts (allies) rather than unhelpful or counter-productive ones (goblins).

10. It is easier to have a healthy mind if your body is healthy. First get the basics right: healthy diet and good hydration; manage alcohol intake, cut out smoking and other "recreational" drugs; good rest and sleep; appropriate physical activity and exercise.

11. You can prepare yourself for stressful situations by practising basic positive responses in a safe environment, and learning some positive self-instructions. You can negotiate stressful situations successfully by stopping your automatic responses, taking your time and choosing an appropriate response, remaining aware, calm, flexible and fair.

12. You can promote relaxation by practising slow abdominal breathing, imagination and visualisation, and voluntary muscle relaxation. This kind of practise will relax you mentally when you feel stressed, relax tight muscles, and promote more general, long-term relaxation.

13. You can learn to change your thought patterns. Get used to asking yourself why you thought a certain thought (meta-thinking). You can replace goblins with allies by knowing yourself, questioning yourself, stopping your habitual thoughts, taking control, reviewing results. You can allow yourself to depart from habit by carrying out behaviour experiments.

14. A better ability to solve problems will reduce your stress. Problem-solving is a skill you can learn. While problem-solving is a rational method, intuitions and strong gut feelings can also provide valuable insights.

15. Chronic stress deadens emotional experience. Emotions have useful functions and enrich our lives. It is not healthy to suppress emotions nor to allow them unbridled free rein. Allow yourself to experience emotions without interpreting them or attaching value judgements to them. It is normal for intense emotions to pass quite quickly. They do so if you do not dwell on them. All head or all heart are not healthy, they need to be balanced.

16. Good communication helps avoid tension and conflict between people. Good communication involves a number of skills which can be learned and perfected through practice. A strong, quiet, balanced ego is an asset in good communication.

17. Help and support from other people is a major buffer against stress. Help may be emotional, practical or material. It is available to everyone. It can come from family, friends, support groups, charities, or government organisations. The Internet is a great resource.

18. Coping has the fundamental goals of reducing, simplifying, and/or sharing the challenges you face. Challenges may be practical and/or emotional, from without and/or from within. Does the challenge require solutions to practical problems or emotional ones? Do you have better leverage acting on the outside situation, or acting within yourself? It is important to use the right tools to act against stress. The six basic strategies are: Organisation, Emotional expression, Modifying responses, Self-nurturing and development, Seeking help, RRE (Rest, Relaxation, Entertainment).

19. Inner strength is a quiet confidence that you possess the capacities and resources to be able to deal effectively with the situations life confronts you with. Inner strength comes from mastery and belief. You can develop it by keeping in good health, practising positive thoughts and optimism, being inspired by positive people, personal development, recognising your affinities, keeping wise words in mind, keeping an inner sanctum, believing in something bigger.

20. Self-awareness empowers all your other efforts to live without stress. Facets of self-awareness include knowledge of your affinities, strengths, limitations, genuine aspirations, and valued principles of living.

Golden rules, precious thoughts, and timeless tips

The top twenty

All the others derive from these:

1. Simplify your life. Avoid complications.

2. Fortify your organisational skills.

3. Strive for realism and balance in assessing situations.

4. Learn from your mistakes.

5. Deal with what you need to deal with, and accept what you cannot change.

6. When dealing with people, first seek harmony and conciliation.

7. Manage your ego. Always be ready to accept with equanimity the possibility that you may be wrong. It is better to be happy than right.

8. Tread lightly on the world and treat it kindly.

9. Learn to say "Yes" and "No".

10. Look after your physical body.

11. Spend time in contact with nature.

12. Be in touch with people who enthuse and inspire you.

13. Let your stress be worthy. Don't stress about unimportant things.

14. Don't expect to go on doing the same things and get different results.

15. Challenge your habits and habitual thoughts, especially the negative ones. Beware of goblins!

16. Take responsibility for your life. Be in control of life, not the other way around.

17. Learn and evolve.

18. Learn to know yourself and have the courage to be true to your nature.

19. Seek out your affinities.

20. Count your blessings.

Practical stuff

1. Simplify your life. Avoid complications.

2. 24/7 is nonsense. Don't be always available. You don't have to be "connected" all the time. Have downtime with the cell phone. Limit dealing with emails to a planned email slot. Be sensible with the Internet.

3. Strive for realism and balance in assessing situations.

4. Fortify your organisational skills (of everything: time, space, money, work). Use them.

5. First thoughts when faced with a problem: "This is the situation. I cannot change what has happened. Let me think what is the best thing I can do to make it better or limit the damage."

6. Learn from your mistakes. Systematically. What went wrong? How could I have managed the situation better? Remember next time.

7. Don't beat around the bush. Don't put off making important decisions, but don't rush them either.

8. End the working day at a certain planned time. Stick to it.

9. Don't expect to go on doing the same things and get different results.

People

1. First seek harmony and conciliation.

2. Listen, don't make assumptions.

3. Don't indulge in the blame game.

4. Do not hate another because he thinks differently to you.

5. Learn to say No and Yes. Cut down on "ifs", "buts" and "maybes".

6. Decide when to be flexible and when to be firm, don't be either just by default.

7. Try to be generous and respectful to others in your attitude and words. Nothing escalates stress like personal conflict.

8. Don't indulge in ego-led arguments.

9. Know when to mind your own business. Don't take on other people's problems if you haven't got the energy for your own.

10. Don't imprison other people with your own beliefs and opinions. Don't over-burden others with advice if not asked for and not wanted. Your example, not your words, is your most powerful tool to influence people.

11. In relationship conflicts, first ask, to what extent am I responsible? To what extent can a change in me benefit both?

12. Always be ready to accept with equanimity the possibility that you may be wrong.

Health

1. Look after your physical body. *Mens sana in corpore sano.*

2. Eat healthily.

3. Get enough rest and sleep.

4. Take physical exercise regularly.

5. Follow the natural rhythms of the days and the seasons.

6. Lose weight if you need to. Don't indulge in making excuses. Just do it. Get help if necessary.

7. Keep an eye on your posture.

8. Breathe properly.

9. Keep well hydrated.

10. Practise moderation.

11. Exercises only work if you do them.

12. Don't depend on substances, or food, to manage stress.

13. Don't indulge in obsessive regimens or fads.

14. Pastimes and activities are for pleasure. They should be done in a relaxed, unhurried way, not obsessively, or to a deadline, or to break a record. Compete if you like, but maintain a sense of proportion.

Mental stuff

1. Let your stress be worthy. Hassles and unknowns are not worthy sources of stress. Difficult stuff is going to happen in your life. You can decide now to stress about it, or you can decide not to.

2. If you are frequently getting upset by mere annoyances, reset your sense of proportion.

3. Don't expect to go on doing the same things and get different results.

4. You *can* change, whatever your age and however firmly ingrained your habits, if you want to.

5. Shrink your ego. Self-righteousness, self-importance, saving face, holding grudges, envy, being judgemental, fear of judgement, feelings of guilt, pretence, wallowing in negative feelings, ruminating about the past, blaming other people or fate, vanity, narcissism, perfectionism, self-pity: these are all ways of indulging the ego. Rise above negative emotions caused by ego-led conflicts.

6. Shift your goals from external ones (material rewards, status) to internal ones (self-development). You will be happier!

7. Lighten up, smile, let your shoulders down, stand tall.

8. Free up your sense of humour. Especially at the silliness of your own ego.

9. It is better to be happy than right. Allow yourself to be wrong. Enjoy it, and learn something!

10. Be in control of life, not the other way around.

11. Challenge your habits and habitual thoughts, especially the negative ones. Beware of goblins!

12. If you suffer from low self-esteem, strive to give yourself positive messages about yourself.

13. Take responsibility for your actions and words. Only then can you assume control of your life.

14. Don't be led by social expectations or others' expectations if they are not in line with your own true priorities.

15. Get neither over-excited nor over-upset about the ups and downs of life. "This, too, will pass". Accept this.

16. Learn realism. Don't be swayed by excessively negative or optimistic assessments. Be suspicious of knee-jerk emotional responses. Be clear of mind and examine things as impartially as you can. Try to develop judgement rather than prejudice. Try to cultivate an attitude of balanced and realistic optimism.

17. Don't get wrapped up in yourself. Show interest in other people.

18. Be in touch with people who enthuse and inspire you, and avoid people who make you feel sad, bad, or angry. (Unless you have enough energy and mastery to enthuse them while at the same time protecting yourself).

19. Create an environment you like to be in, so far as possible, at home and at work.

20. Hope for the best, but be ready for the worst.

21. Do what you can reasonably do. Learn acceptance of situations which you cannot change.

22. Beware of impulsive reactions to tense situations. They can save your life in a split-second, life or death situation. But in complex, long-term situations, they lead to complications.

23. Don't indulge in the blame game: of yourself or others.

24. Learn the skills you lack to cope with stress.

25. Allow yourself to ask for help.

26. A problem shared is a problem halved. Talk about it.

27. Learn tolerance of uncertainty. Cultivate mental flexibility. Banish rigidity.

28. Don't do what you don't want to do, but do what you'd like to do if it weren't for your fear. Take a chance now and again.

29. Don't complain.

30. Don't expect the world to adapt to you. It won't.

31. Don't worry about invented problems, fortune telling, things that may never happen.

32. Give yourself good "I am" messages, not negative ones.

33. Think: Why on earth should I fear criticism?

34. The darkest hour comes just before the dawn.

35. Do not regard a failure as terminal. Regard it as a learning experience. Try again but differently and better. Don't give up at the first obstacle.

36. Don't bet everything on your hopes, expectations or plans coming to the end you desire.

37. Count your blessings.

38. Remember to enjoy today and to learn something from it. It won't come around again.

39. Every evening think: What was the golden moment of today?

Spiritual stuff

1. Learn to know yourself and have the courage to be true to your nature.

2. Try to feel your connection with the social and natural world around you. Take frequent opportunity to be in contact with nature.

3. Tread lightly on the world and treat it kindly - you will have few regrets and your kindness will reflect on you.

4. Remember that if you act true to yourself and at the same time in respect of others, your intrinsic worth is no more and no less than that of any other human being.

5. Remember that everything you do changes the world a tiny bit, for better or for worse. You cannot fully undo what is once done.

6. Learn and evolve, learn and evolve, learn and evolve...

7. Self-knowledge is the greatest treasure.

8. Associate with places or contexts which resonate in you: your affinities.

9. Know your strengths and limitations. (Really know them, don't make them up. Banish your ego from this assessment!) Celebrate your strengths, strengthen your limiting weaknesses.

10. Recognise your genuine aspirations (those which derive from your true nature) and work steadily towards them without hurry or obsession.

11. Do not allow yourself to be imprisoned by your past. If there is anything you need to apologise for or make amends for, do it now, and go forwards.

12. Anything you attempt to do, do it with your full attention, absorb yourself in it and enjoy the feeling of doing things well. Know the difference between a job done well, and obsessively striving for perfection.

13. Develop mastery in something you love to do.

14. Collect wise words.

15. Have a private place of peace and go there often.

16. Recognise that your potential is immense.

17. Let your goals be real. Do not waste your emotions on impossibilities. But do not accept other people's judgements about what is possible for you. Only you can make that judgement. Exercise wisdom.

18. Let your attachments be worthy. Otherwise they are drains on your energy. Relinquish superficial or unwanted attachments, whether material or otherwise.

19. Likewise, leave behind fossilised negative emotions: old anger, grudges, etc. They, too, cause you stress and drain your energy.

20. Don't sling blame around in vain.

21. "Blessed is he who has no expectations" (of self or others). Expectations are different from hopes and goals. Expectations are often a little presumptuous. Be true to yourself, do your realistic best, and take what comes.

22. Be gentle outside and strong inside.

23. Face your fears with courage.

24. All head or all heart are not healthy, they need to be balanced. Faced with a challenge, think whether your mind or your heart should take precedence. It is a choice, not a default.

25. Exercise patience. Don't be extreme. Practise moderation.

26. You are not alone, unless you decide to be.

27. Make every second count. If it's for taking a rest, take a rest, but by decision, not by default.

28. If you are lucky enough to meet a true life companion, love them truly and let yourself be truly loved by them. They are a witness to your life and you to theirs.

29. Don't be in the habit of believing things at face value, or of dismissing them out of hand. But neither should you be racked by doubt and ambivalence. Just observe and don't make premature judgement. Belief is not a simple matter, you cannot truly believe something just because you like the idea. You have to be drawn to it slowly, naturally, organically and inexorably.

Appendices

Appendix 1: Attempts to cope

Ways of coping...	Why...?	Proverbs/sayings/clichés/quotes...
Aggression, e.g. angry outbursts, violence.	It acts as a pressure valve. It exploits the opportunity to release bottled-up resentment.	"Taking it out on somebody else."
Assessing your capabilities and improving your skills, e.g. communication skills, relaxation techniques.	(1) A situation is only seen as threatening if you feel you lack sufficient command over it to ensure a good outcome. (2) Some specific skills can help to reduce the impact of stress in general.	"Don't get out of your depth." "Be prepared."
Assuming responsibility to act.	Helps you feel you are not neglecting your duty to do something. It gives you a sense of control (realistic or otherwise).	"Face the music."
Apportioning blame.	Blaming somebody simplifies a situation. Blaming yourself may invite forgiveness, understanding and sympathy. Blaming somebody or something else takes you off the hook.	"A bad workman always blames his tools." "You made your bed, now lie in it."
Bodily care, e.g. diet, exercise, rest and relaxation.	If you are physically fit and mentally calm and lucid, you are better able to meet a challenge.	*Mens sana in corpore sano.* ("A sound mind in a healthy body.")
Catastrophising: grossly exaggerating the negative aspects of a situation.	It serves several purposes. It asks for sympathy. It helps to express negative emotions. It tells yourself to expect the worst (so any more positive outcome will be more greatly appreciated).	"We're doomed, doomed!"

Changing your expectations, goals or values.	If your expectations are causing you stress, you might decide they are unrealistic and modify them so that they are more easily achievable.	"Be thankful for what you have." "If you can't beat them, join them." "Get real." "Be grateful for small mercies." "Half a loaf is better than none."
Changing your perspective of the situation.	Situations can sometimes appear less threatening if looked at from a different point of view.	"Every cloud has a silver lining." "Look on the bright side." "Two sides to every question." "What's past is past." "This, too, will pass."
Compensations and indulgences, e.g. chocolates, over-eating.	To lift our mood.	"A bellyful is one of meat, drink, or sorrow."
Defensiveness.	If you feel weak in a threatening situation, you may feel safer if you do not expose your weaknesses.	"Keeping up your guard."
Denial or dissociation.	Thinking/saying/acting as if a threatening situation does not exist or has nothing to do with us relieves the stress in the short term.	"Burying your head in the sand." "Out of sight, out of mind."
Distraction and entertainment, e.g. working more than usual, engaging in hobbies, sport, social or cultural activities, zoning out in front of the TV.	To distract the mind, gain temporary relief from stress, and improve your mood.	"Take your mind off things." "A change is as good as a rest." "Eat, drink, be merry, for tomorrow we die."
Drugs, e.g. alcohol, tobacco, prescription medication, illegal drugs.	To temporarily distract the mind, or alter our mood or attitudes.	"Drown your sorrow."
Emotional compensation, e.g. sympathy, cuddles.	Temporarily improves our mood and outlook.	"Tender loving care."

Emotional expression, e.g. shouting, crying, or simply talking about the situation.	It acts as a safety pressure valve. It can also ask for sympathy or understanding.	"Get it off your chest." "Don't keep it bottled up." "Let it out."
Escape and avoidance, e.g. avoiding the people, places, subjects or contexts involved in the threatening situation, procrastination.	It distances us from the source of the threat, and therefore the stress itself, but often only in the short term.	"Don't go there." "Nothing to do with me." "Out of sight, out of mind."
Fatalism.	Passively accepting the inevitability of a situation removes any responsibility you might otherwise feel for it.	"It's destiny." "There's nothing to be done." "It's out of my hands." "It's in the hands of Fate."
Giving deeper meaning to the situation.	Thinking/saying that short-term difficulties are profoundly significant for the greater long-term good makes them easier to bear.	"God moves in mysterious ways." "Everything happens for a reason." "It's a sign." "This is telling me something." "This will make me stronger."
Giving up.	Surrender removes all further responsibility, and hence pressure to act.	"Throwing in the towel."
Humour.	Making jokes out of difficulties acts as a pressure valve and lightens the mood.	"You either laugh or you cry." "Laughter's the best medicine."
Intransigence.	Resolute resistance gives you a sense of strength and command, which may or may not be justified.	"Stand your ground." "Stand up for yourself." "Don't let the bastards grind you down!" "They shall not pass."
Maintaining a heightened state of alert.	Being extra vigilant and careful with respect to any signs of threat might help you be ready to meet it. However, constant vigilance is stressful in itself.	"Once bitten, twice shy."

Organising resources more effectively: time, money, energy, etc.	(1) Planning and organising gives you a sense of control. (2) It may help you save time, money, energy, trouble.	"A stitch in time saves nine." "Look after the pennies and the pounds will look after themselves."
Panic.	Not actually a coping strategy, but the failure of all coping strategies!	"Don't panic, don't panic!"
Problem-solving: analysing the problem, thinking of and assessing possible solutions.	May help to solve or diminish the problem situation.	"I'll mull it over." "I'll sleep on it."
Rationalisation: thinking rationally about the situation.	It removes the distressing emotion from the situation, and may help to see it clearly and in a more realistic light.	"I can't see the wood for the trees." "It's no use crying over spilt milk." "I'm making a mountain of a molehill." "It's a storm in a teacup".
Recklessness: acting impulsively in the hope that all will be well.	Impulsive and optimistic action gives you a (false?) sense of hope. Action makes you believe you have some degree of control.	"Throwing caution to the wind." "In for a penny, in for a pound."
Religion: praying, speaking to a religious authority, attending church, reading religious or spiritual books.	(1) It may help you believe that you are not alone or that a higher being or force will give you strength. (2) It may help you believe that your mundane troubles are unimportant in the grand scheme of things. (3) It may help you believe in ultimate salvation.	"The Lord's my shepherd, I'll not want." "The Lord will provide."
Rest and relaxation. (See also "bodily care" above).	Allows you to recuperate your energy, improve your mood and see things more clearly.	"Sleep on it." "Chill out."
Ritual and superstition.	You may believe that certain words or actions can, by their special power or magic, bring you fortune and prevent misfortune.	"Fingers crossed." "Touch wood."
Seeking information.	Relevant information often helps us to deal more effectively with problem situations.	"Forewarned is fore-armed." "Know your enemy." "Knowledge is power."

217

Seeking social support, e.g. moral or material help from family, friends, social organisations and institutions.	Helps you feel not alone and may give you necessary resources to resolve a problem situation.	"Two heads are better than one." "A friend in need is a friend indeed." "A trouble shared is a trouble halved."
Self-control: giving yourself pre-prepared instructions about how to behave in a current situation.	Avoids impulsive and excessively emotional responses.	"Stiff upper lip." "Chin up!" "Pull yourself together!" "One foot in front of the other." "Relax." "Be positive."
Self-denigration: thinking/saying the situation must have come about because of your general faults.	Like fatalism, passively accepting the inevitability of a situation removes any responsibility you might otherwise feel for it. Like catastrophising, it asks for sympathy, it helps to express negative emotions, it tells you to expect the worst (so any more positive outcome will be more greatly felt).	"Someone up there hates me." "I never do anything right." "It's just my luck." "I'm jinxed."
Self-encouragement: thinking/saying to yourself positive messages about a situation.	It improves your mood and gives you an optimistic outlook. Optimists generally experience more success in life.	"It'll be a doddle." "You can do it." "It's not as bad as it looks." "This time tomorrow, it'll all be over."
Self-justification.	It may persuade people you are not to blame, and therefore take the pressure off you.	"It's not my fault."

Withdrawal (emotional and social), e.g. not going out, not being with people, sleeping too much. More generalised than escape/avoidance.	It eliminates any possibility of being directly confronted by threats or thoughts of threats.	"I just want to be alone." "To be or not to be?"
Worrying.	Constantly thinking about what may go wrong.	"It is not work that kills, but worry."

Appendix 2: Stretching for stress

Preliminaries

1. Before you do any of these exercises, please read the disclaimer at the beginning of this book.

2. Stress makes the muscles tense and tense muscles heighten our vulnerability to stress. This makes a vicious cycle. Thus stretching tense muscles is a way to reduce stress. The first 11 exercises in this series may be done as a general routine, for example to complement the muscle relaxation exercise outlined in Chapter 12. The last exercise, exercise 12, is useful to do frequently during the day if you have a desk job.

3. The muscles most affected by stress are those of the shoulders and upper back, neck, and jaw. For this reason, the exercises I suggest here focus on these areas.

4. It is best to do the exercises in a warm environment, and when your body is warm. Do not do them as soon as you wake up – get up and walk around for a few minutes first. If you feel cold, have a warm shower before you exercise.

5. Exercises done in the lying position can be done on your bed or on an exercise mat on the floor.

6. Before doing each exercise, check your body position. With seated and standing exercises, "think tall": neck straight (many people will need to tuck in their chin very slightly), shoulders relaxed but not hanging forwards. If seated, make sure you are not slouching. If standing, many people will need to tuck their pelvis slightly (bring your "tail bone" in). If lying on your back, make sure your head, trunk and legs are aligned.

7. All your movements should be slow and quite gentle. Do not move stretch your body beyond a comfortable limit. During the exercises breathe in a relaxed way and with a normal rhythm. Unless specified in the instructions for the exercises, do not hold your breath or try to time your breathing with your movements.

8. It is suggested that you do the exercises in the order in which they are presented here. With exercises that you do on both sides, it does not matter which side you start on.

9. Exercises only work if you do them! (That means every day, or nearly.)

Exercise 1 - Trunk rotation stretch

This is a particularly good exercise to stretch the muscles of the trunk, neck and chest and to free up stiffness at the top of the back.

Lie down on your right side, legs bent to 90°, together. Stretch your arms out in front of you, fingers straight. Stretch your upper arm and shoulder as far forwards as you can, while breathing in deeply. Then, while slowly breathing out, bring the straight upper arm in a wide arc over you and round to the other side. While you do this allow your upper body, neck and head to rotate round with the arm. When you've gone as far round as possible, stretch out both straight arms. Come back to the initial position and get ready to start again. Repeat 3 times. Then do the same while lying on your left side.

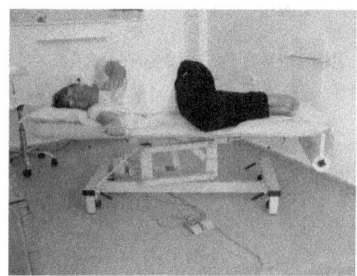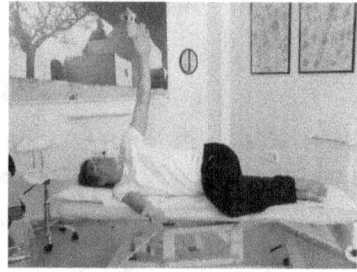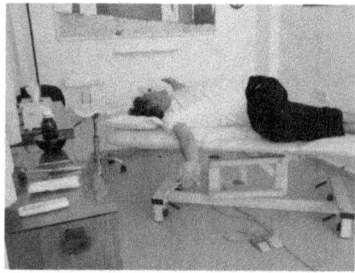

Trunk rotation stretch

Exercise 2 - The cat stretch

Another excellent exercise to stretch and mobilise the spine and the muscles that run along it. There are many versions of this exercise. This one is very simple, but some people have difficulty coordinating the movements of the head, back and pelvis. To help, think of making an "n" shape with your body (head and bottom lower than your back), followed by a "u" shape (head and bottom higher than your back).

Get onto all fours (hands and knees). Arch your back upwards, while bringing your head down and tucking your bottom in. Maintain the position for 5 seconds. Then create a downwards curve in your back, while raising your head and sticking your bottom out. Maintain the position for 5 seconds. Repeat 3 times. During the exercise do not bend your elbows or move your body backwards or forwards.

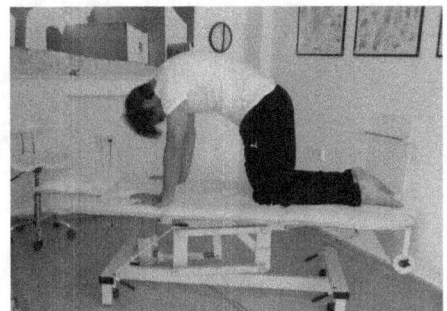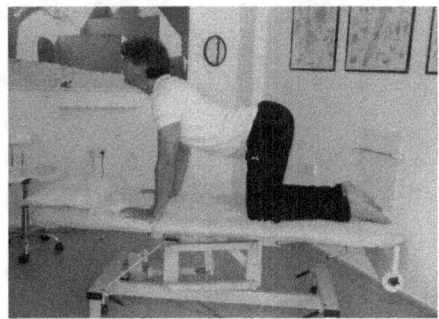

"The cat" stretch

Exercise 3 - Back of neck stretch

This is an exercise to stretch the muscles at the back of the neck and the upper part of the back.

Seated with your back straight, and not resting against the chair back. Make sure your shoulders are relaxed but not falling forwards. Put your hands behind your head and interlock your fingers. Bring your head down in front to stretch the muscles at the back of your neck. While you bring your head down in front, bring your elbows to the front to let your arms weigh on your head. Do not actively pull with your arms, the weight of your relaxed arms is sufficient. Do not raise your shoulders or allow your body to bend forwards. Maintain the position for 5 seconds. Return to the starting position. You will do this 3 times, but in a cycle including some or all of exercises 4, 5, 6 and 7.

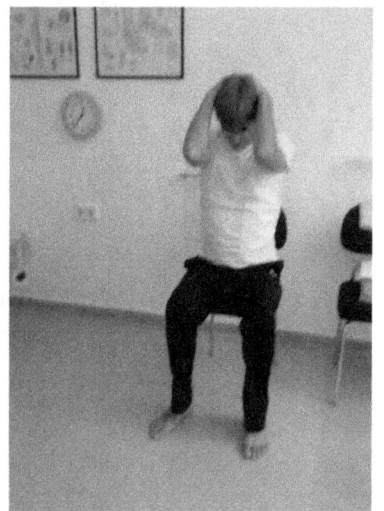 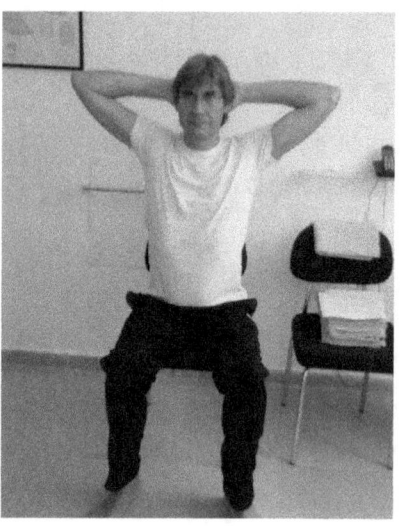

Back of the neck stretch

Exercise 4 - Oblique back of neck stretch

This exercise really gets into the number one stress muscle: the superior trapezius, which runs from the back of your head to your shoulder on both sides.

Seated with your back straight, and not resting against the chair back. Make sure your shoulders are relaxed but not falling forwards. Turn your head 40° to your left (that's almost half way). Put the hand on the same side (the left) on the top of your head so that the fingers can grip the back of your head. Your elbow should be in front of your face. Bring your head down in that direction to stretch the muscles at the back of your neck on the opposite side. Help by pulling just a little with your arm so that you feel the stretch, not so much that you feel pain. The right shoulder should be relaxed, not raised. Do not allow your body to bend forwards or sideways. Maintain the position for 5 seconds. Return to the starting position. Then do the same on the opposite side. You will do this 3 times, but in a cycle including some or all of exercises 3, 5, 6 and 7.

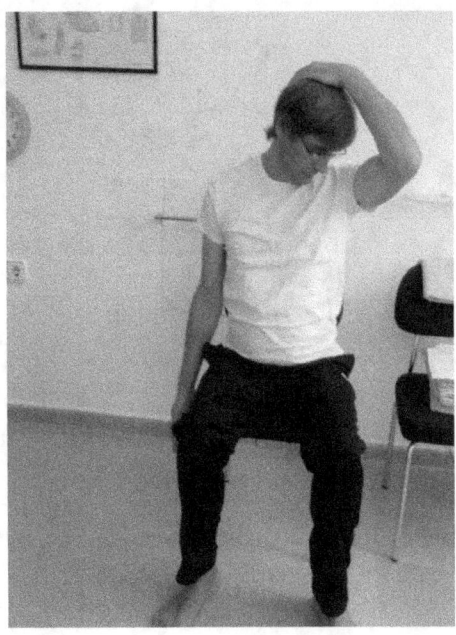

Oblique back of the neck stretch

Exercise 5 - Side of neck stretch

Seated with your back and neck straight, and not resting against the chair back. Make sure your shoulders are relaxed but not falling forwards. Bring your head down to one side (ear to shoulder) while still looking forwards, to stretch the muscles on the opposite side of the neck. You should feel the stretch but not pain. The shoulder on the stretched side should stay relaxed, and not raised. Do not allow your body to bend sideways. Maintain the position for 5 seconds. Return to the starting position. Then do the same on the opposite side. You will do this 3 times, but in a cycle including some or all of exercises 3, 4, 6 and 7.

Side of neck stretch

Exercise 6 - Neck rotation stretch

Seated with your back and neck straight, and not resting against the chair back. Make sure your shoulders are relaxed but not falling forwards. Slowly turn your head completely to one side. Your eyes should follow an imaginary horizon. Do not raise or lower your chin or bend your neck. Maintain the position for 5 seconds. Return to the starting position. Then do the same on the opposite side. You will do this 3 times, but in a cycle including some or all of exercises 3, 4, 5 and 7.

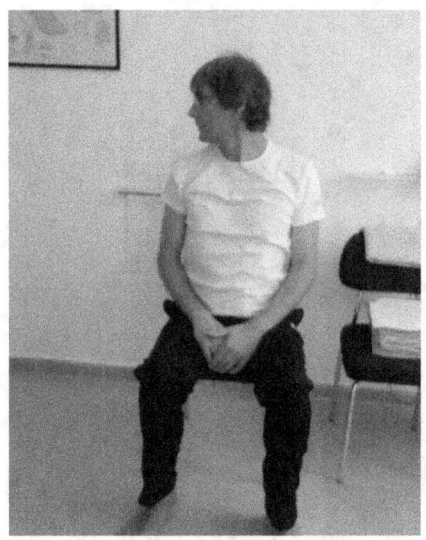

Neck rotation stretch

Exercise 7 - Front of neck stretch

An exercise to stretch the scalene muscles at the front of your neck, which are commonly involved in a dysfunctional upper-chest breathing pattern.

Seated with your back and neck straight, and not resting against the chair back. Make sure your shoulders are relaxed but not falling forwards. Slowly turn your head completely to one side (the final position of exercise 6). Now look upwards. Maintain this position for 5 seconds. Return to the starting position. Then do the same on the opposite side. You will do this 3 times, but in a cycle including some or all of exercises 3, 4, 5 and 6.

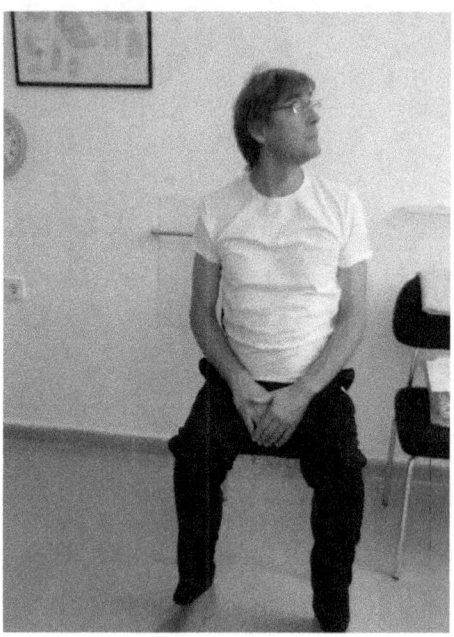

Front of neck stretch

Exercise 8 - Head retraction

By bringing the neck straight and tucking in the chin you stretch the small muscles that connect the back of your skull to the top of the spine, muscles which are often responsible for stress-related headaches. Many people habitually assume a "head forward" posture, which can cause these muscles to become chronically shortened. This exercise will help to eliminate this habit.

Seated with your back and neck straight, and not resting against the chair back. Make sure your shoulders are relaxed but not falling forwards. Lengthen the back of your neck by sitting tall, aiming the crown of your head (not your forehead) at the ceiling. Tuck and lower your chin slightly, until you feel tension at the back of the neck. Maintain this position for 5 seconds. Return to the starting position. Repeat the exercise 3 times. The first picture below shows a bad "head forward" posture. The second shows the position held in the exercise, with the neck straightened and lengthened, and the chin drawn in and down a little.

Head retraction

Exercise 9 - Jaw release

The jaw muscles are very commonly affected by stress, causing headaches, nocturnal jaw clenching, and problems with the teeth. This is a good stretch to do before bed, to help prevent clenching during the night.

For this exercise you first need to locate two parts of your anatomy. The first is the fleshy bulge on the palm of your hand at the base of your thumb. This is called the "thenar eminence". The second is the part of your jaw between the ear and the angle of the jaw, known as the "ramus" of the mandible (plural: rami). These are shown in the pictures below.

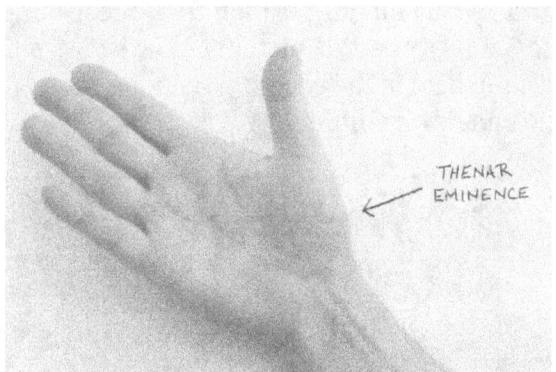 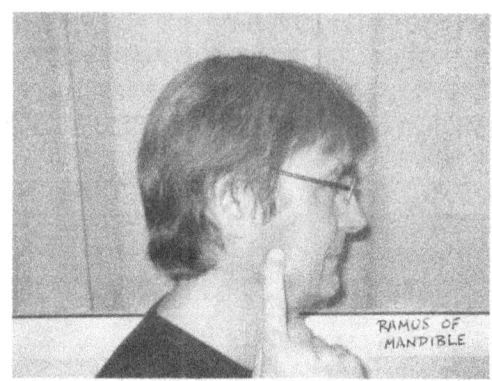

Now, sit with your back and neck straight, and not resting against the chair back. Open your mouth wide briefly, then let it relax in a slightly opened position. Put both hands to your cheeks with the thenar eminences (see pictures above) in contact with the rami of the mandible. Your elbows should be pointing downwards. If you relax your arms and shoulders completely, you will find that their weight creates a stretching tension felt below the ears. Do not actively pull down with your arms, their relaxed weight is sufficient. Maintain this for 2 minutes, making sure you keep your mouth and arms completely relaxed.

Jaw release

Exercise 10 - Shoulder backwards circling

This exercise is best done together with (and before) exercise 11. Together they will help to free up and release tension from the shoulder girdles.

Standing with your back and neck straight, and your shoulders relaxed but not falling forwards. The circling is done with four consecutive directions of movement rolled into one fluid cycle:

1 First raise your shoulders (shrug).

2 Then bring your shoulders back.

3 Then bring your shoulders down.

4 Then bring your shoulders forwards.

Go on in the same way for about 10 cycles.

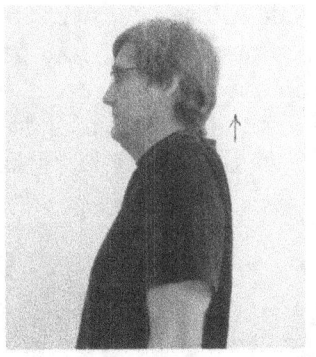

Position 1

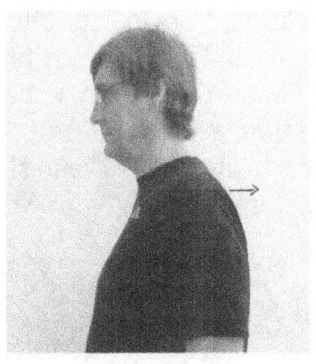

Position 2

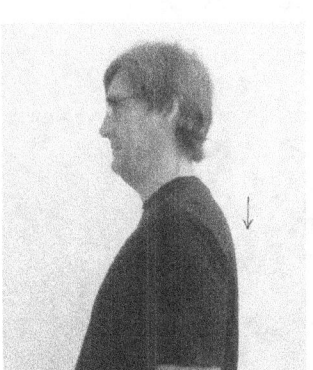

Position 3

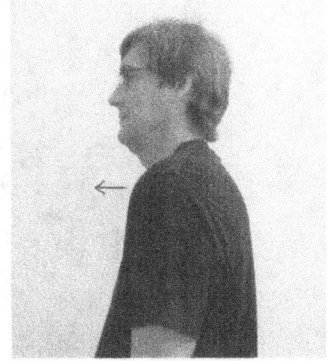

Position 4

Exercise 11 - Arm shaking

This exercise is best done together with (and after) exercise 10.

Standing, with your arms hanging loosely down, simply shake your arms and hands as if shaking water off your hands for a few seconds.

Exercise 12 - Brugger relief position

This exercise is designed to offer relief from stress and muscular tension at your office desk. You can do it several times during the working day.

Put everything down and move your chair back from the desk. Sit on the front edge of your chair with your feet placed firmly on the ground, hip-width apart. Sit up tall, with your back and neck straight and your chin slightly tucked. Your shoulders should be relaxed but not dropped forwards. Let your arms hang down naturally at either side. Close your eyes. Take a slow, deep breath from the abdomen and at the same time, rotate your arms so that your palms are facing forwards and slightly outwards. When you breath out, do not blow the air out, just let it flow out naturally. At the same time, relax your arms – they will naturally rotate back to a neutral position with the palms facing inwards and slightly backwards. Repeat in a relaxed, unhurried way about six times before resuming your work.

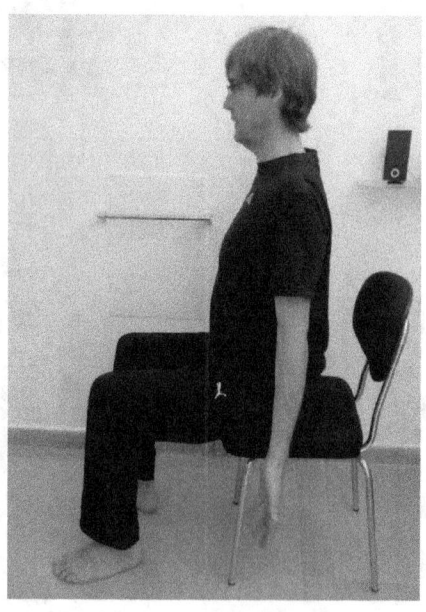

Brugger relief position

232

Appendix 3: Complex chronic stress scenarios

In Chapter 18 I gave some simple examples to illustrate how stressful scenarios can be considered in terms of (a) whether the situation is more a practical or emotional one; and (b) whether the challenge is from without or from within. The reality is often not so clear cut. Here are some examples to illustrate that.

1. Your long-term spouse or partner wants to separate from you because he or she has become involved with another person. Here we can say that, if your partner/spouse has made up his/her mind, the challenge to you is primarily an emotional one. There may well be practical implications, but to begin with these are secondary. Now, the challenge appears to have come from events outside yourself, and those seem at this stage to be entirely beyond your control. As such, the only way forward is within yourself. That is, to the question, "Is it more reasonable for me to attempt to change the outside pressures affecting me, or to change myself so that I can face them more easily?", you are compelled to answer the latter. You have greater leverage on your emotional stress by facing the challenge within.

2. You have been made redundant at the age of 55 and are having great difficulty finding another job. Losing your job was simply due to the economic circumstances of the time, but your challenges now are to face both the emotional impact of not earning your living and the practical one of supporting yourself and your family. You have to work both within and without, by learning to come to terms with your situation, as well as actively seeking work or, in the meantime, other sources of income such as government benefits. You need to act practically to solve the problem, but you need to face the challenge to your self-esteem as well.

3. You feel unable to cope with the practical problems brought by living with a loved one with an incapacitating illness. There will be your emotional response to face, but first and foremost there are the practicalities of the situation itself. You will have to manage it by sharing the necessary tasks with other family members, or consider other options, such as hiring a professional carer. You will also need to keep as healthy and capable in mind and body as you can ("developing and nurturing yourself").

4. You are suffering from emotional burn-out because of working with several intense and harrowing cases in your job in a caring profession. Here we have pressures from without generating a problem within you, affecting your health, particularly at an emotional level. This is a challenge from without because you are doing a job you love and under normal circumstances you handle it well. But an unusually intense period has pushed you too far and you feel jaded and unenthusiastic about going to work, making it also a challenge within. You need to share your emotions by talking to colleagues who have experienced burn-out, at the same time as managing your workload, reducing it even to

the point of taking a break. You have leverage on this problem both by acting on the external factors that triggered it (reduce your workload), and working on yourself (recharge your batteries by getting more rest and relaxation, or taking a break, and having counselling to learn specific skills in avoiding burn-out).

5. Your grown-up son or daughter will have nothing more to do with you on account of a past conflict, and because of this you cannot see your grandchildren. Your challenges are both emotional and practical. But there will always be sadness so long as you cannot see your grandchildren, so you need primarily to address this practicality. You need to assess realistically to what extent a reconciliation is possible, at least so far as an accord be reached to allow you contact with your grandchildren. You could involve a professional counsellor as an intermediary. To this extent, you act upon the problem situation. Until such time as the situation is resolved, you are going to have to exercise acceptance and patience. To this extent, you act to manage your own responses.

6. Since the break-up of a long-term relationship, you have been consumed by feelings of hopelessness and worthlessness. This is "the shadow of a past events". You will have to seek help to allow you to understand (and internalise the understanding) that your feelings are unreasonable, that you indeed have worth and are far from being without hope. You will face the challenge within.

Appendix 4: Principles of Living ("Virtues")

Acceptance

Adaptability

Authenticity

Beauty

Benevolence

Care

Charity

Clear thinking

Commitment

Compassion

Contentment

Courage

Courtesy

Detachment

Determination

Dignity

Diligence

Enthusiasm

Equality

Excellence

Fairness

Faith

Forgiveness

Freedom

Friendship

Frugality

Generosity

Gentleness

Grace

Graciousness

Gratitude

Harmony

Helpfulness

Honesty

Honour

Hope

Humanity

Humility

Idealism

Integrity

Joyfulness

Judgement

Justice

Kindness

Knowledge

Leadership

Love

Loyalty

Moderation

Modesty

Open-mindedness

Openness

Optimism	Serenity
Order	Service
Passion	Sincerity
Patience	Solidarity
Peace	Spirituality
Perseverance	Strength
Piety	Tact
Preparedness	Tenacity
Purpose	Thoroughness
Purity	Thoughtfulness
Rectitude	Tolerance
Reliability	Trust
Resilience	Truth
Respect	Understanding
Responsibility	Unity
Reverence	Vision
Sacrifice	Vitality
Scepticism	Wisdom
Self-discipline	Work

Glossary

Acute stress	Intense stress of recent onset.
Adaptation	The process of adapting to a change in the environment.
Adaptive	Refers to adaptation. In the context of stress, an adaptive response is functional, it benefits the organism. See also "maladaptive".
Adrenaline (Adrenalin)	A hormone secreted by the inner part (the medulla) of the adrenal glands. It acts rapidly to make the body ready to respond to sudden emergencies.
Alarm stage/mode (of the GAS)	The first stage/mode of the stress response, characterised by alarm, and the urge rapidly to confront or escape from a situation ("fight or flight").
Allostasis	The process of bodily adaptation to long-term changes in the environment. It involves a shift in the homoeostatic balance.
Anabolism	The metabolic process of making larger molecules from smaller ones and thus building up bodily tissues.
Appraisal	Assessment.
Autonomic nervous system (ANS)	The part of the nervous system that controls all involuntary bodily functions.
Avoidance	In psychology, it is the behaviour of avoiding situations which trigger anxiety.
Behaviour experiment	An experiment you do to see what happens if you behave in a certain way.
Behavioural	To do with behaviour.
Catabolism	The metabolic process of breaking down larger molecules into smaller ones, for example in liberating chemically stored energy to produce heat or movement.
Catastrophise	To interpret a situation in a dramatically and unrealistically negative way.
Challenge	A demand you have to satisfy which presents a certain amount of difficulty.
Chronic stress	Long-term stress.
Cognition	Mental processes involved in processing information, e.g. awareness, knowledge, understanding, and thinking.
Cognitive	To do with cognition.
Cognitive-behavioural therapy	A kind of psychological therapy focussing on thoughts and behaviour.
Conditioning	The mental process by which we learn to produce automatic responses to particular stimuli.

Coping	Our attempts to respond to situations in order to bring about satisfactory outcomes. This may mean a return to the *status quo,* or an improvement in one's life, or even "least bad" damage limitation.
Coping resources	The things and attributes that you have which help you to cope.
Coping responses	Emotions, thoughts and behaviour whose objective is the reduction of stress.
Corticosteroids	A group of hormones secreted from the outer part (the cortex) of the adrenal glands. Cortisol is one of these.
Cortisol	One of the corticosteroid hormones, important in the body's response to chronic stress.
Demands	Things that are asked of you by the situation or by people.
Denial	Refusing to acknowledge a situation.
Dis-stress	See "negative stress".
Dissociation	In psychology, it means a mental detachment from reality. It may involve a wide range of experiences from mild to severe.
Dysfunctional	An adjective used to describe things, processes or behaviours, which are not working well. See also "functional".
Emotional intelligence	The ability to identify, understand and manage emotions in positive and enhancing rather than detrimental ways.
Endocrine system	The hormones, their interactions, and the glands that secrete them.
Escape	In psychology, it is the behaviour of removing oneself from situations which trigger anxiety.
Eustress	See "positive stress".
Exhaustion stage/mode (of the GAS)	The third and last mode of the stress response, characterised by rapid bodily and mental decline and the onset of illness.
Fatalism	The general belief or attitude that events are determined by forces beyond one's control, so that it is pointless to try to influence them.
Functional	An adjective used to describe things, processes or behaviours, which are working well. See also "dysfunctional".
GAS	See "General Adaptation syndrome".
General Adaptation Syndrome (GAS)	A three-stage theory of the body's response to stress, developed by Hans Selye.
Glycogen	The form of storage sugar that the body uses for rapid energy release. It is stored in the liver and muscles.
Hassles	Small but annoying sources of stress in daily life.
Homoeostasis	The physiological process by which the body is able to maintain a stable internal environment in response to short-term changes in the wider environment.
Homoeostatic	To do with homoeostasis.
Hyperventilation	Over-breathing. It is characterised by rapid, shallow breathing, and

	may be associated with anxiety and panic.
Maladaptive	Refers to adaptation. In the context of stress, a maladaptive response is dysfunctional, it is deleterious to the organism. See also "adaptive".
Major life changes	This term is used to describe important events in people's lives which are the source of severe stress.
Mastery	The state of having learned a skill to an advanced level of proficiency.
Material resources	Money, tools, materials, etc. that help you to meet a demand.
Metabolism	The bodily process of transforming chemical substances from one kind to another.
Meta-thinking	Thinking about one's thoughts and thought processes.
Mindfulness	The state or practice of heightened awareness and absence of judgement of what we are experiencing in the present.
Mindset	A set of beliefs and attitudes, usually about a specific subject. Stress mindsets are sets of beliefs and attitudes about stress, for example, whether one sees stress as being enhancing or harmful to health and performance.
Negative stress	Stress which harms us. The imbalance between demands and our ability to cope is excessive, with deleterious results for our health or state of mind. It has been called "dis-stress".
Neurotransmitters	Chemicals that convey information between nerve cells.
Parasympathetic nervous system (PNS)	The branch of the autonomic nervous system that stimulates regenerative processes in the body. It works in opposite but complementary ways to the sympathetic nervous system.
Personal characteristics	Personality traits and attributes.
Personal resources	Those mental and physical attributes that we can draw on to help us cope with challenges.
Personality	One's individual set of characteristics relating to behaviour, cognition and emotion.
Physiology	Bodily processes.
Positive stress	Stress which stimulates us and aids our personal development. It has been called "Eustress".
Primary appraisal	The first mental assessment of a situation. "Is this a threat?"
Rationalisation	The process of finding a rational explanation or meaning in a situation.
Resistance stage/mode (of the GAS)	The second stage/mode of the stress response, characterised by a series of low-grade but long-term adaptations that gradually drain the organism's resources.
Resources	See "coping resources".
Responses	The emotions, thoughts, actions and physiological adaptations that occur in order to cope with an event or situation.

Secondary appraisal   The second mental assessment of a challenge. "Can I deal with it?"

Self-instructions   Instructions which we give ourselves in order to exert self-control.

Social support   Help from people or organisations.

Somatisation   The process by which psychological problems are experienced as physical symptoms.

Stress   How our mind and body respond to challenges. In everyday speech, it is often associated with negative feelings and effects. According to Lazarus and Folkman's (1984) Transactional Model, stress is the result of *"an imbalance between the demands imposed on the organism, and the capacity of the organism to cope with those demands"*.

Symptoms   Abnormal sensations or signs indicating disorder or disease.

Sympathetic nervous system (SNS)   The branch of the autonomic nervous system that primes the body for rapid action. It works in opposite but complementary ways to the parasympathetic nervous system.

Threat   A challenge which is perceived as being dangerous to one's welfare (mental, physical, social, economic, etc.).

Thrive   To grow, develop positively, and attain fulfilment.

Index

www.ingramcontent.com/pod-product-compliance
Lightning Source LLC
Chambersburg PA
CBHW081655120626
46550CB00010B/2904